JANE AUSTEN: *Emma* David Lodge
JANE AUSTEN: *'Northanger Abbey'* & *'Persuasion'* B.C. Southam
JANE AUSTEN: *'Sense and Sensibility'*, *'Pride and Prejudice'* & *Mansfield Park'*
 B.C. Southam
BECKETT: *Waiting for Godot* Ruby Cohn
WILLIAM BLAKE: *Songs of Innocence and Experience* Margaret Bottrall
CHARLOTTE BRONTË: *'Jane Eyre'* & *'Villette'* Miriam Allott
EMILY BRONTË: *Wuthering Heights* Miriam Allott
BROWNING: *'Men and Women'* & *Other Poems* J.R. Watson
CHAUCER: *Canterbury Tales* J.J. Anderson
COLERIDGE: *'The Ancient Mariner'* & *Other Poems* Alun R. Jones &
 William Tydeman
CONRAD: *'Heart of Darkness'*, *'Nostromo'* & *'Under Western Eyes'* C.B. Cox
CONRAD: *The Secret Agent* Ian Watt
DICKENS: *Bleak House* A.E. Dyson
DICKENS: *'Hard Times'*, *'Great Expectations'* & *'Our Mutual Friend'* Norman Page
DICKENS: *'Dombey and Son'* & *'Little Dorrit'* Alan Shelston
DONNE: *Songs and Sonets* Julian Lovelock
GEORGE ELIOT: *Middlemarch* Patrick Swinden
GEORGE ELIOT: *'The Mill on the Floss'* & *'Silas Marner'* R.P. Draper
T.S. ELIOT: *Four Quartets* Bernard Bergonzi
T.S. ELIOT: *'Prufrock'*, *'Gerontion'*, *'Ash Wednesday'* & *Other Shorter Poems*
 B.C. Southam
T.S. ELIOT: *The Waste Land* C.B. Cox & Arnold P. Hinchliffe
T.S. ELIOT: *Plays* Arnold P. Hinchliffe
HENRY FIELDING: *Tom Jones* Neil Compton
E.M. FORSTER: *A Passage to India* Malcolm Bradbury
WILLIAM GOLDING: *Novels 1954–64* Norman Page
HARDY: *The Tragic Novels* R.P. Draper
HARDY: *Poems* James Gibson & Trevor Johnson
HARDY: *Three Pastoral Novels* R.P. Draper
GERARD MANLEY HOPKINS: *Poems* Margaret Bottrall
HENRY JAMES: *'Washington Square'* & *'The Portrait of a Lady'* Alan Shelton
JONSON: *Volpone* Jonas A. Barish
JONSON: *'Every Man in his Humour'* & *'The Alchemist'* R.V. Holdsworth
JAMES JOYCE: *'Dubliners'* & *'A Portrait of the Artist as a Young Man'* Morris Beja
KEATS: *Odes* G.S. Fraser
KEATS: *Narrative Poems* John Spencer Hill
D.H. LAWRENCE: *Sons and Lovers* Gamini Salgado
D.H. LAWRENCE: *'The Rainbow'* & *'Women in Love'* Colin Clarke
LOWRY: *Under the Volcano* Gordon Bowker
MARLOWE: *Doctor Faustus* John Jump
MARLOWE: *'Tamburlaine the Great'*, *'Edward the Second'* & *'The Jew of Malta'*
 John Russell Brown
MARLOWE: *Poems* Arthur Pollard
MAUPASSANT: *In the Hall of Mirrors* T. Harris
MILTON: *Paradise Lost* A.E. Dyson & Julian Lovelock
O'CASEY: *'Juno and the Paycock'*, *'The Plough and the Stars'* & *'The Shadow of a*
 Gunman' Ronald Ayling
EUGENE O'NEILL: *Three Plays* Normand Berlin
JOHN OSBORNE: *Look Back in Anger* John Russell Taylor
PINTER: *'The Birthday P*
POPE: *The Rape of th*
SHAKESPEARE: *A M*
SHAKESPEARE: *Anto*

Charlotte Brontë

Jane Eyre and *Villette*

A CASEBOOK

EDITED BY

MIRIAM ALLOTT

MACMILLAN

First published 1973 by
THE MACMILLAN PRESS LTD
Houndmills, Basingstoke, Hampshire RG21 2XS
and London
Companies and representatives
throughout the world

ISBN 0–333–13657–8

Printed in Hong Kong

7th reprint 1992

CONTENTS

To Jim and Livvie

ACKNOWLEDGEMENTS

The author and publishers wish to thank the following, who have kindly given permission for the use of copyright material: David Cecil, 'Charlotte Brontë' from *Early Victorian Novelists* by permission of David Higham Associates; Robert Colby, 'Lucy Snowe and the Good Governess' from *Fiction With a Purpose* by permission of Indiana University Press; D. W. Crompton, 'The New Criticism: A Caveat' from *Essays in Criticism*, July 1960, by permission of *Essays in Criticism: A Quarterly Journal of Literary Criticism*; Robert B. Heilman, *Charlotte Brontë's New Gothic*; R. B. Martin, *The Accents of Persuasion* reprinted by permission of the Sterling Lord Agency; Roy Pascal, 'The Autobiographical Novel' from *Essays in Criticism*, ix April 1959, by permission of *Essays in Criticism: A Quarterly Journal of Literary Criticism*; M. H. Scargill, 'All Passion Spent: A Revaluation of Jane Eyre' reprinted from *University of Toronto Quarterly*, vol. 19 (1950) by permission of University of Toronto Press; Kathleen Tillotson, 'Jane Eyre' from *Novels of the Eighteen-Forties* by permission of the Clarendon Press, Oxford.

GENERAL EDITOR'S PREFACE

The Casebook series, launched in 1968, has become a well-regarded library of critical studies. The central concern of the series remains the 'single-author' volume, but suggestions from the academic community have led to an extension of the original plan, to include occasional volumes on such general themes as literary 'schools' and genres.

Each volume in the central category deals either with one well-known and influential work by an individual author, or with closely related works by one writer. The main section consists of critical readings, mostly modern, collected from books and journals. A selection of reviews and comments by the author's contemporaries is also included, and sometimes comment from the author himself. The Editor's introduction charts the reputation of the work or works from the first appearance to the present time.

Volumes in the 'general themes' category are variable in structure but follow the basic purpose of the series in presenting an integrated selection of readings, with an Introduction which explores the theme and discusses the literary and critical issues involved.

A single volume can represent no more than a small selection of critical opinions. Some critics are excluded for reasons of space, and it is hoped that readers will pursue the suggestions for further reading in the Select Bibliography. Other contributions are severed from their original context, to which some readers may wish to turn. Indeed, if they take a hint from the critics represented here, they certainly will.

A. E. DYSON

ABBREVIATIONS

The Brontës: Their Lives, Friendships and Correspondence, in Four Volumes, The Shakespeare Head Brontë, ed. T. J. Wise and J. A. Symington (1849–52)	*LL* (Life and Letters)
Elizabeth Gaskell, *The Life of Charlotte Brontë* (1857)	Mrs Gaskell's *Life*

INTRODUCTION

Of Charlotte Brontë's four novels, three, *Jane Eyre* (1847), *Shirley* (1849) and *Villette* (1853), were published in her lifetime, and one, *The Professor* (1857), posthumously, although it was finished and sent on its unsuccessful tour of the publishers during 1846 to 1847. In 1853 as approving reviews of *Villette* began to accumulate, Charlotte recognised that it was with this third novel and with *Jane Eyre* that she had kindled her readers' strongest interest and admiration. *Shirley* had been in general respectfully received, but most people had found it a disappointment after the riveting narrative of its best-selling predecessor. This preference for *Jane Eyre* and *Villette* still persists, though critical opinion about their relative merits has varied over the years. By the 'ordinary' reader, however, *Jane Eyre* is unquestionably better known and more warmly liked. The qualities which ensured its early success still ensure responsive audiences for the numerous adaptations which have been made of it for the stage, the cinema and television. It has been read in instalments over the air and studied regularly at school. Most people at least know it by name, as they know the title of *Wuthering Heights,* the single novel published by Charlotte's sister Emily. It continues to command popular attention because of the skill of its first-person narrative, the brusque appeal of its larger-than-life hero, Mr Rochester, and the Cinderella-like triumph of its 'plain, poor and little' but still passionate governess-heroine Jane.

Villette is an unlikely candidate for this kind of popularity, for it substitutes for that novel's strong colouring the self-discipline of a heroine whose destiny it is always to suffer in silence, and ruthlessly holds in check any tendency to indulge the more genial *Märchen* elements with which so many novelists have soothed their readers. But sombre as it is, Lucy Snowe's autobiographical narrative has its own powerful appeal. A recent television adaptation has shown that the characters and the setting of the story can still compel a modern audience. It is easy to see why Charlotte's more serious-minded admirers welcomed this book, which restored to them the narrative skills of *Jane Eyre* but eliminated melodrama in the interests of sobriety and self-discipline. Some later Victorian readers thought less highly of *Villette* than their predecessors had done (see below, pp. 31, 143, 154), but it has regained its importance for many modern students of the Brontës, who see in it the successful outcome of its author's struggle to come to terms with 'reality' as against 'romance'. Such a struggle is a characteristic expression of one kind of romanticism, and it is with the work of the Brontës as writers in the Romantic tradition that modern professional critics, as distinct from non-literary enthusiasts, have so often been concerned. Their differences of opinion about *Jane Eyre* and *Villette* – and about Charlotte's literary standing generally – are frequently linked with this interest.

Charlotte was born on 21 April 1816, as the third child of the Reverend Patrick Brontë and his wife Maria. Her two elder sisters, Maria and Elizabeth, died in childhood; she was to commemorate Maria in *Jane Eyre* as Helen Burns, a portrait which impressed many of her earliest readers. There were three other children: Patrick Branwell Brontë, the only son, born in 1817; Emily Jane Brontë, born on 30 July 1818, the most puzzling and for many readers the most original member of the family; and Anne Brontë, born on 17 January 1820, whose two novels, *Agnes Grey* (1847) and *The Tenant of Wildfell Hall* (1848), reflect the Brontë image faintly in a mirror of piety. The six young children lost their mother in the autumn of 1821, and less than four years afterwards Maria and Elizabeth were dead too; so Charlotte had only just reached her teens when she shouldered family responsibilities. In the subsequent course of their short lives (the family disease of tuberculosis killed Emily in December 1848 and Anne in the following May), it was she who planned for herself and her sisters, trying to get them adequately equipped to earn their living by teaching, and later spurring them on to make something of their unique creative gifts by seeking a publisher for their various literary enterprises.

Their father was not appealed to for practical help, since he remained a remote and somewhat eccentric figure who usually spent his time in his study at the parsonage preparing his sermons and reading his books. But he transmitted to his talented children the imaginative inheritance of his Irish Celtic ancestry and his feeling for the value of self-education and things of the mind. He was to become deeply proud of his eldest surviving daughter, gathering together in later years all the reviews of her novels and reading them over to himself in his solitary room. He had a long while in which to reflect sadly upon her, for he died in 1861 aged eighty-four, while she died in March 1855 aged thirty-nine, having managed in the eight years since publishing Jane Eyre to complete two further novels and to experience a few months of marriage to the Reverend Arthur Nicholls, her father's curate since 1845. He had first proposed in 1852, but there were delays because of her own misgivings and her father's disapproval. At last the old man was persuaded to relent and the marriage took place in June 1854. Within the year, Charlotte succumbed to a painful illness associated with her pregnancy. Some time during that year, she read aloud to her husband the fragment of a new story, now known to us as 'Emma'. It was first published in the *Cornhill Magazine* for April 1860, with an introduction by Thackeray, whom she had so greatly admired and to whom she had dedicated the second edition of *Jane Eyre*.

Charlotte's staunch struggles against odds reached an important stage when she began to cast about for the means of making a livelihood for herself and her sisters. They had little money, a common want in the families of most country clergymen. They were

not physically robust – Charlotte herself was undersized, subject
to nervous headaches and depression, and, in particularly bad
times, managed to keep going, one feels, only because of the
indomitable will and sense of principle which she shared with her
sisters. Above all, a *farouche* reserve and unworldliness existed in
each sister side by side with remarkable creative gifts. Their limitations were linked with their genius. The sisters' reserve and unworldliness, for example, were heightened by the very conditions
which helped to stimulate their creative imagination, that is the
wild beauty and isolation of the Yorkshire moors which surrounded their parsonage home at Haworth and where they spent
the happiest and freest hours of their childhood and youth. Moreover their physical seclusion helped to foster their intellectual
activity. They read widely, drawing on their father's store of
books; on the library in the Yorkshire town of Keighley, some few
miles away; and on the regularly arriving newspapers and
periodicals, notably *Blackwood's Magazine,* which kept them up
to date with its articles, reviews and stories (many of these stories
appearing throughout the 1830s and 1840s were strongly
'Gothick' in feeling). They knew most of the older authors, including Shakespeare, and were strongly affected by the writers of the
period of Romanticism into which they were born, especially
Wordsworth, Byron and Scott – 'For fiction – read Scott alone',
Charlotte once told her school friend Ellen Nussey.[1] Romantic
influences are pronounced in their celebrated childhood fantasies :
the cycle of stories centred on the imaginary kingdom of Angria
and its 'burning clime', which Charlotte and her brother Branwell
created together, and which continued to absorb her in her early
twenties, and the companion cycle centred on the imaginary realm
of Gondal, created by Emily and Anne, and of which only poems
ascribed by Emily to various wildly passionate inhabitants of that
colourful region now survive.[2] We know too that by the 1830s
Charlotte had extended her reading to take in contemporary
French fiction. She found, it is true, many of these French novels
'unprincipled', but they interested her deeply, especially those by
George Sand (see below, pp. 161–2), whose dithyrambic cele-

brations of freedom moved many Victorian readers besides the
Brontës. Several of Charlotte's early reviewers found in her
heroines resemblances to those of George Sand, and various
French elements in her manner and style were singled out by
critics of the Brontës throughout the nineteenth century.
It was, indeed, to a French-speaking country that Charlotte
turned in 1842, when – after each sister had experienced loneliness
and hardship while teaching in school or filling the post of governess in a private family – she decided to take Emily with her to the
Pension Heger in Brussels as a preparation for their cherished but
unrealistic project of setting up their own school in the parsonage
at Haworth. The decision to go abroad had far-reaching effects,
for her experiences during the two years which she spent there as
pupil and teacher were to provide staple materials for her four
novels. Her strongest emotions were aroused by the arresting personality of M. Heger himself, for whom she conceived an un-
reciprocated passion. His qualities she worked and reworked in her
principal male figures, from her early sketches in *The Professor* to
the mature recreation of this first novel in *Villette*.
What happened when the sisters were together again at the
parsonage in 1845 is a well known story. The facts were first
recorded by Charlotte herself in her Biographical Notice for the
memorial edition of *Wuthering Heights* and *Agnes Grey*, published in 1850, which outlines the sequence of events from her acci-
dental discovery of Emily's poems in the autumn of 1845 to the
transformation of Charlotte, Emily and Anne Brontë into 'Currer,
Ellis and Acton Bell', jointly authors of the little volume of *Poems*
which appeared in 1846, and individually of *Jane Eyre, Wuthering Heights* and *Agnes Grey*, which were published towards the
end of 1847. Charlotte recognised that Emily's poetry deserved
to be published, fought – with Anne's quiet support – to overcome
Emily's fierce distaste for publicity by setting out for inspection
her own and Anne's verses, and took every practical measure to
ensure that the three sisters should together realise their 'early
cherished . . . dream of one day becoming authors'. They chose
their 'ambiguous' pseudonyms, she tells us in the same 'Notice',

because they had scruples about 'assuming Christian names positively masculine' and at the same time,

... did not like to declare ourselves women, because ... we had a vague impression that authoresses are liable to be looked on with prejudice; we had noticed how critics sometimes use for their chastisement the weapon of personality, and, for their reward, a flattery which is not true praise ...

It was Charlotte, again, who found out about publishing procedures, conducted the correspondence and managed the financial arrangements connected with the bringing out of their *Poems* (they subsidised the publication themselves), and in April 1846 inaugurated their new project,

... a work of fiction, consisting of three distinct and unconnected tales which may be published either together as a work of three volumes of the ordinary novel size, or separately as single volumes . . .[3]

Charlotte's account differs slightly from Mrs Gaskell's over the precise length of time and the number of publishers who were approached before two of the 'volumes', *Wuthering Heights* and *Agnes Grey,* were accepted by Thomas Newby in the summer of 1847. We have it on Charlotte's authority that her own volume, *The Professor,* was rejected six times before arriving at the publishing house of Smith, Elder on 15 July 1847.[4] It was refused once more, but few refusals in publishing history can have had such encouraging effects on a would-be writer. It was courteously explained by the firm's sympathetic literary adviser, W. S. Williams,[5] that the story was too short and too colourless to sell on its own, but that literary promise was displayed and 'a work in three volumes would meet with careful attention'. Charlotte promptly replied that she had a narrative of this length in hand '. . . to which I have endeavoured to impart a more vivid interest . . . In about a month I hope to finish it . . .'[6]

The 'narrative' was *Jane Eyre.* Charlotte was better than her word, for she posted the MS. on 24 August, just one year after she had begun work on it,[7] and less than three weeks after her letter.

With equally impressive speed, George Smith, who was immediately enthusiastic, brought the book out on 16 October – a mere
six weeks later – in a three-volume edition entitled *Jane Eyre. An
Autobiography. Edited by Currer Bell.* He thus launched the new
book and its author into fame while the proofs of her sisters' novels
were still languishing on Newby's shelves. It was 'Currer Bell's'
success which at last spurred Newby into getting 'Ellis's' and
'Acton's' novels ready in time for the following December.

The facts about the rest of Charlotte's writing career are soon
told. A second edition of *Jane Eyre* was called for by the end of the
year and a third by the spring of 1848. For the second edition the
title was altered to *Jane Eyre. An Autobiography. By Currer Bell,*
the fiction about the editor being dropped at the risk of a certain
oddity in the new wording. Charlotte also wrote a preface thank-
ing everyone for their welcome to a new author, and added her
celebrated dedication to Thackeray. The third edition carried an
author's note disclaiming all title to any novels other than this one,
a statement which points to the immense confusion then current
about the separate identities of 'the Bells'. The confusion had been
added to by the sharp practice of Thomas Newby, who promoted
'Ellis' and 'Acton' by wording his advertisements to make it seem
that their books were written by Smith's 'celebrated new author'.

Charlotte's second novel, *Shirley,* which she had begun to think
about in December 1847, took her nearly two years to write. The
first two volumes ran well until the black period from September
1848 to May 1849 when the deaths of Branwell, Emily and Anne
followed each other in rapid succession. But she toiled on, and the
book appeared on 26 October 1849. It was reissued in a one-
volume edition on 19 August 1852. She began her last novel,
Villette, early in 1851, worked on it laboriously with many inter-
missions of ill-health and depression and by November 1852 had
despatched it to Smith's, who brought it out on 24 January 1853.
As to *The Professor,* after two unsuccessful attempts to interest her
publishers in bringing out a revised version, she gave up hope of
seeing it in print, yielding 'with ignoble facility', as she put it in a
letter to George Smith of February 1851.[8] It was not until 1856,

when Mrs Gaskell was preparing her biography, *The Life of Charlotte Brontë*, and had triumphantly secured the MS. from Charlotte's husband, that it was decided that the book should be published. It appeared in the following years shortly after the *Life*, the timing being agreed upon by Mrs Gaskell and George Smith as the most likely to meet the interest of Charlotte's admirers.[9]

The Early Reception of Jane Eyre

From the first, there was no question about the popular success of 'Currer Bell's' first novel. It rapidly became a topic of conversation in fashionable literary circles, and also a target for a few self-appointed guardians of public morality who warned against its 'improprieties'. It is hard to separate the reasons for early misgivings about its moral values from those which made it so attractive to the majority of readers. The radical *Examiner*, though it could be shrewd about her weaknesses, approved of her, as she approved of it; the high-and-dry 'organs of the High Church Party', as she called the *Guardian* and the *Christian Remembrancer*,[10] were discerning about her literary gifts, but took exception to her unsettling individualism; and the *Spectator*, anxious for the 'respectable families' for whom it catered, maintained its customary chilliness until satisfied by *Villette* that 'Currer Bell' was unlikely to bring a blush to the domestic cheek. At least one reviewer – Elizabeth Rigby in the *Quarterly Review*, whose opinions were at odds with those of the editor, John Lockhart – seems to have been antagonised by what she took to be an intransigent voice from a less than respectable part of society (pp. 56, 67).

For everyone, *Jane Eyre* was 'new'. 'Power', 'freshness', 'originality', 'vigour', 'truth' – such terms recur in the early reviews. Moreover the book was reviewed everywhere; even by the generous standards of the day, *Jane Eyre* received lavish attention. (Victorian reviewers devoted many pages to new novels, outlining the story in detail and incorporating long extracts.) Among the large number of newspapers and periodicals not represented below, the *Weekly Chronicle* of 23 October, one week after *Jane Eyre*'s publication, found it 'the most extraordinary pro-

duction that has issued from the press for years'. That Charlotte's
success with her first novel owed much to its timing becomes clear
from the comparisons which it provoked. *Jane Eyre*, in other
words, made its dramatic appearance in the grey interval which
separates the years of Jane Austen and Scott from the opening of
the most lively period in the history of the English novel. It could
hardly be called a novel at all, felt the reviewer in the *Era* for
November 1847, so widely did it differ from other modern
fiction. There was 'no high life glorified' nor 'low life elevated to
an enviable state of bliss'; 'all the serious novels of the day lose in
comparison' for in place of their 'morbid excitement' and 'defiance of probability' *Jane Eyre* offered 'the strength of true feeling
. . . and robust common sense'. The *Era*'s list of 'serious' writers is
headed by Bulwer Lytton and G. P. R. James, prolific and once
popular novelists who are now barely names to most of today's
readers. From the 1850s onwards it became increasingly common in criticism to compare the rise of the Victorian novel to the
flowering of Elizabethan drama. The range and variety which
prompted the comparison began to emerge in the three years
following the publication of *Jane Eyre*, for in this brief period
came Thackeray's masterpiece, *Vanity Fair* (1847–8); Trollope's
first novels, *The Macdermots of Ballycoran* (1847) and *The
Kellys and the O'Kellys* (1848); Mrs Gaskell's first novel, *Mary
Barton* (1848); Dickens's *David Copperfield* (1849–50); and
Charles Kingsley's social novels, *Yeast* (1848) and *Alton Locke*
(1850). All the Brontë novels, except *Villette*, belong to this same
short period. Within a decade, these writers, who were by then
household names, were joined by George Eliot, whose major
achievement spans the mid-Victorian years and has its part to play
in the partial eclipse of Charlotte's work from the 1860s onwards.

Charlotte's 'new' quality – namely the observation of everyday
reality heightened by intense feeling, the whole being thrown into
relief by the freshness and immediacy of her autobiographical
narrative – proclaims her affinity with one kind of Romanticism.
Not until 1899, in Mrs Humphry Ward's admirable commentaries on the Brontës for the Haworth Edition of their works

(p. 158), was there to be any close attempt to analyse the Brontës' relationship to the whole movement of European Romanticism, but early reviewers did glance at Byronic elements in Charlotte's work (for example, the *Examiner* on *Shirley*, 3 November 1849) and several linked her with George Sand. The *Dublin University Magazine* for May 1848 found a resemblance between Jane Eyre and George Sand's heroine, Consuelo. G. H. Lewes, in many ways the most interesting of the Brontës' early reviewers, was profoundly impressed by this affinity, and opened one of his many reviews of her novels by declaring, 'In Passion and Power – those noble twins of Genius – Currer Bell has no living rival except George Sand...' (p. 78).

Lewes was representative in his delight in the new writer's individual voice, truth of characterisation, lively descriptive powers and command of a vigorous English style. He was also representative in singling out the 'improbabilities' which marred the 'truth' of her writing. It was to counter this tendency that he recommended to Charlotte a course of Jane Austen's novels, thus provoking from her a lively outburst on Jane Austen's limitations.[11] Lewes was not alone in attempting to strike a balance between Charlotte's weaknesses and strengths. Albany Fonblanque of the *Examiner*, whom Charlotte bracketed with the French critic Eugène Forçade as the most perceptive of her reviewers,[12] tried to explain what was meant by the 'coarseness' which had been so often and so woundingly mentioned. 'We have it in a less degree in *Shirley*,' he said in the *Examiner* for 3 November 1849, 'but here it is. With a most delicate and intense perception of the beautiful, the writer combines a craving for stronger and rougher stimulants. ...' She has, he finds, vigour, truth, reality, but lacks the qualities, including humour, with which 'to soften and relieve the habit of harsh delineation...'.

'Coarseness' was a term which, in effect, meant different things to different reviewers. Fonblanque was thinking in 1849 apparently of the provincial setting, speech and behaviour of Charlotte's Yorkshire characters. For others, it referred to the indecorous presentation of her characters' love affairs, which were conducted in an unusually outspoken manner and in unconventional settings. It was sufficiently disconcerting to find a heroine who was 'plain, poor and little' but still passionate; it was still more unsettling to find her living under the same roof with Mr Rochester, himself no polished hero of conventional romance, in a situation which invited misunderstanding.

For others again, 'coarseness' had to do with the sardonic handling of such 'upper class' characters as Blanche Ingram and her mother (Charlotte was particularly vulnerable here for she lacked a light hand with satire). For still others, 'coarseness' was associated with the manner in which she dealt with Church matters and religion, whether she was castigating the curates in *Shirley,* or shuddering away from 'Romanism' in *Villette.*

The quality recognised by the *Christian Remembrancer* in its review of *Jane Eyre* (p. 57) perhaps best explains the misgivings behind this kind of censure. 'Currer Bell', the reviewer felt, was 'a good hater'; 'moral Jacobinism burns in every page', and 'unjust, unjust is the burden of every reflection upon the things and powers that be'. This impassioned individualism so similar in feeling though not in belief to that 'proud, rugged, intellectual republicanism . . . bidding cant and lies be still', for which Froude in 1849 felt that the 'clergy gentlemen and the Church turned respectable could be no match'[13] – was, on the other hand, the quality most admired by Charlotte's favoured critic, Eugène Forçade (p. 61).

The same quality probably helped to provoke the special animosity animating the few strongly hostile attacks on *Jane Eyre,* notably Elizabeth Rigby's snobbish piece in the *Quarterly Review* (p. 67), which, while expressing admiration for scenes of truly tragic passion, condemned the heroine's 'vulgarity'. Mr Rochester's coarseness and brutality, the author's ignorance of fashionable dress and behaviour, and the 'anti-Christian' nature of the book as a whole. If the author was female, then she must have 'for some sufficient reason long forfeited the society of her own sex', and if male, then the writer was no artist (the peculiar logic was immediately pounced upon by the deeply offended

Charlotte). Lockhart, as editor of the *Quarterly* and an enthusiast for the unknown 'Bells' (a copy of whose *Poems* he had received in 1847), had passed on to Elizabeth Rigby with the review assignment the rumour that the 'brothers' were Lancashire weavers,[14] one of the bizarre speculations then current, and it would appear that this had had its effect.

Elizabeth Rigby's review appeared towards the close of 1848, more than a year after *Jane Eyre*'s publication, and provided talking points in further notices of the same book, which were, remarkably, still coming out in 1849, and also for the first reviews of *Shirley* towards the end of that year. The points about 'vulgarity' and lack of principle were usually taken up only to be dismissed or else placed in a reasonable critical context. But it could not be denied that 'the Bells' presented problems, a fact which became even more apparent after 'Acton', whose *Agnes Grey* had seemed reassuringly normal in comparison with its astonishing companion, *Wuthering Heights,* had in the summer of 1848 followed up her first novel with *The Tenant of Wildfell Hall,* an outspoken story about the miseries attending profligacy and alcoholism.

The Early Reception of Villette
By the time *Villette* appeared in 1853, the mystery about 'the Bells' was solved, and almost everyone now knew who 'Currer Bell' was and what her life had been. Charlotte had herself revealed in 1850 the surprising fact that the 'brothers' who had been taken to task so often for their 'coarseness', 'brutality' and want of principle, were in fact three retiring young women who had been brought up in a remote country parsonage and two of whom were now dead, cut off in the early prime of life by the fatal family disease. Since then she had ventured a little into society, visited London, and become friendly with some leading literary figures, among them the happier and healthier Elizabeth Gaskell, whose quick sympathies immediately drew her to this lonely gifted woman. Her personal reputation, then, helped to create a sympathetic atmosphere for the arrival of her new work. It was also the case that she had less to lose with her third novel than with her second,

for the successor to a best-selling first book almost inevitably courts reactions of disappointment.

With the appearance of *Villette* most doubts were removed. Even when the author (who still signed herself 'Currer Bell') was taken to task for the prevailing sombreness of Lucy's story, it was in sorrow rather than anger, and with exhortations not to yield to unrelieved gloom. Apart from two reviews, both written by women and in their various ways as upsetting as the *Quarterly*'s review of *Jane Eyre*, there was little serious condemnation. 'Coarseness' was barely mentioned, and pleasure was taken in Charlotte's return to her absorbing autobiographical method, her sustained feeling for persons and places, and the welcome elevation of her general moral tone. The reality of the Brussels scenes was universally admired and the characters surrounding Lucy were each singled out as vital, marvellously observed and 'true', from Paulina as a child (who was warmly praised) to Ginevra Fanshawe and the formidable Madame Beck. Above all, everyone was intrigued, and many captivated, by the vivacious presentation of the eccentric and irascible little hero, Paul Emanuel. Even the two reviews by women proclaimed the book's skill and power, and one of them found that from the somewhat ambiguous materials which went to the making of Mr Rochester had evolved at last a hero who was 'even loveable'.

The two reviews in question were Harriet Martineau's in the *Daily News* and Anne Mozley's in the *Christian Remembrancer* (pp. 75, 105). Both were unsigned, but Charlotte recognised Harriet's authorship :

'Extremes meet', says the proverb . . . Miss Martineau finds with *Villette* nearly the same fault as the *Puseyites* – She accuses me with attacking Popery 'with virulence' – of going out of my way to assault it 'passionately'. In other respects she has shown . . . a spirit . . . strangely and unexpectedly acrimonious . . . [15]

Harriet was a staunch freethinker. Her 'Puseyite' opposite number in this case was Anne Mozley, sister of John Mozley, editor of the *Christian Remembrancer*. In her long and frequently admiring article, Anne Mozley recalled the periodical's earlier attack on the 'outrages on decorum' in *Jane Eyre*, found some improvements in this respect in *Villette*, but deplored the narrowness displayed in the author's views on 'Romanism'. She ended by attacking the author's support for feminine independence, for it is in the 'daily round of simple duties and pure pleasures' that 'true happiness and satisfaction lie'. From her diametrically opposite point of view, Harriet also attacked Charlotte's view of women. She disliked the novel's overwhelming 'subjective misery' and the obsessive concern of the female characters with the need for love – women, she argued, do have other interests, and the failure to allow for this is a limiting weakness in an otherwise splendid, even Balzacian, tale.

Charlotte could not readily forgive either reviewer. She wrote a pained letter to the editor of the *Christian Remembancer*[16] and felt betrayed by Harriet, with whom – different as they were in temperament and outlook – she had been friendly since December 1849, and to whom she had gone for advice when bewildered by repeated references to the indelicate behaviour of her heroes and heroines. 'She could not make it out at all', Harriet records, 'and wished that I could explain it' :

... I had not seen that sort of criticism then ... but I had heard *Jane Eyre* called 'coarse'. I told her that love was treated with unusual breadth, and that the kind of intercourse was uncommon, and uncommonly described, but that I did *not* consider the book a coarse one ... [17]

Later Charlotte again begged Harriet to tell her the truth about *Villette*. Harriet did so, in a private letter as well as in her review. The 'truth' was too much for Charlotte, who broke off the correspondence and put an end to the friendship.

1857–1899

There are two striking features in the development of the Brontës' critical reputation during the later part of the nineteenth century. One is the movement of feeling which gradually swept Charlotte's novels from the centre of the stage to place there instead the handful of poems and the single novel, *Wuthering Heights,* left behind by her sister Emily. The other is the growth of interest in 'the Brontë story', as distinct from interest in the Brontës' literary achievement, an interest which then and since has often done the family a disservice by drawing attention away from their quality as writers in order to concentrate on the everyday details of their lives. Both these tendencies were firmly established by the 1890s, when Emily's primacy for so many Brontëans was acknowledged by Clement Shorter and Mrs Humphry Ward, the two most distinguished late-Victorian students of the Brontës, and when the personal interest taken in the three sisters culminated in the founding of the Brontë Society. Both tendencies are first manifest in the 1850s, when the identity of 'the Bells' became known and the still impenetrable mystery surrounding Emily and her strange work – which Mrs Gaskell's *Life* did little more than Charlotte's Biographical Notice to dispel – fired the enthusiasm of leading writers who responded ardently to her poetic power, among them Matthew Arnold, D. G. Rossetti, G. H. Lewes and Swinburne (his allegiance to both sisters dated from long before his celebrated essays of 1877 and 1883). But until the 1870s, Charlotte was still always discussed at greater length than either of her sisters.

The warmth of feeling felt for Charlotte after 1850 was renewed at her death in 1855, when the obituaries expressed a universal sense of personal loss (the ruptured friendship did not prevent Harriet Martineau from writing one of the leading tributes) and was revived again two years later with the appearance of Mrs Gaskell's masterly commemoration of her friend in *The Life of Charlotte Brontë.* The prestige of both the biographer and her subject ensured a wide and well-informed reception for Mrs Gaskell's work, which was reviewed as extensively as *Jane Eyre* had been ten years earlier. The biographical emphasis in all the reviews was, naturally, pronounced, but many of the major periodicals – as we can see from the contributions to *Fraser's Magazine, Blackwood's Magazine* and the *National Review* – rose to the occasion by securing reviews from prominent men of letters, who took the opportunity to attempt, for the first time, some evaluation of the

Brontës' total literary achievement. These critics were no longer confused by the mystery of 'the Bells'. They could look at their work as a whole instead of piecemeal – even *The Professor* came out in time to be included in their reappraisals and to be compared with *Villette*, on which it shed new light. Again, Mrs Gaskell's skill in evoking the Brontës' Yorkshire setting quickened their sense of the 'wilder' world in which Charlotte and her sisters had grown up and enabled them to dispose of the narrower moral issues raised in the old controversies about 'coarseness' and 'immorality'.

At the same time, this fresh critical perspective encouraged some of the commentators, among them John Skelton, W. C. Roscoe and E. S. Dallas (pp. 123, 129, 131), to consider the artistic risks incurred by the narrow range of tone and subject-matter which is so closely bound up with the Brontës' 'passion and power'. The close influence of environment and personal experience upon the Brontës' work, an influence which Mrs Gaskell's study had shown to be profoundly important, did not, it it true, prevent these critics from recognising, in Skelton's words, that 'the experience can never entirely explain the work'. But they went further than Charlotte's enthusiastic French critic, Émile Montégut, for whom the direct reflection of Charlotte's personal life in *Jane Eyre* and *Villette* was one source of her strength in these novels. Such '*amour de soi*', which later critics were to identify as the most important expression of the Brontës' individual romantic temper,[18] was associated with powerful intensity of feeling, but it could also be held to account for certain weaknesses, notably the lack of universality in their portrayals of life, and, in Charlotte's case, the substitution in her characterisations of meticulous personal observation for sympathetic intuition. This absence of 'negative capability' is a quality noticed by W. C. Roscoe (pp. 28, 30, 130–1), who felt that while character 'is her forte', she 'never fully comprehends it', and that even in her liveliest figures, not excluding Jane Eyre and Paul Emanuel, there is a certain dislocation and a general want of progression and development.

Some decline of interest in the Brontës inevitably took place in the decade following these reassessments, for attention was drawn in the 1860s to major new literary events, especially the prestigious opening of George Eliot's career as a novelist. Mrs Oliphant pointed out in 'The Literature of the Last Fifty Years', a Jubilee article for *Blackwood's Magazine* of January 1887, that another woman than Charlotte had been the first 'to attain the highest place in literature. The position of George Eliot is unique'. Mrs Oliphant's other pronouncements on this occasion were less accurate. Charlotte's 'impassioned revelation of feminine distresses', she thought, had won her merely a temporary fame, while Anne and Emily (the author of 'an extraordinary and feverish romance') probably owed their 'former' reputations chiefly to Mrs Gaskell, 'herself also worthy of note as a novelist'. They all belonged, 'beginning and end to the Victorian period . . . when society was purer and manners better', and, since that age had gone beyond recall, the only places where one could 'bring oneself once more under the powerful spell of Lucy Snowe and Jane Eyre' were private libraries and 'the old-fashioned circulating libraries of our youth'

Mrs Oliphant notwithstanding, interest in Charlotte and her sisters had been gathering fresh strength in the 1870s and 1880s. Even in the 1860s, the study by 'Camille Selden', *L'Esprit des femmes de notre temps* (1865), which contains 'Charlotte Brontë et la vie morale en Angleterre', was reviewed at length in the *Catholic Herald*; Harper's *New Monthly Magazine* carried in 1863 a tribute to 'Charlotte Brontë's Lucy Snow'; and Alexander Smith, in his 'Novels and Novelists of the Day', for the *North British Review* of February 1863, was representative in using Charlotte as a measure of comparison when discussing George Eliot, who had

. . . less than Charlotte Brontë of lyrical impulse and impetuosity; – fewer of those unexpected passionate and intense sentences . . . which readers of *Jane Eyre* and *Villette* know so well – she has quite as much passion, only . . . in equally diffused heat rather than sparkles of fire . . .

Mrs Oliphant herself, in *Blackwood's Magazine* for November
1867, had helped to keep Charlotte in the public mind by presenting her once more (cp. p. 117) as the originator of a new kind of
heroine, whose debased descendants now excitedly awaited the
heroes' 'flesh and muscles . . . strong arms . . . and warm breath' in
the sensational novels of Annie Thomas, Rhoda Broughton and
'Ouida'.

But the coming-of-age of criticism of Charlotte dates from the
response in 1877 to Thomas Wemyss Reid's short biographical
study, *Charlotte Brontë*, which breaks little new ground in itself.
It is a sign of the times that his principal departure from Mrs
Gaskell lies in his substantial celebration of Emily as an incompar-
ably gifted writer. But his book touched off two sharply contrasted
essays, which along with Mrs Ward's prefaces and a handful of
twentieth-century essays, are among the *loci classici* of studies of
Charlotte. The first is Swinburne's monograph, *A Note on
Charlotte Brontë* (1877), and the second, Leslie Stephen's reply,
'Charlotte Brontë', published in the *Cornhill Magazine* for December 1877 and reprinted in 1879 in the third edition of his *Hours
in a Library* (pp. 144, 148).

Swinburne was delighted by Reid's attentiveness to both Charlotte and Emily, but the tone of his essay was affected by what he
regarded as the unspeakably inadequate praise for Charlotte
offered by Reid's reviewer in the *Spectator*. In his own verbose
eulogy (his projected 'Note' expanded uncontrollably into a short
book) he prophesied that Charlotte would survive all the 'female
immortals' of the hour and would be read '. . . when even Daniel
Deronda has gone the way of all waxworks, and even Miss
Broughton no longer cometh up as a flower, and even Mrs
Oliphant is at length cut down like the grass . . .'. For him, her
quality of 'genius' outshines even George Eliot's intellectual distinction, and each word and action of her characters compels
absolute acceptance and conviction of its truth, a view over which
W. C. Roscoe, for example, would have demurred. It was this
unusual exaltation of Charlotte at the expense of George Eliot
– whose 'exceptional intellectual power' was exactly what made

the cultivated reader set her above every other contemporary novelist – that seemed so extraordinary to Leslie Stephen. His cool, measured, penetrating reply, which was based on the view that 'if criticism cannot boast of being a science, it ought to aim at something like a scientific basis', separates Charlotte's strengths from her weaknesses. The latter include her want of general ideas, the lack of universality in her major figures, including Paul Emanuel, whose success Swinburne proclaims but does not analyse (Stephen in any case admired *Villette* less than *Jane Eyre*), and, above all, the crucial flaw in her processes of thinking and feeling, which led her to protest against conventionality while adhering to society's conventions. These weaknesses ensure – as George Smith found in 1873 (p. 141) and Peter Bayne in 1881 – that she cannot be placed in the highest rank. She is foremost among those who have suffered unresolved emotional conflicts, have felt passionately 'the necessity of consolation', and have drawn their readers to use them by their powerful expression of human distress.

If we disregard the coolness of temper which made it difficult for Leslie Stephen to appreciate Emily's reflection of 'the mood of pure passion', his essay can stand as one of the most illuminating nineteenth-century statements about Charlotte to appear before Mrs Humphry Ward's. His judgements about Emily were not usually shared by his successors in the 1880s, when the growing concern with her, strongly reflected in Peter Bayne's chapters about the Brontës in his *Two Great Englishwomen* (1881),[19] reached a climax in 1883 with Mary Robinson's *Emily Brontë,* the first full-length biography. This prompted Swinburne's second major Brontë essay, his seminal 'Emily Brontë' written as a review of Mary Robinson's book for the *Athenæum* of 16 June 1883. By 1896, Clement Shorter was able to write of Emily as 'the sphinx of our literature' whose 'cult . . . started with Mr Sidney Dobell (p. 115) . . . found poetic expression in Mr Matthew Arnold's fine lines on her and culminated in an enthusiastic eulogy of Mr Swinburne who placed her in the very forefront of English women of genius.'[20]

The whole movement of feeling, in which the merits of Char-

lotte and Emily were more and more searchingly weighed and
fell more and more in favour of Emily, finds its ultimate nineteenth-century expression in Mrs Ward's commentaries for the
Haworth Edition of the Brontës' work which came out, in seven
volumes, in 1899–1900, as *The Life and Works of Charlotte
Brontë and her Sisters* (p. 164). Mary Ward undertook the task
at the request of Charlotte's publisher, George Smith. Her breadth
and sense of proportion (which would have pleased her uncle,
Matthew Arnold), her familiarity with French, German and even
Russian literature, and her own feeling for the novelist's processes
of recreating actual experience, brought her as close as anyone has
come to understanding the quality of the Brontë sisters' artistic
achievement and their particular brand of romanticism. She
understood Charlotte well, appreciating the effects on her work
of her hereditary Celtic strain, her Yorkshire Pennine environment
and her response to contemporary French literature. She notes the
enormous weight of contemporary interest in 'the Brontë story'
and recognises that while the remarkable biographical facts do
not alone account for the sisters' current fame, it is still true that
the most compelling elements in their work derive from the powerful impress of their own personality – a personality in Charlotte's
case, fresh, strong, 'surprising' and, in the end, compensating for
all her improbabilities, weaknesses and absurdities. She recognises
in both Charlotte and Emily, in spite of the dithyrambs and
amateurish 'lack of literary reticence' of the one, and the occasional crudities of the other, a 'similar *fonds* of stern and simple
realism' and a 'similar faculty of observation at once shrewd and
passionate'; and she finds in the end that the differences between
them are 'almost wholly in Emily's favour'.

Charlotte Brontë in the Twentieth Century
There is an obvious continuity of critical opinion linking Mrs
Ward's view of Charlotte's work with assessments of her achieve-
ment in the twentieth century. For one thing, the movement of
allegiance away from 'Charlotte's more simple certainties to
Emily's more wild and puzzling questions'[21] has continued

throughout most of the period, as a glance at any serious biblio-
graphical survey will show. Three of the six columns of small print
in the section devoted to the Brontës in the *Cambridge Bibliography of English Literature* (Nineteenth Century, 1969 edition)
cover most of the studies which have appeared since 1940. These
columns indicate the intense activity in Brontë studies that has
taken place even since Mrs Ward wrote in 1899 of the vast number of books which had recently appeared about the Brontës' life
and work.[22] The same columns also show that at least until the
mid-1950s the majority of these modern studies have been devoted
to Emily, and that it is only since then that any serious attempts
have been made to restore Charlotte to a position of primacy
among the three sisters. Even so, the amount of material is still
considerable and this attempt to survey the course of modern
critical opinion about Charlotte must be content to indicate the
broader movements and single out some of the principal commentators associated with them.

The most influential of the Brontës' modern critics in confirming Mrs Ward's view of their relative achievements is Lord David
Cecil in the chapters, 'Charlotte Brontë' (p. 167) and 'Emily
Brontë', included in his *Early Victorian Novelists* (1934). Like Mrs
Ward, he sees that Charlotte's novels are crippled by weaknesses
which in any writer less passionate would be fatally damaging,
that they are transfigured by this passionate intensity of feeling,
and that their undoubted power is in the end a matter of the
inescapable impress of her own personality. Again like Mrs Ward,
he has no doubt that Emily is the greater writer.

As with so many commentaries on the Brontës since the later
nineteenth century, the shadow more or less inadvertently cast
upon Charlotte in David Cecil's study owes much to the nature
and quality of what is said about Emily. Original as she was in
her time, Charlotte lacks the arresting unconventionality which
readers of *Wuthering Heights* have found imaginatively stimulat-
ing. Emily's single novel has prompted more detailed exegesis –
too much of it, one feels now – than all Charlotte's novels put
together. There has been no continuous and absorbing debate

B

about the 'correct' reading of any of her books as there has been
about *Wuthering Heights*.[23] The issue most canvassed in the 1950s,
when fresh attempts to assess Charlotte's work began to accumulate, concerns the relative merits of *Jane Eyre* and *Villette,* which
were still universally agreed to represent her most successful
achievement. Even when ostensibly devoted to one novel, many
essays tend to review her whole development from *The Professor*
to *Villette.* Towards the end of the decade, some of the new
apologias are based on the claim that to be properly appreciated
Charlotte's novels must be read in the same way as *Wuthering
Heights,* that is, as 'poetic' or 'symbolic' novels, illustrating the
imaginative organisation and structural complexity which have
encouraged many of Emily's readers to refer in the same breath
to her novel and to the poetic dramas of Webster and Shakespeare.
The singular inappropriateness of this approach to Charlotte's
work is D. W. Crompton's theme in his note, 'The New Criticism :
A Caveat' (p. 211). The road towards this 'new criticism' of Charlotte had been indicated some ten years earlier in M. H. Scargill's
influential 'All Passion Spent; A Revaluation of *Jane Eyre*' (p.
175), which takes the extreme view that Charlotte in this novel
had broken completely with naturalistic tradition : 'The conventions have become symbols : the fictional lover has become The
Lover; the mad woman of the Gothic novel has been put to
allegorical use', and the novel as a whole records 'an intense spiritual experience' comparable with the 'ordeal of purgation in *King
Lear*'.

Happily this critic's concern with abstractions does not prevent
him from noticing Charlotte's vivid particularity in individual
episodes. Her interplay of reason and feeling, the source of this
kind of strength, is investigated at some length by R. B. Heilman
in his now well known 'Charlotte Brontë's "New" Gothic' of 1958
(p. 195), later supplemented by 'Charlotte Brontë, Reason and
the Moon' (*Nineteenth Century Fiction,* 1960). For Mr Heilman,
Charlotte, by her tart humour and dry factuality, deliberately
reduces what he calls the 'primitive Gothic' elements in her work,
namely those which seek 'a relatively simple thrill or momentary

intensity of feeling'. At the same time, she finds her own way of achieving the ends served by this 'primitive' Gothicism, for example by the use of frightening symbolic dreams, surrealistic descriptive effects and the explorations of new regions of feeling in the relations between men and women. In the essay represented below, these qualities are traced from *The Professor* to *Villette*, the latter turning out to be the novel most richly 'saturated' with both the 'old' Gothic and the 'new'. In his other essay, Mr Heilman explores Charlotte's mingling of reason and intuition in *Jane Eyre* through her use of moon imagery; according to Charles Burkhart's supplementary piece for the same periodical, 'Another Key Word for *Jane Eyre*' (*Nineteenth Century Fiction*, 1961), her use of the word 'Nature' acts as an additional guide to this interplay.

In these various inquiries into Charlotte's attempt to discipline her indulgence of romantic feeling, interest oscillates between *Jane Eyre* and *Villette*, with *Villette* exercising the stronger pull for many critics in the later 1950s and the 1960s. Mrs Tillotson in her *Novels of the Eighteen-Forties* (1954), concentrates on *Jane Eyre* (p. 183) because she is interested in the historical circumstances which contributed to Charlotte's success as well as in the conflict in her work between 'realism' and 'romance'. Mrs Tillotson situates *Jane Eyre* firmly in its decade, where, she finds, circumstances were right for the book to get off to a flying start. It would have been too 'low' for 1837, too outspoken for 1857 (though the championing of Charlotte against charges of 'coarseness' at this time seems not to fit this part of her thesis), and, if 'fresh', had no more novelty than was welcome at the time. Its perennial appeal is partly due to Charlotte's technical skills, especially her handling of the first-person narrative. It is also due to the self-discipline first practised by Charlotte in *The Professor*, whose conscientious down-to-earth truthfulness and greyness were necessary first stages in the journey from her Angrian fantasies towards a more ordered and complex achievement.

The latter argument is taken up and expanded, this time with the emphasis on *Villette*, in R. A. Colby's 'Villette and the Life of

the Mind' (*PMLA*, 1960), another important contribution to
Brontë studies. Here Charlotte is presented as a writer in whom
the romantic imagination at last, in her third novel, 'reconciles
itself to real life'. *Villette* is thus very highly regarded, and the
various elements making for its success are seen to include the
mingling of the strains of English and French romanticism with
mid-Victorian realism, a diagnosis with which Mrs Ward would
largely have agreed. The argument as a whole is designed to shed
light both on Charlotte's artistic development and on *Villette's*
place in the general evolution of the English novel.

Villette, again is selected by Roy Pascal, along with Lawrence's *Sons and Lovers* and Joyce's *A Portrait of the Artist as a
Young Man*, to illustrate his arguments about the fictionalising of
personal experience (p. 205), a subject of peculiar interest for
students of the Victorian novel and one which has not yet, perhaps, received as much attention as it deserves. Mr Pascal joins
those who see in *Villette* the final stage in Charlotte's progress to
maturity, finding that she now uses her heroine 'to get nearer to
the truth about her own character', whereas in *The Professor* she
had 'sidled away' from the pressing emotional problems associated
with her Brussels teacher M. Heger.

A more central position is taken in Norman Sherry's short but
pithy *The Brontës: Charlotte and Emily* (1969), in which the
author excludes Anne from consideration, finds Emily unquestionably the most original of the sisters, and distinguishes Charlotte for the intensity with which she dramatises individual
passion, her weaknesses becoming apparent when in *The Professor*
and *Shirley* she deliberately subdued this concern to divide the
honours with public or social themes. The family achievement is,
again, Mrs Ewbank's preoccupation in *Their Proper Sphere*
(1966), which has the sub-title 'A study of the Brontë Sisters as
Early-Victorian Female Novelists'. In keeping with this brief, the
author points to thematic parallels in novels by early nineteenth-
century women writers, especially those concerned with governesses. The study offers alert descriptive analysis of the
novels, rather than evaluation of their relative merits, and it is
clear regarding Charlotte's preoccupation with the 'master-

pupil' relationship which impressed even early readers as an important component in her treatment of the passionate relationships between her men and women. The literary context explored in this study is extended by R. A. Colby in his second major essay on *Villette*, 'Lucy Snowe and the Good Governess' (p. 229), which forms part of his book, *Fiction with a Purpose* (1967). Mr Colby's survey of the religious, political and 'educational' climate of opinion in the late 1840s and early 1850s adds considerably to the thorough investigations which have already been made into the literary and biographical background of Charlotte's work.

Among those critics who have attempted to redress the balance of interest in this kind of background material by concentrating as far as possible on a purely critical approach, the two best known are R. B. Martin and Mrs Wendy Craik, writers who share what is nowadays an unusual belief in the primacy of Charlotte over her sister Emily. Mr Martin in *Accents of Persuasion* (1966) omits all biographical material and steadily examines each of Charlotte's novels in turn, exploring her major themes, her success in giving them 'artistic life', and 'the self-reliant Protestant ethic that so dominated her life'. His principal conclusions emphasise the maturing in each novel of the principal character, who eventually reaches the point where reason and passion can be reconciled, the technical importance for Charlotte of sustaining a consistent 'point of view', and the major success of *Villette*, which he sees as a clear-eyed 'autumnal' novel of acceptance and resignation. Mrs Craik, in *The Brontë Novels* (1968), again eschews biographical material as far as possible, and offers a closely argued revaluation of the work of the three sisters, which, regretfully, cannot be justly reproduced in the space available here. Her views about Anne's novels are warmer than those of many of her predecessors and she admires Emily's originality in *Wuthering Heights*, but she has no doubts about Charlotte's equal artistic importance and regards her as a major novelist in her own right. She also takes an independent line over the relative merits of *Jane Eyre* and *Villette* : the scope of the latter 'breaks new ground for the novel', but 'one must conclude that it is not so perfect a whole as *Jane Eyre* . . . it takes in less than the full range of human experience . . . much has been lost . . . the faults . . . are not loss of skill, but loss of power . . .'.

It is worth adding in conclusion that whatever the risks of over-emphasising the autobiographical sources of the work of Charlotte and her sisters, such sources cannot, in the case of these strongly personal writers, be lightly overlooked. The writers who have done most to bring together all the biographical facts about them in this century are Winifred Gérin (see Bibliography), who has produced detailed biographies of all the Brontë sisters, and Phyllis Bentley, herself a Yorkshire woman and a lifelong Brontëan, who has vividly evoked the atmosphere of the Brontës' Yorkshire Pennine home in the most recent of her many studies, *The Brontës and their World* (1969), a splendid picture book, containing a useful biographical commentary, which brings before us some of the central visual images which helped to stimulate their creative imagination.

NOTES

1. Letter of 4 July 1834 (*LL* I 122).
2. For F. E. Ratchford's study of these fantasies see Bibliography, p. 244.
3. Letter to Aylott and Jones, 6 April 1846 (*LL* II 87).
4. Letter to George Smith, 5 February 1851 (*LL* III 206).
5. William Smith Williams (1800–75), the mild-mannered older man whom George Smith had recently brought into the firm, had been involved in literary affairs since his days as an apprentice with Keats's publishers, Taylor and Hessey. He possessed considerable literary discernment, was active in promoting *Jane Eyre* once it was out, shrewdly singling out recipients of presentation copies from among prominent literary personalities (including Thackeray and G. H. Lewes), and kept up a correspondence with Charlotte throughout 1847–53. He thus stimulated most of her exclusively 'literary' letters and her lively running commentary on her own critics and reviewers.

6. Mrs Gaskell's *Life of Charlotte Brontë* (1857), chap. 16 (Haworth Edition, 327–8).

7. That is to say during her short stay in Manchester in 1846; she was attending her father, who required treatment for cataract of the eye, and she began writing the first chapter in their lodgings while he lay upstairs recovering from the operation.

8. *LL* iii 206.

9. Mrs Gaskell's *Letters,* ed. J. A. V. Chapple and Arthur Pollard (1966), pp. 410, 417.

10. See Charlotte's letter to Margaret Wooler, '. . . the majority of the reviews have been favourable . . . there is a minority . . . which views the work with no favourable eye. Currer Bell's remarks on Romanism have drawn on him the condign displeasure of the High Church Party – which displeasure has been unequivocally expressed through their principal organs the *Guardian,* the *English Churchman* and the *Christian Remembrancer'* (*LL* iv 58).

11. See her letters to G. H. Lewes of 12 and 18 January 1848 (*LL* ii 178–81).

12. See below, pp. 52, 67.

13. J. A. Froude, *The Nemesis of Faith* (1849) 153.

14. C. K. Shorter, *Charlotte Brontë and her Circle* (1896) p. 349.

15. Letter to Margaret Wooler, 14 April 1853 (*LL* iv 58).

16. Dated 18 July 1853 (*LL* iv 79; a fuller version appears in the *Christian Remembrancer*'s review of Mrs Gaskell's *Life* in the summer of 1857).

17. First printed in Mrs Gaskell's *Life,* chap. 26 (Haworth Edition, pp. 595–8), reproduced *LL* iv 43.

18. For example, Mrs Humphry Ward in her preface to the Haworth Edition of *Jane Eyre* and Jacques Blondel in his detailed study, *Emily Brontë: expérience spirituelle et création poétique* (Paris, 1956).

19. Peter Bayne (1830–96), journalist and critic, had long been an enthusiast for the Brontës. His study of 1881 (which ostensibly deals exclusively with Charlotte Brontë and Elizabeth Barrett Browning) is in effect an expansion of his already elaborately detailed essay, 'Ellis, Acton and Currer Bell' (*Essays in Biography and Criticism,* 1857); he was especially fascinated by Emily, whose work he found as troubling as it was attractive.

20. Clement Shorter, *Charlotte Brontë and her Circle* (1896), pp. 145–6.

21. See Judith O'Neill, *Critics on Charlotte and Emily Brontë* (1968), p. 7.

22. See her Introduction to *Jane Eyre*: 'Judging by the books that have been written and read in recent years, by the common verdict as to the Brontë sisters, their story, and their work, which prevails, almost without exception, in the literary criticism of the present day; by the tone of personal tenderness, even of passionate homage, in which many writers speak of Charlotte and of Emily; and by the increasing recognition which their books have obtained abroad, one may say that the name and memory of the Brontës were never more alive than now . . . ' (Haworth Edition, p. x).

23. Some attempt is made to trace the ins and outs of this debate in the present editor's *Wuthering Heights: Casebook* (1970).

PART ONE

Early Opinions of *Jane Eyre* and *Villette*

1. THE EARLY RECEPTION OF
JANE EYRE (1847–1848)

w. m. thackeray: 'Exceedingly moved and pleased by *Jane Eyre*'

I wish you had not sent me *Jane Eyre*. It interested me so much that I have lost (or won if you like) a whole day in reading it at the busiest period with the printers I know waiting for copy. Who the author can be I can't guess, if a woman she knows her language better than most ladies do, or has had a 'classical' education. It is a fine book, though, the man and woman capital, the style very generous and upright so to speak. I thought it was Kinglake[1] for some time. The plot of the story is one with which I am familiar.[2] Some of the love passages made me cry, to the astonishment of John, who came in with the coals. St John the Missionary is a failure I think, but a good failure, there are parts excellent. I don't know why I tell you this but that I have been exceedingly moved and pleased by *Jane Eyre*. It is a woman's writing, but whose? Give my respects and thanks to the author, whose novel is the first English one (and the French are only romances now) that I've been able to read for many a day...

source: Letter to W. S. Williams, 23 October 1847.

NOTES

For Thackeray's later views about Charlotte's work, see his comments on *Villette*, p. 93 below. For Charlotte's enthusiasm for Thackeray, their meetings in 1849 and 1851 and George Smith's gift to her in 1853 of a portrait of Thackeray see Mrs Gaskell's *Life*, chapters 18–19, 23–4, 26.

1. Presumably A. W. Kinglake (1809–91), author of *Eothen* (1844) and the article on 'The Rights of Women' for the *Quarterly Review*, vol. 75 (1845).

2. Thackeray may have been reminded of his own marital tragedy, but see below, p. 45 n., and also the parallel with Mrs Radcliffe's *A Sicilian Romance*, referred to p. 239 below.

H. F. CHORLEY : Preferable 'to philosophy, pedantry, or Puseyite controversy'

There is so much power in this novel as to make us overlook certain eccentricities in the invention, which trench in one or two places on what is improbable, if not unpleasant. Jane Eyre is an orphan thrown upon the protection – or, to speak correctly, the cruelty – of relations living in an out-of-the-way corner of England; who neglect, maltreat, chastise, and personally abuse her. She becomes dogged, revengeful, superstitious : and, at length, after a scene – which we hope is out of nature now that 'the Iron Rule' is overruled and the reign of the tribe Squeers ended,[1] – the child turns upon her persecutors with such precocious power to threaten and alarm that they condemn her to an *oubliette* – sending her out of the house to a so-called charitable institution. There she has again to prove wretchedness, hard fare and misconstruction. The trial, however, is this time not unaccompanied by more gracious influences. Jane Eyre is taught, by example, that patience is nobler than passion; and so far as we can gather from her own confessions, grows up into a plain, self-sustained young woman, with a capital of principle sufficient to regulate those more dangerous gifts which the influences of her childhood had so exasperated. Weary of the monotonous life of a teacher, she advertises for the situation of a governess; and is engaged into an establishment – singular, but not without prototype – to take care of the education of the French ward of a country gentleman; which said girl proves, when called by her right name, to be the child of an opera *danseuse*. The pretty, frivolous little fairy Adèle, with her hereditary taste for dress, coquetry and pantomimic grace, is true to life. Perhaps too – we dare not speak more positively – there is truth in the abrupt, strange clever Mr Rochester; and in the fearless original way in which the strong man and the young governess travel over each other's minds till, in a puzzled and uncomfortable manner enough, they come to a mutual understanding. Neither is the mystery of Thornfield an exaggeration of reality. We, ourselves, know of a large mansion-house in a distant county where, for many years, a miscreant was kept in close confinement, – and his existence, at best, only darkly hinted in the neighbourhood. Some such tale as this was told in a now-forgotten novel – *Sketches of a Seaport Town*. We do not quarrel with the author of *Jane Eyre* for the manner in which he has made the secret explode at a critical juncture of the story. From that point forward, however, we think the heroine too outrageously tried, and too romantically assisted in her difficulties. – until arrives the last moment, at which obstacles fall down like the battlements of *Castle Melodrame* ... No matter, however :– as exciting strong interest, of its old-fashioned kind, *Jane Eyre* deserves high praise, and commendation to the novel-reader who prefers story to philosophy, pedantry, or Puseyite controversy.[2]

SOURCE: *Athenæum*, 23 October 1847.

NOTES

Hugh Fothergill Chorley reviewed widely for the *Athenæum* throughout 1833–68, including reviews of *Jane Eyre* and *Wuthering Heights* (L. A. Marchand, *The Athenæum: A Victorian Mirror of Culture* (1941) p. 192). He was also the author of *Sketches of a Seaport Town* (1834), ruefully referred to in this review as 'a now-forgotten novel'.

1. Alluding to Dickens's *Nicholas Nickleby*, published 1838–9.

2. For a lively account of novels inspired by the Oxford Movement see Margaret Maison's *Search Your Soul, Eustace* (1961).

The Critic: 'a story of surpassing interest'

Our readers will probably remember a volume of poems, the joint production of three brothers Bell, which, albeit little noticed by our critical brethren, took our fancy so much, as seeming to be freighted with promise, that we dedicated several columns to a review,[1] and, as we are informed, thereby contributed mainly to establish for the authors a reputation which we hope was something more than nominal.

The performance before us, by one of the brothers, proves the justice of those anticipations. Currer Bell can write prose as well as poetry. He has fertile invention, great power of description, and a happy faculty for conceiving and sketching character. *Jane Eyre* is a remarkable novel, in all respects very far indeed above the average of those which the literary journalist is doomed every season to peruse, and of which he can say nothing either in praise or condemnation, such is their tame monotony of mediocrity. It is a story of surpassing interest, riveting the attention from the very first chapter, and sustaining it by a copiousness of incident rare indeed in our modern English school of novelists, who seem to make it their endeavour to diffuse the smallest possible number of incidents over the largest possible number of pages. Currer Bell has even gone rather into the opposite extreme, and the incidents of his story are, if anything, too much crowded. But this is a fault which readers, at least, will readily pardon.

Jane Eyre is an orphan, dependent upon relations, who heap upon her all sorts of ill-treatment, until her spirit rebels instead of breaking, and as a punishment, or rather to be rid of her, she is sent to a Charitable Institution, whose wretched fare, exacting tyranny, puritanical pretension, and systematic hypocrisy are painted with a vividness which shews them to be no fiction, but a copy from the life, and it is evident that the author has aimed a well-directed blow at actually existing charities in more than one county, of which this one is a type.

When this sort of a slow torture can be endured no longer, she seeks a situation as governess, and finds it in the house of a gentleman, who entrusts to her care his ward, as she is called, but who is, in fact, the child of an opera-dancer. There is exquisite delicacy in the drawing of this young creature : it is a perfect picture of a little girl, such as we do not know where to parallel in the whole range of literature – so rare it is to find childhood naturally depicted. If the author had done no more than this, he would have entitled himself to a high place among the novelists of his day. The mystery which attaches to Thornfield, so well preserved, is not so happily revealed. The denouement is too abrupt, and there has been an evident effort to bring matters to a conclusion at a point prescribed rather by the printer than by the progress of the story.

This, however, is the consequence of our absurd three volumed system, which compels improper curtailment as well as needless expansion. The character of Mr Rochester is brought out with consummate skill, learned, as in real life, not by telling it but by shewing it, as events display the various features of his mind. Here the mystery is revealed, and the trials and troubles that follow thereupon, and the end of all, so entirely unexpected, and so different from the established usage of novelists, we leave the reader to explore, without marring the pleasure of the search by anticipating the plot. Among the personages most ably drawn are those who figure in the charity-school at Lowood, especially the patron, so pious and so hard-hearted, so firm in faith, so failing in worth, so good a Christian in precept, so bad an one in practice. The heroine also is very well sustained : she is not faultless, but human – a woman and not an angel; on which account we feel all the more interested in her fortunes.

Being such, we can cordially recommend *Jane Eyre* to our readers, as a novel to be placed at the top of the list to be borrowed, and to the circulating-library keeper as one which he may with safety order. It is sure to be in demand.

S O U R C E : *The Critic, Journal of British and Foreign Literature,* 30 October 1847.

N O T E

1. *The Critic,* 4 July 1846, pp. 6–8. The reviewer welcomed the *Poems* and recognised the primacy of Emily's poetic gifts; Charlotte remembered it in 1847 as 'unexpectedly and generously eulogistic' (*LL* II 147–8) and was always pleased by this periodical's reception of her own and her sisters' work.

The Spectator: 'the whole is unnatural'

Essentially, *Jane Eyre, an Autobiography,* has some resemblance to those sculptures of the middle ages in which considerable ability both mechanical and mental was often displayed upon subjects that had no existence in nature, and as far as delicacy was concerned were not pleasing in themselves. There is, indeed, none of their literal impossibilities or grotesqueness – we do not meet the faces of foxes or asses under clerical hoods; neither is there anything of physical grossness. But, with clear conceptions distinctly presented, a metaphysical consistency in the characters and their conduct, and considerable power in the execution, the whole is unnatural, and only critically interesting. There is one fault, too, in *Jane Eyre,* from which the artists of the middle ages were free – too much of artifice. Their mastery of their art was too great to induce them to resort to trick to tell their story. In the fiction edited by Currer Bell there is rather too much of this. Dialogues are carried on to tell the reader something he must know, or to infuse into him some explanations of the writer; persons act not as they would probably act in life, but to enable the author to do a 'bit o' writing'; everything is made to change just in the nick of time; and even the 'Returned Letter Office' suspends its laws that Jane Eyre may carry on her tale with 'effect'.

The fiction belongs to that school where minute anatomy of the mind predominates over incidents; the last being made subordinate to description or the display of character [outlines the 'three acts' of the story : Jane Eyre as an orphan, as governess to Mr Rochester's 'protégé', and as mistress to a private charity school; refers in passing to the 'hardly "proper" conduct between a single man and a maiden in her teens'; and concludes that 'the close is the best-managed part of the book'].

A story which contains nothing beyond itself is a very narrow representation of human life. *Jane Eyre* is this, if we admit it to be true; but its truth is not probable in the principal incidents, and still less in the manner in which the characters influence the incidents so as to produce conduct. There is a low tone of behaviour (rather than of morality) in the book; and, what is worse than all, neither the heroine nor hero attracts sympathy. The reader cannot see anything loveable in Mr Rochester, nor why he should be so deeply in love with Jane Eyre; so that we have intense emotion without cause. The book, however, displays considerable skill in the plan, and great power, but rather shown in the writing than the matter; and this vigour sustains a species of interest to the last.

Although minute and somewhat sordid, the first act of the fiction is the most truthful; especially the scenes at the philanthropic school. There are many parts of greater energy in *Jane Eyre*, but none equal to the following [quotes from chapter 9 the death of Helen Burns].

S O U R C E : *The Spectator,* 6 November 1847.

N O T E

The first cool review. Charlotte feared that 'the way to detraction has been pointed out ... this turn of opinion will not improve the demand for the book' (*LL* II 153, 154). See Introduction, p. 20.

A. W. FONBLANQUE: 'a book of decided power'.

This book has just been sent to us by the publishers. An accident caused the delay, and is responsible for what might else have seemed a tardy notice of the first effort of an original writer. There can be no question but that *Jane Eyre* is a very clever book. Indeed it is a book of decided power. The thoughts are true, sound, and original; and the style, though rude and uncultivated here and there, is resolute, straightforward, and to the purpose. There are faults, which we may advert to presently; but there are also many beauties, and the object and moral of the work is excellent. Without being professedly didactic, the writer's intention (amongst other things) seems to be, to show how intellect and unswerving integrity may win their way, although oppressed by that predominating influence in society which is a mere consequence of the accidents of birth or fortune. There are, it is true, in this autobiography (which though relating to a woman, we do not believe to have been written by a woman), struggles, and throes, and misgivings, such as must necessarily occur in a contest where the advantages are all on one side; but in the end, the honesty, kindness of heart, and perseverance of the heroine, are seen triumphant over every obstacle. We confess that we like an author who throws himself into the front of the battle, as the champion of the weaker party; and when this is followed up by bold and skilful soldiership, we are compelled to yield him our respect.

Whatever faults may be urged against the book, no one can assert that it is weak or vapid. It is anything but a fashionable novel. It has not a Lord Fanny for its hero, nor a Duchess for its pattern of nobility. The scene of action is never in Belgrave or Grosvenor Square ... On the contrary, the heroine is cast amongst the thorns and brambles of life; – an orphan; without money, without beauty, without friends; thrust into a starving charity school; and fighting her way as governess, with few accomplishments. The hero, if so he may be called, is (or becomes) middle-aged, mutilated, blind, stern, and wilful. The sentences are of simple English; and the only fragrance that we encounter is that of the common garden flower, or the odour of Mr Rochester's cigar.

Taken as a novel or history of events, the book is obviously defective; but as an analysis of a single mind, as an elucidation of its progress from childhood to full age, it may claim comparison with any work of the same species. It is not a book to be examined, page by page, with the fictions of Sir Walter Scott or Sir Edward Lytton or Mr Dickens, from which (except in passages of character where the instant impression reminds us often of the power of the latter writer) it differs altogether. It should rather be placed by the side of the autobiographies of Godwin[1] and his successors, and its comparative value may be then reckoned up, without fear or favour. There is less eloquence, or rather there is less rhetoric, and perhaps less of that subtle analysis of the inner human history, than the author of *Fleetwood* and *Mandeville* was in the habit of exhibiting; but there is, at the same time, more graphic power, more earnest human purpose, and a more varied and vivid portraiture of men and things.

The danger, in a book of this kind, is that the author, from an extreme love of his subject, and interest in the investigation of human motives, may pursue his analysis beyond what is consistent with the truth and vitality of his characters . . .

The writer of *Jane Eyre* has in a great measure steered clear of this error (by no means altogether avoiding it), and the book is the better for it. But it is time to introduce the reader a little into the secrets of the story . . .

SOURCE: *The Examiner*, 27 November 1847.

NOTES

Albany William Fonblanque edited the radical *Examiner* (launched 1808 by John and Leigh Hunt) during 1830–47 and continued to con-

tribute reviews after his replacement by John Foster; his reviews
were unsigned but Charlotte knew of his authorship from W. S.
Williams and often mentioned him admiringly in her letters (e.g.
LL II 160, III 37).

1. William Godwin (1756–1836), Shelley's father-in-law, published
The Adventures of Caleb Williams (1794), *St Leon* (1799), *Fleetwood*
(1805) and *Mandeville, a Tale of the Times of Cromwell* (1817).

G. H. LEWES: 'Reality – deep, significant reality – is the great
characteristic of the book.'

... This, indeed, is a book after our own heart; and, if its merits
have not forced it into notice by the time this paper comes before
our readers, let us, in all earnestness, bid them lose not a day in
sending for it. The writer is evidently a woman, and, unless we
are deceived, new in the world of literature. But, man or woman,
young or old, be that as it may, no such book has gladdened our
eyes for a long while. Almost all that we require in a novelist she
has : perception of character, and power of delineating it; pic-
turesqueness; passion; and knowledge of life. The story is not only
of singular interest, naturally evolved, unflagging to the last, but
it fastens itself upon your attention, and will not leave you. The
book closed, the enchantment continues. With the disentangle-
ment of the plot, and the final release of the heroine from her
difficulties, your interest does not cease. You go back again in
memory to the various scenes in which she has figured; you linger
on the way, and muse upon the several incidents in the life which
has just been unrolled before you, affected by them as if they were
the austere instructions drawn from a sorrowing existence, and
not merely the cunning devices of an author's craft. Reality –
deep, significant reality – is the great characteristic of the book.
It is an autobiography, – not, perhaps, in the naked facts and
circumstances, but in the actual suffering and experience. The
form may be changed, and here and there some incidents invented; but the spirit remains such as it was. The machinery of

the story may have been borrowed, but by means of this machinery the authoress is unquestionably setting forth her own experience. This gives the book its charm : it is soul speaking to soul; it is an utterance from the depths of a struggling, suffering, much-enduring spirit : *suspiria de profundis*!

When we see a young writer exhibiting such remarkable power as there is in *Jane Eyre*, it is natural that we should ask, Is this experience drawn from an abundant source, or is it only the artistic mastery over small materials? Because, according as this question is answered, there are two suggestions to be made. Has the author seen much more and felt much more than what is here communicated? Then let new works continue to draw from that rich storehouse. Has the author led a quiet secluded life, uninvolved in the great vortex of the world, undisturbed by varied passions, untried by strange calamities? Then let new works be planned and executed with excessive circumspection; for, unless a novel be built out of real experience, it can have no real success. To have vitality, it must spring from vitality. All the craft in the circulating-library will not make that seem true which is not true – will not affect the reader after his curiosity is satisfied.

It is too often forgotten, that the most ignorant reader is a competent judge of truth in this sense, that he is always powerfully influenced by it, and always feels the absence of it. *Hamlet, Don Quixote, Faust,* marvellous creations as they are, with roots diving deep into the profoundest regions, and with branches rising into the highest altitudes of thought, do, nevertheless, powerfully interest even the foolishest readers. There is a chord in the human breast which vibrates sympathetically whenever it be touched; and no artist need fear that, if he touch it with skill, his skill will be thrown away . . . we often hear professed novel-readers declare, that however stupid, trashy, and absurd the novel, they must finish it, 'to see what becomes of the hero and heroine'! They are compelled to finish; but they never go back to it, never think of it afterwards. Whereas, if to that curiosity about the story there are added scenes which, being transcripts from the book of life, affect the reader as all truth of human nature must affect him, then the

novel rises from the poor level of street-conjuring into the exalted
region of art.

Of this kind is *Jane Eyre*. There are some defects in it – defects
which the excellence of the rest only brings into stronger relief.
There is, indeed, too much melodrama and improbability, which
smack of the circulating library – we allude particularly to the
mad wife and all that relates to her, and to the wanderings of Jane
when she quits Thornfield; yet even those parts are powerfully
executed. But the earlier parts – all those relating to Jane's childhood and her residence at Lowood, with much of the strange love
story – are written with remarkable beauty and truth. The characters are few, and drawn with unusual mastery : even those that
are but sketched – such as Mr Brocklehurst, Miss Temple, Mrs
Fairfax, Rosamond, and Blanche – are sketched with a vividness
which betrays the cunning hand : a few strokes, and the figure
rises before you. Jane herself is a creation. The delicate handling
of this figure alone implies a dramatic genius of no common order.
We never lose sight of her plainness; no effort is made to throw
romance about her – no extraordinary goodness or cleverness
appeals to your admiration; but you admire, you love her, – love
her for the strong will, honest mind, loving heart, and peculiar
but fascinating person. A creature of flesh and blood, with very
fleshly infirmities, and very mortal excellencies; a woman, not a
pattern : that is the Jane Eyre here represented. Mr Rochester is
also well drawn, and from the life; but it is the portrait of a man
drawn by a woman, and is not comparable to the portrait of Jane.
The way in which the authoress contrives to keep our interest in
this imperfect character is a lesson to novelists. St John Rivers,
the missionary, has a touch of the circulating-library, but not
enough to spoil the truth of the delineation; there is both art and
artifice in the handling, and, although true in the main, and
very powerful in parts, one feels a certain misgiving about him :
it is another example of the woman's pencil. Helen Burns is lovely
and lovable; true, we believe, even in her exalted spirituality and
her religious fervour : a character at once eminently ideal and
accurately real.

The story is so simple in its outlines yet so filled out – not spun out – with details, that we shall not do it the injustice of here setting down the mere plot. It is confined to few characters, and is easily, naturally evolved (with exceptions always of those melodramatic incidents before alluded to), carrying the reader on with it to the end. We have spoken of the reality stamped upon almost every part; and that reality is not confined to the characters and incidents, but is also striking in the descriptions of the various aspects of Nature, and of the houses, rooms, and furniture. The pictures stand out distinctly before you : they *are* pictures, and not mere bits of 'fine writing'. The writer is evidently painting by words a picture that she has in her mind, not 'making up' from vague remembrances, and with the consecrated phrases of 'poetical prose'. It would be exceedingly easy to quote many examples, but we will content ourselves with this very brief passage [quotes from chapter 1, 'Folds of scarlet drapery . . . long and lamentable blast'].

Is not that vivid, real, picturesque? It reads like a page out of one's own life and so do many other pages in the book . . . This faculty for objective representation is also united to a strange power of subjective representation . . . we select . . . the punished child shut up in the old bed-room . . . The passage about the looking-glass, towards the close, strikes us as singularly fine [quotes from chapter 2 'The red room . . . I returned to my stool'] . . . .

We have no space to go on quoting charming passages, though our pencil has been freely employed in marking them. We have already given enough to make both the authoress and the reader understand what we mean by our praise. To her we emphatically say, Persevere; keep reality distinctly before you, and paint it as accurately as you can, invention will never equal the effect of truth.

The style of Jane Eyre is peculiar; but, except that she admits too many Scotch or North-country phrases, we have no objection to make to it, and for this reason : although by no means a fine style, it has the capital point of all great styles in being *personal* –

the written speech of an individual, not the artificial language
made up from all sorts of books . . .

s o u r c e : 'Recent Novels, French and English', *Fraser's Magazine*, December 1847.

N O T E

On Lewes and Charlotte Brontë see Introduction, p. 22.

J O H N G I B S O N L O C K H A R T : 'Worth fifty Trollopes, Martineaus, Dickenses and Bulwers'

. . . I have finished the adventures of Miss Jane Eyre, and think
her far the cleverest that has written since Austen and Edgeworth
were in their prime. Worth fifty Trollopes and Martineaus rolled
into one counterpane, with fifty Dickenses and Bulwers to keep
them company; but rather a brazen Miss. The two heroines
exemplify the duty of taking the initiative, and illustrate it under
the opposite cases as to worldly goods of all sorts, except wit. One
is a vast heiress, and beautiful as angels are everywhere but in
modern paintings. She asks a handsome curate, who will none
of her, being resolved on a missionary life in the Far East. The
other is a thin, little, unpretty slip of a governess, who falls in love
with a plain stoutish Mr Burnand, aged twenty years above herself, sits on his knee, lights his cigar for him, asks him flat one fine
evening, and after a concealed mad wife is dead, at last fills that
awful lady's place . . .

s o u r c e : Letter to Mr and Mrs Hope, 29 December 1847, in
Life and Letters of John Gibson Lockhart, ed. Andrew Lang
(1897), II 307–9.

NOTE

John Gibson Lockhart (1794–1854), author of the *Life of Burns* (1828) and the *Life of Scott* (1837–8), edited the *Quarterly Review* 1825–53. He was among those singled out by Charlotte in June 1847 (others were Tennyson, Wordsworth and De Quincey) to receive a presentation copy of *Poems* (1846), of which only two copies had been sold since publication (*LL* II 307–9). His opinion of 'the Bells' – whom he had heard were 'Lancashire weavers' (see Introduction, p. 24) – is more warm-hearted than that of his chosen reviewer of *Jane Eyre* for the *Quarterly* (p. 67, below). 'Trollopes' is a reference to the novelist Frances Trollope (1780–1830), mother of Anthony Trollope (p. 157, below); her books include *The Widow Barnaby* (1838). *The Vicar of Wrexhill* (1837) and *Domestic Manners of the Americans* (1832), a candid record of her visit to America.

Christian Remembrancer: 'Every page burns with moral Jacobinism'

Since the publication of *Grantley Manor*,[1] no novel has created so much sensation as *Jane Eyre*. Indeed, the public taste seems to have outstripped its guides in appreciating the remarkable power which this book displays. For no leading review has yet noticed it, and here we have before us the second edition. The name and sex of the writer are still a mystery. Currer Bell (which by a curious Hibernicism appears in the title-page as the name of a female autobiographer) is a mere *nom de guerre* – perhaps an anagram. However, we, for our part, cannot doubt that the book is written by a female, and, as certain provincialisms indicate, by one from the North of England. Who, indeed, but a woman could have ventured, with the smallest prospect of success, to fill three octavo volumes with the history of a woman's heart? The hand which drew Juliet and Miranda would have shrunk from such a task.

That the book is readable, is to us almost proof enough of the
truth of our hypothesis. But we could accumulate evidences to
the same effect. Mr Rochester, the hero of the story, is as clearly
the vision of a woman's fancy, as the heroine is the image of a
woman's heart. Besides, there are many minor indications of a
familiarity with all the mysteries of female life which no man can
possess, or would dare to counterfeit . . . Yet we cannot wonder
that the hypothesis of a male author should have been started,
or ladies especially should still be rather determined to uphold it.
For a book more feminine, both in its excellence and defects, it
would be hard to find in the annals of female authorship. Throughout there is masculine power, breadth and shrewdness, combined
with masculine hardness, coarseness, and freedom of expression.
Slang is not rare. The humour is frequently produced by a use
of Scripture at which one is rather sorry to have smiled. The love-
scenes glow with a fire as fierce as that of Sappho, and somewhat
more fuliginous. There is an intimate acquaintance with the worst
parts of human nature, a practised sagacity in discovering the
latent ulcer, and a ruthless rigour in exposing it, which must
command our admiration, but are almost startling in one of the
softer sex. *Jane Eyre* professes to be an autobiography, and we
think it is likely that in some essential respects it is so. If the
authoress has not been, like her heroine, an oppressed orphan, a
starved and bullied charity-school girl, and a despised and slighted
governess (and the intensity of feeling which she shows in speaking
of the wrongs of this last class seems to prove that they have been
her own), at all events we fear she is one to whom the world has
not been kind. And, assuredly, never was unkindness more cordially repaid. Never was there a better hater. Every page burns
with moral Jacobinism. 'Unjust, unjust', is the burden of every
reflection upon the things and powers that be. All virtue is but well
masked vice, all religious profession and conduct is but the whiten-
ing of the sepulchre, all self-denial is but deeper selfishness. In
the preface to the second edition, this temper rises to the transcendental pitch. There our authoress is Micaiah, and her generation
Ahab; and the Ramoth Gilead, which is to be the reward of dis-

regarding her denunciations, is looked forward to with at least as much of unction as of sorrow . . .

We select the following extract as an illustration of our remarks [quotes from chapter 21, ' "I am very ill I know . . ." ' to 'Neither of us had dropt a tear'] . . . All the expressions of tenderness and forgiveness, on the part of the injured Jane, are skilfully thrown in so as to set off to the utmost the unconquerable hardness of the dying sinner's heart. They are the pleadings of the good angel, made audible, and rejected to the last. We are compelled to see and acknowledge beyond the possibility of doubt, that Mrs Read dies without remorse, without excuse, and without hope.

The plot is most extravagantly improbable, verging all along upon the supernatural, and at last running fairly into it. All the power is shown and all the interest lies in the characters . . .

The character of Mr Rochester, the hero, the lover, and eventually the husband, of Jane Eyre, we have already noticed as being, to our minds, the characteristic production of a female pen. Not an Adonis, but a Hercules in mind and body, with a frame of adamant, a brow of thunder and a lightning eye, a look and voice of command, all-knowing and all-discerning, fierce in love and hatred, rough in manner, rude in courtship, with a shade of Byronic gloom and appetising mystery – add to this that when loved he is past middle age, and when wedded he is blind and fire-scarred, and you have such an Acis as no male writer would have given his Galatea, and yet what commands itself as a true embodiment of the visions of a female imagination. The subordinate characters almost all show proportionate power. Mr Brocklehurst, the patron and bashaw of Lowood, a female orphan school, in which he practises self-denial, alieno centro, and exercises a vicarious humility, is a sort of compound of Squeers and Pecksniff, but more probable than either, and drawn with as strong a hand . . . Mrs Reed is a good type of the 'strong-minded' and odious woman. Excellent too, in an artistic point of view, is the character of St John Rivers, the Calvinist clergyman and missionary, with all its complex attributes and iridescent hues – self-denial strangely short with selfishness – earthly pride and restless ambition blend-

ing and alternating with heaven-directed zeal, and resignation to the duties of a heavenly mission. The feeblest character in the book is that of Helen Burns, who is meant to be a perfect Christian, and is a simple seraph, conscious moreover of her own perfection. She dies early in the first volume, and our authoress might say of her saint, as Shakespeare said of his Mercutio, 'If I had not killed her, she would have killed me.' In her, however, the Christianity of Jane Eyre is concentrated, and with her it expires, leaving the moral world in a kind of Scandinavian gloom . . .

In imaginative painting Jane Eyre is very good [quotes from chapter 9, 'I discovered . . . wild primrose plants'].

The rather ambitious descriptions of manners and social life which the book contains are, we are bound to say, a most decided failure. Their satire falls back with accumulated force upon the head of the satirist. It is 'high life below stairs' with a vengeance; the fashionable world seen through the area railings, and drawn with the black end of the kitchen poker [quotes from chapter 17 Blanche Ingram's exchanges with her mother and with Rochester] . . .

To say that *Jane Eyre* is positively immoral or antichristian, would be to do its writer an injustice. Still it wears a questionable aspect . . . The authoress of *Jane Eyre* will have power in her generation, whether she choose to exercise it for good or evil. She has depth and breadth of thought – she has something of that peculiar gift of genius, the faculty of discerning the wonderful in and through the commonplace – she has a painter's eye and hand – she has great satiric power, and, in spite of some exaggerated and morbid cynicism, a good fund of common sense. To this common sense we would appeal. Let her take care that while she detects and exposes humbug in other minds, she does not suffer it to gain dominion in her own . . . Let her cease, if she can, to think of herself as Micaiah, and of society as Ahab. Let her be a little more trustful of the reality of human goodness, and a little less anxious to detect its alloy of evil. She will lose nothing in piquancy, and gain something in healthiness and truth. We shall look with some anxiety for that second effort which is proverbially decisive

of a writer's talent, and which, in this case, will probably be decisive of the moral question also.

SOURCE: *Christian Remembrancer,* April 1848.

NOTES

On the views of this periodical see Introduction, pp. 20, 23, 25–6.
1. *Grantley Manor: a Tale* (1847) by the Roman Catholic biographer, novelist and playwright, Lady Georgina Fullerton (1812–85). Her other novels include *Ellen Middleton* (1844) and *Lady-Bird* (1852).

GEORGE ELIOT: 'one would like ... a somewhat nobler cause'

I have read Jane Eyre, mon ami, and shall be glad to know what you admire in it. All self-sacrifice is good – but one could like it to be in a somewhat nobler cause than that of a diabolical law which chains a man body and soul to a putrefying carcase. However the book *is* interesting – only I wish the characters would talk a little less like the heroes and heroines of police reports.

SOURCE: Letter to Charles Bray, 11 June 1848.

NOTE

For George Eliot's increased enthusiasm in 1853 see below, p. 112.

EUGÈNE FORCADE: 'Swift, vehement, vigorously personal and completely English'

... the vicissitudes and sorrows of the present time lend a particular interest to romantic literature. The events which have inter-

rupted numbers of careers, have consigned a host of distinguished
people to that life of retirement, rest and contemplation which is,
as it were, the environment in which this kind of literature most
readily flourishes. When the finest actors turn spectator, when
public offices condemn to idleness men who have held the highest
ranks in the life of the nation, the life of the intellect and the
imagination is of necessity enriched by all that is lost to the world
of affairs. Imagine – and the February revolution has realised this
hypothesis over and over again – imagine a mind formerly
absorbed in externals, in superficial business, in all the mechanical
activities associated with public office, suddenly thrown back on
the meditations of unoccupied solitude, on the intimacy of a
narrow circle, on that kind of quiet self-communion in which one
enters into full possession of oneself, and in which one can feel
and see oneself living ... The mind and heart regain a certain
elasticity, a sensibility, a power of making a fresh approach to
matters of thought and feeling, which in itself constitutes a rejuve-
nation full of unexpected charms ... I see lofty minds and loving
hearts unite, band together – so to speak – to protect one another
against the tempest loosed on the world; I see them arrange to
spend together these moments of torment, happy to have discovered or re-discovered one another, as the members of a family
enjoy gathering, as the winter evenings draw in, round the table
before the fire, while the rain beats on the windows and the wind
howls mournfully across the bare garden. Now, surely, is the time
for a novel, for long readings interpreted by the inner voices of the
soul.

It seems to me that such conditions and such a mood should call
forth their own novelist and inspire creations of new sympathy and
colour, something more than works of pure entertainment or mere
literary craft ... We demand more nowadays. More than ever
before, we want the novelist to be a moralist ... What is the sickness of our time? Utopia, the false ideal that makes an absurd and
untrue image of man, that realises the dictum of Montaigne and
Pascal: in seeking to make man an angel, it intoxicates and
degrades him to the level of a beast. Utopia dreams of a mech-

anical perfection for man, a perfection that is monotonous and
stupid . . . What do men seek from utopia? A social device to save
them from the struggle with life and spare them pain – that is,
effort, work and action, or in other words, all that constitutes
human virtue and glory. The socialist utopia is thus the aim and
outward expression of lazy minds, debased imaginations and
cowardly natures . . . Poetry, that flame of human liberty . . .
would die in the geometric, mechanical humanity that the
utopians wish to construct with rule and compass . . . The most
powerful weapon of poetry is the philosophy of the passions, whose
intimate depths it alone can plumb and which it alone can express
with its irresistible eloquence. And this is where the novel has a
part to play, for the novel is the form of poetry devoted to the
individual history of human emotion and it is therefore for the
novel above all to formulate the protest of society and art against
socialism and to force the lay figure of humanitarianism to make
way for the breathing reality of man himself.

These thoughts came to mind as I read the book, which has
attracted a good deal of notice in England and which is the sub
ject of this essay. *Jane Eyre* is the first novel of a writer whose
identity is concealed from the curious by a pseudonym. Who has
written these swift and vehement pages? A young man, some say;
others, a woman . . . Internal evidence and certain details of the
book do strongly suggest that *Jane Eyre* is in fact the work of a
woman; but whoever the author of this novel may be and whatever the qualities that have singled it out for attention and brought
it immediate success, one thing struck me about *Jane Eyre* and
that is the eminently and vigorously personal character of the
book. *Jane Eyre,* I must warn you, is not at all a story of universal
interest, one of those tales independent of place which may be
read with the same pleasure in Paris, Madrid or Moscow. Nor is
Jane Eyre a literary work of deep significance, but it is a highly
curious and engaging moral study for those who, like myself,
cannot – even though they are French – bring themselves to turn
socialist. It is a book that is completely English in the moral sense
of the word. One feels all through it the spirit of that Anglo-

Saxon race, crude if you will – you Frenchmen who still imagine
yourselves Athenians in 1848 – but masculine, inured to suffering
and hardship. Their novels are not endless variations on the *Carte
du Tendre*. They firmly implant in the hearts of their children the
feeling for freedom and responsibility; they have given the world
not Saint-Simon and Fourier but William Penn, Daniel Defoe
and Benjamin Franklin. This is the aspect that interests me in the
story told us by the author of *Jane Eyre*, the story of a child, an
orphan, cast alone on the world and fighting a solitary battle. The
account vibrates with a feeling which seems sometimes to bear the
accent of a personal confession and it has that passion and anima-
tion which always inspire the beginner in the zest of a first work.
But what especially charmed me was that the author has relied
solely on the eloquence of the emotions depicted and has not for a
moment thought of calling down a fiery judgment on society in a
drama in which society nevertheless plays more or less the cruel
and tyrannical role assigned to fate in the tragedies of antiquity.

And the author of *Jane Eyre* is all the more to be admired for
having disdained the declamatory resources offered by the subject
in that she has systematically created other and singular difficulties
for herself ... Jane Eyre is not one of those beautiful, smiling
young ladies pursued by elegant suitors, idealised in the golden
light of girlish dreams. If you make the acquaintance of the hero
and heroine of *Jane Eyre* you will certainly be able to take an
interest in their adventures but the desire to be like them will
never enter your head. The novelist has taken the bold step of
making his hero and heroine decidedly ugly, allowing them to
catch here and there as best they may under the influence of
emotion, that chance beauty which we call the beauty of the devil.
There is another resource in common use among English novelists
which is likewise eschewed in *Jane Eyre* : I mean the depiction of
life in high society which of itself has guaranteed the success of a
number of fashionable novels. In its setting *Jane Eyre* is quite
simply a novel of country life. This book contains not a hint of a
description of a London season, a stay in a watering-place, or a
point-to-point race; no social lions appear, not even the briefest

sketch of the Beau Brummell or the Comte d'Orsay of the day : no
stroll in the park, no dinner at Richmond, not a trace of fashionable ranting. Everything takes place in the country just as though
drawing-rooms, watering-places, and spring in London had never
existed. It is a sober and serious tale concerned to bring to life the
poor and dependent situation of a highly interesting class of person
and one that is very numerous among women in England. And for
us, the foreigners, the romantic attraction of such a picture is perhaps nothing more than an inquisitive interest in scenes of everyday life in another country... In England, the old order [of primo-
geniture] still exists with all the vicissitudes and contrasts to which
it gives rise in the history of particular families and the aristocracy
still offers up its own children in a human sacrifice to poverty, in
order to preserve intact in a single line the family name and fortune. The political, colonial and mercantile activities of the English
people, that spirit of enterprise that takes Anglo-Saxons to every
corner of the world, do it is true redress, for men, the effects of the
law of primogeniture. They seem even to draw from this law a
continual stimulus... It is not quite the same for women; they
have not the same means of getting a place in the sun. Among the
middle classes especially, how many girls belonging to the junior
branch of the family, must decline through poverty to dependence
and destitution! How often must one find, especially among these
Englishwomen, that inner conflict, that fatality arising from their
situation, so cruelly felt by our needy middle classes, and which
grows out of a disharmony between birth, education and fortune.
It is in this class that our author has chosen the heroine of her
novel [Forçade follows this with a minute descriptive analysis of
the story, probably the longest of its kind to appear; his subsequent
apology for its brevity reads oddly in context] ...

After the wrong I have done this novel by this necessarily abbre-
viated account, I will not commit the further injustice of submitting it to the dissection of minute criticism. A novel is made up of
three things : situation, characters and plot. The author of *Jane
Eyre* has chosen a really interesting and romantic situation. This
young girl, orphaned, educated on charity, entering the world

c

with a cultivation of mind second to none but in a subordinate and inferior station, brought into contact with everything that her intelligence and feeling equip her to understand, merit and desire but that fate denies her, receiving at last through love full entry into life – this story will always be touching ... Nor have I any reproach to level at the characters in *Jane Eyre* : they are energetic and emphatic rather than delicate; but they are true, that of Jane especially, and every scene in the novel gives them in the smallest details a solidity which is full of life. But the plot, here is the weak side of the work. I cannot understand why the author of *Jane Eyre* could not have found a simpler action through which to develop her situation and characters; I cannot understand why she should have thought she needed to have such complicated and disjointed incidents, often improbably linked. Yet the author of *Jane Eyre* had quite enough talent to create a complete and irreproachable work.

But what I shall never cease to praise is the vigorous, healthy, moral spirit that informs every page of *Jane Eyre*. Whatever our novelists may say, this book proves once more that there are infinite resources for fiction in the depiction of the upright morals and straightforward events of real life and the simple and open development of the passions. When will we French stop investigating in our novels with such obsessive relentlessness the metaphysics, the subtle and sometimes profound politics of depraved instincts, corrupt emotions, monstrous attachments, of everything bred of the fermentation of evil in human nature? ...

s o u r c e : *Revue des Deux Mondes,* October 1848.

NOTE

Eugène Forçade, regular contributor to this influential French journal, won Charlotte's warm approval for his reviews of her two first novels. His '*Jane Eyre* : Autobiographie' is excessively long and reflects his concern with current political troubles in France, against which he measures Charlotte's staunch individualism. Charlotte wrote, 16 November 1848, 'The notice is one of the most able, the most acceptable to the author of any that has yet appeared. Eugène Forçade understood and enjoyed *Jane Eyre* ... The censures are as well-founded as the commendations' (*LL* ii 271). See also p. 162 below.

ELIZABETH RIGBY: '... combining such genuine power with such horrid taste ...'

... *Jane Eyre*, as a work, and one of equal popularity, is, in almost every respect, a total contrast to *Vanity Fair*. The characters and events, though some of them masterly in conception, are coined expressly for the purpose of bringing out great effects. The hero and heroine are beings both so singularly unattractive that the reader feels they can have no vocation in the novel but to be brought together; and they do things which, though not impossible, lie utterly beyond the bounds of probability. On this account a short sketch of the plan seems requisite; not but it is a plan familiar enough to all readers of novels – especially those of the old school and those of the lowest school of our own day. For Jane Eyre is merely another Pamela, who, by the force of character and the strength of her principles, is carried victoriously through great trials and temptations from the man she loves. Nor is she even a Pamela adapted and refined to modern notions; for though the story is conducted without those derelictions of decorum which we are to believe had their excuse in the manners of Richardson's time, yet it is stamped with a coarseness of language and laxity of tone which have certainly no excuse in ours. It is a very remarkable book : we have no remembrance of another combining such genuine power with such horrid taste. Both together have equally assisted to gain the great popularity it has enjoyed; for in these days of extravagant adoration of all that bears the stamp of novelty and originality, sheer rudeness and vulgarity have come in for a most mistaken worship.

The story is written in the first person. Jane begins with her earliest recollections and at once takes possession of the reader's intensest interest by the masterly picture of a strange and oppressed child she raises up in a few strokes before him. She is an orphan, and a dependant in the house of a selfish, hard-hearted aunt, against whom the disposition of the little Jane chafes itself in natural antipathy, till she contrives to make the unequal struggle as intolerable to her oppressor as it is to herself. She is therefore, at eight years of age, got rid of to a sort of Dothegirls Hall,[1] where she continues to enlist our sympathies for a time with her little pinched fingers, cropped hair, and empty stomach. But things improve : the abuses of the institution are looked into [outlines the rest of the story, noting the 'scenes of truly tragic power' following the interrupted wedding] . . .

Such is the outline of a tale in which, combined with great materials for power and feeling, the reader may trace gross inconsistencies and improbabilities, and chief and foremost that highest moral offence a novel writer can commit, that of making an unworthy character interesting in the eyes of the reader. Mr Rochester is a man who deliberately and secretly seeks to violate the laws both of God and man, and yet we will be bound half our lady readers are enchanted with him for a model of generosity and honour. We would have thought that such a hero had had no chance, in the purer taste of the present day; but the popularity of *Jane Eyre* is a proof how deeply the love of the illegitimate romance is implanted in our nature. Not that the author is strictly responsible for this. Mr Rochester's character is tolerably consistent. He is made as coarse and as brutal as can in all conscience be required to keep our sympathies at a distance. In point of literary consistency the hero is at all events impugnable, though we cannot say as much for the heroine.

As to Jane's character – there is none of that harmonious unity about it which made little Becky[2] so grateful a subject of analysis – nor are the discrepancies of that kind which have their excuse and response in our nature. The inconsistencies of Jane's character lie mainly not in her own imperfections, though of course she has her share, but in the author's . . . The error in Jane Eyre is, not that her character is this or that, but that she is made one thing in the eyes of her imaginary companions, and another in that of the actual reader . . . We hear nothing but self-eulogiums on the perfect tact and wondrous penetration with which she is gifted, and yet almost every word she utters offends us, not only with the absence of these qualities, but with the positive contrasts of them, in either her pedantry, stupidity, or gross vulgarity . . . Even in that *chef-d'œuvre* of brilliant retrospective sketching, the description of her early life, it is the childhood and not the child that interests you. The little Jane, with her sharp eyes and dogmatic speeches, is a being you neither could fondle nor love. There is a hardness in her infantine earnestness, and a spiteful precocity in her reasoning, which repulses all our sympathy. One sees that she is of a nature to dwell upon and treasure up every slight and unkindness, real or fancied, and such natures we know are surer than any others to meet with plenty of this sort of thing. As the child, so also the woman – an uninteresting, sententious, pedantic thing; with no experience of the world, and yet with no simplicity or freshness in its stead [quotes from chapter 13 her 'governessy effusions' about *'cadeaux'*] . . .

Let us take a specimen of her again when Mr Rochester brings home his guests to Thornfield. The fine ladies of this world are a new study to Jane, and capitally she describes her first impression of them as they leave the dinner table and return to the drawing-room – nothing can be more gracefully graphic than this . . . But now for the reverse. The moment Jane Eyre sets these graceful creatures conversing, she falls into mistakes which display not so much a total ignorance of the habits of society, as a vulgarity of mind inherent in herself. They talked together by her account like parvenues trying to show off. They discuss the subject of governesses before her very face, in what Jane affects to consider the exact tone of fashionable contempt. They bully the servants in language no lady would dream of using to her own – far less to those of her host and entertainer – though certainly the 'Sam' of Jane Eyre's is not precisely the head servant one is accustomed to meet with in houses of the Thornfield class . . . But the crowning scene is the offer – governesses are said to be sly on such occasions, but Jane out-governesses them all – little Becky would have blushed for her . . . Although so clever in giving hints, how wonderfully slow she is in taking them ! Even when, tired of his cat's play, Mr Rochester proceeds to rather indubitable demonstrations of affection – 'enclosing me in his arms, gathering me to his breast, pressing his lips on my lips' – Jane has no idea what he can mean. Some ladies would have thought it high time to leave the Squire alone with his chestnut tree; or, at all events, unnecessary to keep up that tone of high-souled feminine obtusity which they are quite justified in adopting if gentlemen will not speak out – but Jane again does neither. Not that we say she was wrong, but quite the reverse, considering the circumstances of the case – Mr Rochester was her master, and 'Duchess or nothing' was her first duty – only she was not quite so artless as the author would have us suppose . . . A little more, and we should have flung the book aside to lie for ever among the trumpery with which such scenes ally it; but it were a pity to have halted here, for wonderful things lie beyond – scenes of suppressed feeling, more fearful to witness than the most violent tornadoes of passion – struggles with such intense sorrow and suffering as it is sufficient misery to know that any one should have conceived, far less passed through; and yet with that stamp of truth which takes precedence in the human heart before actual experience. The flippant fifth-rate, plebeian actress has vanished, and only a noble, high-souled woman, bound to us by the reality of her sorrow, and yet raised above us by the strength of the will, stands in actual life before us. If this be Jane Eyre, the author has done her injustice hitherto, not we. Let us look at her in the first recognition of her sorrow after the discomfiture of the marriage [quotes from chapter 26, 'Only the clergyman stayed . . . the floods overflowed me'] . . .

We have said that this was the picture of a natural heart. This, to our view, is the great and crying mischief of the book. Jane Eyre is throughout the personification of an unregenerate and undisciplined spirit, the more dangerous to exhibit from that prestige of principle and self-control which is liable to dazzle the eye too much for it to observe the inefficient and unsound foundation on which it rests. It is true Jane does right, and exerts great moral strength, but it is the strength of a mere heathen mind which is a law unto itself. No Christian grace is perceptible upon her. She has inherited in fullest measure the worst sin of our fallen nature – the sin of pride . . . she looks upon all that has been done for her not only as her undoubted right, but as falling far short of it. The doctrine of humility is not more foreign to her mind than it is repudiated by her heart. It is by her own talents, virtues, and courage that she is made to attain the summit of human happiness, and, as far as Jane Eyre's own statement is concerned, no one would think that she owed anything either to God above or to man below. She flees from Mr Rochester, and has not a being to turn to. Why was this? . . . Jane had lived for eight years with 110 girls and fifteen teachers. Why had she formed no friendship among them? Other orphans have left the same and similar institutions, furnished with friends for life, and puzzled with homes to choose from. How comes it that Jane had acquired neither? . . .

Altogether the autobiography of Jane Eyre is pre-eminently an anti-Christian composition. There is throughout it a murmuring against the comforts of the rich and against the privations of the poor, which, as far as each individual is concerned, is a murmuring against God's appointment – there is a proud and perpetual assertion of the rights of man, for which we find no authority either in God's word or in God's providence . . . [refers to the auhorship] Jane Eyre is sentimentally assumed to have proceeded from the pen of Mr Thackeray's governess, whom he had himself chosen as his model of Becky, and who, in mingled love and revenge, personified him in return as Mr Rochester. In this case, it is evident that the author of *Vanity Fair,* whose own pencil makes him grey-haired, has had the best of it . . . To this ingenious rumour the coincidence of the second edition of *Jane Eyre* being dedicated to Mr Thackeray has probably given rise. For our parts, we see no great interest in the question at all. The first edition of *Jane Eyre* purports to be edited by Currer Bell, one of a trio of brothers or sisters, or cousins, by names Currer, Acton and Ellis

Bell, already known as the joint-authors of a volume of poems. The second edition of the same is dedicated, however, 'by the author', to Mr Thackeray; and the dedication (itself an indubitable chip of Jane Eyre) signed Currer Bell . . . Whoever it be, it is a person who, with great mental powers, combines a total ignorance of the habits of society, a great coarseness of taste, and a heathenish doctrine of religion . . . We do not hesitate to say that the tone of the mind and thought which has overthrown authority and violated every code human and divine abroad, and fostered Chartism and rebellion at home, is the same which has also written *Jane Eyre*.[3]

Still we say again this is a very remarkable book. We are painfully alive to the moral, religious, and literary deficiencies of the picture, and such passages of beauty and power as we have quoted cannot redeem it, but it is impossible not to be spellbound with the freedom of the touch. It would be mere hackneyed courtesy to call it 'fine writing'. It bears no impress of being written at all, but is poured out rather in the heat and hurry of an instinct, which flows ungovernably on to its object, indifferent by what means it reaches it, and unconscious too. As regards the author's chief object, however, it is a failure – that, namely, of making a plain, odd woman, destitute of all the conventional features of feminine attraction, interesting in our sight. We deny that he had succeeded in this. Jane Eyre, in spite of some grand things about her, is a being totally uncongenial to our feelings from beginning to end. We acknowledge her firmness – we respect her determination – we feel for her struggles; but for all that, and setting aside higher considerations, the impression she leaves on our mind is that of a decidedly vulgar-minded woman – one whom we should not care for as an acquaintance, whom we should not seek as a friend, whom we should not desire for a relation, and whom we should scrupulously avoid for a governess.

There seem to have arisen in the novel-reading world some doubts as to who really wrote this book; and various rumours, more or less romantic, have been current in Mayfair, the metropolis of gossip . . . though we cannot pronounce that it appertains to a real Mr Currer Bell and to no other, yet that it appertains to a

man, and not, as many assert, to a woman, we are strongly inclined
to affirm ... No woman – a lady friend, whom we are always
happy to consult, assures us – makes mistakes in her own métier –
no woman trusses game and garnishes dessert-dishes with the same
hands, or talks of so doing in the same breath. Above all, no
woman attires another in such fancy dresses as Jane's ladies
assume – Miss Ingram coming down, irresistible, 'in a morning
robe of sky-blue crape, a gauze azure scarf twisted in her hair'!!
No lady, we understand, when suddenly roused in the night,
would think of hurrying on 'a frock'. They have garments more
convenient for such occasions, and more becoming too.[4] This
evidence seems incontrovertible. Even granting that these incon-
gruities were purposely assumed, for the sake of disguising the
female pen, there is nothing gained; for if we ascribe the book to a
woman at all, we have no alternative but to ascribe it to one who
has, for some sufficient reason, long forfeited the society of her own
sex.

And if by no woman, it is certainly also by no artist. The
Thackeray eye has had no part there. There is not more disparity
between the art of drawing Jane assumes and her evident total
ignorance of its first principles, than between the report she gives
of her own character and the conclusions we form for ourselves.
Not but what, in another sense, the author may be classed as an
artist of very high grade. Let him describe the simplest things in
nature – a rainy landscape, a cloudy sky, or a bare moorside, and
he shows the hand of a master; but the moment he talks of the art
itself, it is obvious that he is a complete ignoramus.

We cannot help feeling that this work must be far from bene-
ficial to that class of ladies whose cause it affects to advocate. Jane
Eyre is not precisely the mouthpiece one would select to plead the
cause of governesses, and it is therefore the greater pity that she
has chosen it: for there is none we are convinced which, at the
present time, more deserves and demands an earnest and judicious
befriending ...

s o u r c e : *Quarterly Review*, December 1848.

NOTES

Elizabeth Rigby (1809–93), authoress, married in 1849 Sir Charles
Lock Eastlake, President of the Royal Academy (1850–65); apart
from regular contributions to the *Quarterly*, she published *A Residence on the Shores of the Baltic* (1841) and many works on painters
and painting. An account of her varied life and her generally unstuffy
literary reviews appears in Marion Lockhead's *Elizabeth Rigby, Lady
Eastlake* (1961). Her authorship of this unsigned review, in which
Jane Eyre is discussed together with Thackeray's *Vanity Fair* (1847–
8) and the Report for 1847 of the Governesses' Benevolent Institution, became known to Charlotte in February 1849 (*LL* ii 314, iii 12),
but was not generally known until the 1890s. See further, Introduction, pp. 23–4.

    1. Another allusion to *Nicholas Nickleby*; see above, p. 44 n.

    2. Becky Sharp in *Vanity Fair*; see above.

    3. See Introduction, p. 23.

    4. Elizabeth Rigby had written a learned article on 'Dress' for the
Quarterly Review, March 1847.

2. THE EARLY RECEPTION OF *VILLETTE* (1853)

HARRIET MARTINEAU: 'Two faults ... all else is power, skill, interest'

Everything written by 'Currer Bell' is remarkable. She can touch nothing without leaving on it the stamp of originality. Of her three books, this is perhaps the strangest, the most astonishing, though not the best. The sustained ability is perhaps greater in *Villette* than in its two predecessors, there being no intervals of weakness, except in the form of a few passages, chiefly episodical, of over-wrought writing, which though evidently a sincere endeavour to express real feeling, are not felt to be congenial, or very intelligible, in the midst of so much that is strong and clear. In regard to interest, we think that this book will be pronounced inferior to *Jane Eyre* and superior to *Shirley*. In point of construction it is superior to both; and this is a vast gain and a great encouragement to hope for future benefits from the same hand which shall surpass any yet given. The whole three volumes are crowded with beauties – with the good things for which we look to the clear sight, deep feeling and singular, though not extensive, experience of life which we associate with the name of 'Currer Bell'. But under all, through all, over all, is felt a drawback, of which we were anxious before, but which is terribly aggravated here – the book is almost intolerably painful. We are wont to say, when we read narratives which are made up of the external woes of life, such as may and do happen every day, but are never congregated in one experience – that the author has no right to make readers so miserable. We do not know whether the right will be admitted in the present case, on the ground of the woes not being external; but certainly we ourselves have felt inclined to rebel against the pain, and, perhaps on account of protraction, are disposed to deny its necessity and truth. With all her objectivity, 'Currer Bell' here afflicts us with an amount of subjective misery which we may fairly remonstrate against; and she allows us no respite – even while treating us with humour, with charming description and the presence of those whom she herself regards as the good and gay. In truth, there is scarcely anybody that is good – serenely and cheerfully good, and the gaiety has pain in it. An atmosphere of pain hangs about the whole, forbidding that repose which we hold to be essential to the true presentment of any large portion of life and experience. In this pervading pain, the book reminds us of Balzac; and so it does in the prevalence of one tendency, or one idea, throughout the whole conception and action. All the female characters, in all their thoughts and lives, are full of one thing, or are regarded by the reader in the light of that one thought – love. It begins with the child of six years old, at the opening – a charming picture – and it closes with it at the last page; and, so dominant is this idea – so incessant is the writer's tendency to describe the need of being loved, that the heroine, who tells her own story, leaves the reader at last under the uncomfortable impression of her having either entertained a double love, or allowed one to supersede another without notification of the transition. It is not thus in real life. There are substantial, heartfelt interests for women of all ages, and under ordinary circumstances, quite apart from love : there is an absence of introspection, an unconsciousness, a repose in women's lives – unless under peculiarly unfortunate circumstances – of which we find no admission in this book; and to the absence of it, may be attributed some of the criticism which the book will meet from readers who are not prudes, but whose reason and taste will reject the assumption that events and characters are to be regarded through the medium of one passion only.

And here ends all demur. We have thought it right to indicate clearly the two faults in the book, which it is scarcely probable that

anyone will deny. Abstractions made of these, all else is power,
skill and interest. The freshness will be complete to readers who
know none but English novels. Those who are familiar with Balzac
may be reminded, by the sharp distinction of the pictured life,
place and circumstance, of some of the best of his tales : but there
is nothing borrowed; nothing that we might not as well have had
if 'Currer Bell' had never read a line of Balzac – which may very
likely be the case. As far as we know, the life of a foreign *pension*
(Belgian, evidently) and of a third-rate capital, with its half provincial population and proceedings, is new in purely English
literature; and most lifelike and spirited it is. The humour which
peeps out in the names – the court of Labassecour, with its heir-
apparent, the Duc of Dindoneau – the Professors Boissec and
Rochemorte – and so forth – is felt throughout, though there is
not a touch of lightheartedness from end to end. The presence of
the heroine in that capital and *pension* is strangely managed; and
so is the gathering of her British friends around her there; but, that
strangeness surmounted, the picture of their lives is admirable.
The reader must go to the book for it; for it fills two volumes and a
half out of the three. The heroine, Lucy Snowe, tells her own story.
Every reader of *Jane Eyre* will be glad to see the autobiographical
form returned to. Lucy may be thought a younger, feebler sister
of Jane. There is just enough resemblance for that – but she has
not Jane's charm of mental and moral health, and consequent
repose. She is in a state of chronic nervous fever for the most part;
is usually silent and suffering; when she speaks, speaks in enigmas
or in raillery, and now and then breaks out under the torture of
passion; but she acts admirably – with readiness, sense, conscience
and kindliness. Still we do not wonder that she loved more than
she was beloved, and the love at last would be surprising enough,
if love could ever be so. Perhaps Pauline and her father are the
best-drawn characters in the book, where all are more or less
admirably delineated. We are not aware that there is one failure.

A striking peculiarity comes out in the third volume, striking
from one so large and liberal, so removed from ordinary social
prejudices as we have been accustomed to think 'Currer Bell'. She

goes out of her way to express a passionate hatred of Romanism.
It is not the calm disapproval of a ritual religion, such as we should
have expected from her, ensuing upon a presentment of her own
better faith. The religion she invokes is itself but a dark and doubt-
ful refuge from the pain which impels the invocation; while the
Catholicism on which she enlarges is even virulently reprobated.
We do not exactly see the moral necessity for this (there is no
artistical necessity) and we are rather sorry for it, occurring as it
does at a time when catholics and protestants hate each other
quite sufficiently; and in a mode which will not affect conversion.
A better advocacy of protestantism would have been to show that
it can give rest to the weary and heavy laden; whereas it seems to
yield no comfort in return for every variety of sorrowful invocation. To the deep undertone of suffering frequent expression is
given in such passages as this – beautiful in the wording but otherwise most painful [quotes *Villette*, chap. 24, 'Now, a letter like this
. . . comprehend him'].

We cannot help looking forward still to other and higher gifts
from this singular mind and powerful pen. When we feel that
there is no decay or power here and think what an accession there
will be when the cheerfulness of health comes in with its bracing
influence, we trust we have only to wait to have such a boon as
Jane Eyre gives us warrant to expect, and which 'Currer Bell'
alone can give.

s o u r c e : *Daily News,* 3 February 1853.

G . H . L E W E S : 'Passion and Power'

In Passion and Power – those noble twins of Genius – Currer Bell
has no living rival, except George Sand. Hers is the passionate
heart to feel, and the powerful brain to give feeling shape; and
that is why she is so original, so fascinating. Faults she has, in
abundance; they are so obvious, they lie so legible on the surface,
that to notice them with more insistance than a passing allusion is

the very wantonness of criticism. On a former occasion, and in
another place, we remonstrated with her on these said faults, but
we now feel that the lecture was idle. Why wander delighted
among the craggy clefts and snowy solitudes of the Alps, complain-
ing of the want of verdure and of flowers? In the presence of real
Power why object to its not having the quiet lineaments of Grace?
There is a Strength clothed with Gentleness, but there may also
be Strength rugged, vehement – careless of beauty . . . Is it not
enough for us to accept her *as* she is?

One may say of Currer Bell that her genius finds a fitting illustration in her heroes and heroines – her Rochesters and Jane
Eyres. They are men and women of deep feeling, clear intellects,
vehement tempers, bad manners, ungraceful, yet loveable persons.
Their address is brusque, unpleasant, yet individual, direct, free
from shams and conventions of all kinds. They outrage 'good
taste', yet they fascinate. You dislike them at first, yet you learn to
love them. The power that is in them makes its vehement way right
to your heart. Propriety, ideal outline, good manners, good
features, ordinary thought, ordinary speech, are not to be
demanded of them. They are the Mirabeaus[1] of romance; and the
idolatry of a nation follows the great gifts of a Mirabeau, let
'Propriety' look never so 'shocked'. It is the triumph of what is
sterling over what is tinsel, of what is essential to human worth
over what is collateral. Place a perfectly well-bred, well-featured,
graceful considerate gentleman – a hero of romance, vague and
ideal – beside one who is imperious, coarse, ill-tempered, ill-
featured, but who, under this husk of manner and of temper contains the kernel of what is noble, generous, loving, powerful, and
see how in the long run human sympathies will detach themselves
from the unsatisfying hero, and cling to the man whose brain and
heart are powerful! It is like placing a clever agreeable novel
beside *Jane Eyre.* Janet captured all our hearts; not because she
was lovely, lady-like, good, but because she was direct, clear, upright, capable of deep affections, and of bravely enduring great
affliction. If any one pointed out her faults, we admitted them, but
never swerved a line from our admiration. We never thought her

perfect, we loved her for what was loveable, and left the rest to be set down to human imperfection.

And so of this story we have just read. *Villette* has assuredly many faults, and novel readers, no less than critics, will have much to say thereon. More adroit 'construction', more breathless suspense, more thrilling incidents, and a more moving story, might easily have been manufactured by a far less active, inventive, passionate writer; but not such a book. Here, at any rate, is an *original book*. Every page, every paragraph, is sharp with *individuality*. It is Currer Bell speaking to you, not the Circulating Library reverberating echoes. How *she* has looked at life, with a saddened, yet not vanquished soul; what *she* has thought, and felt, not what she thinks others will expect her to have thought and felt; *this* it is we read of here, and this it is which makes her writing welcome above almost every other writing. It has held us spell-bound.

Descending from generals to particulars, let us say that, considered in the light of a novel, it is a less interesting story than even *Shirley*. It wants the unity and progression of interest which made *Jane Eyre* so fascinating; but it is the book of a mind more conscious of its power. *Villette* is meant for Brussels. The greater part of its scenes pass in the Netherlands, not unhappily designated as *Labassecour*. People will wonder why this transparent disguise was adopted. We conjecture that it was to prevent personal applications on the reader's part, and also to allow the writer a greater freedom as to details. The point is, however, very unimportant . . .

SOURCE: *The Leader*, 12 February 1853.

NOTES

The Leader : this progressive weekly paper was founded in 1850 by G. H. Lewes and Thornton Hunt; it included Hubert Spencer and A. W. Kinglake among its staff and ran until 1866 (Lewes left in 1854).

1. The colourful career of Honoré-Gabriel de Riquetti, Comte de

Mirabeau (1749–91), Revolutionary orator and statesman, was a current topic of conversation since the publication of John Stores Smith's *Mirabeau: A Life History* (1848), which Charlotte read shortly after it came out (*L* II 224–5).

The Spectator : 'Morbid sensibility' accompanies 'resolution . . . power . . . discretion . . . good sense'

Villette is Brussels, and Currer Bell might have called her new novel 'Passages from the Life of a Teacher in a Girls' School at Brussels, written by herself'. Of plot, strictly taken as a series of coherent events all leading to a common result, there is none; no more, at least, than there would be in two years of any person's life who had occupations and acquaintances, and told us about them. Of interesting scenes, and of well-drawn characters, there is, on the other hand, abundance; and these, though they fail to stimulate the curiosity of the reader like a well-constructed plot, sustain the attention, and keep up a pleasant emotion, from the first page to the last.

All the emotions excited by art are pleasant, even though their subject-matter be in itself painful; otherwise we should have hesitated in applying the term to the emotions caused by this book. For while the characters are various, happily conceived, and some of them painted with a truth of detail rarely surpassed, the centre figure – the girl who is supposed to write the book – is one who excites sympathies bitter-sweet, and in which there is little that is cheerful or consoling. Like Jane Eyre in her intense relish for affection, in her true-heartedness, in her great devotion to the small duties of her daily life, there is nothing about her of the real inward strength that made Jane's duties something of a compensation for the affection denied her. If it were not too harsh a word to be used of so good a girl as Miss Lucy Snowe, one might almost say that she took a savage delight in refusing to be comforted, in a position indeed of isolation and hardship, but one still that a large experience of mankind and the miseries' incident to the lot of humanity would hardly pronounce to be by comparison either a miserable or a degraded lot. But this book, far more than *Jane Eyre*, sounds like a bitter complaint against the destiny of those women whom circumstances reduce to a necessity of working for their living by teaching, and who are debarred from the exercise of those affections which are indeed the crown of a woman's happiness, but which it is unwise and untrue to make indispensable to a calm enjoyment of life and to an honourable and useful employment of it. Nor do we think that the morbid sensibility attributed to Lucy Snowe is quite consistent with the strength of will, the daring resolution, the quiet power, the discretion and good sense, that are blended with it in Currer Bell's conception. Still less, perhaps, is such a quality, involving as it does a constant tormenting self-regard, to be found in common with clear insight into the characters and motives of others, and with the habit of minute observation, which, resulting in admirable and clear delineation, makes Lucy Snowe's autobiography so pleasant a book in all respects except the spasms of heart-agony she is too fond of showing herself in – we will not venture to hint of showing herself off in, for there is a terrible feeling of reality about them, which seems to say that they are but fictitious in form, the transcripts of a morbid but no less real personal experience.

But for this one fault in the central character – and even this may be true to nature, though to that exceptional nature which would prevent many persons from recognising its truth – we have nothing but praise to bestow upon the characterisation of this book ... Mrs Bretton and her son Dr John, Madame Beck the mistress of the pensionnat at Brussels, M. Paul Emanuel professor of belles lettres, M. Home de Bassompierre and his charming little daughter, worthless pretty Ginevra Fanshawe – we shall henceforth know them as if we had lived among them; and, bad or good, they are people worth knowing, for the skill of the painter if not for their own qualities. But the curious thing is, that the morbid feeling so predominant in the writer – the hunger of the heart which cannot obtain its daily bread, and will not make-

believe that a stone is bread – does not in the least reflect itself
upon these characters. They are as distinctly drawn, as finely
appreciated, as if the soul of the writer were in perfect harmony
with itself and with the world, and saw men and things with
correct glance of science, only warmed and made more piercing by
a genial sympathy. It may therefore be conjectured, that the mind
of Miss Lucy Snowe in writing the book had changed from the
mood in which she passed through the scenes described in it; that
a great calm had settled down upon the heart once so torn by
storms; that a deep satisfaction, based upon experience and faith,
had succeeded to the longing and distress of those earlier days.

Faith is indeed a very prominent feature in Miss Snowe's mind;
more a religious than a theological faith; more a trust, a sentiment,
and a hope, than a clearly-defined belief that could be stated in
propositions. But truth is another feature, and she will not sacrifice truth to faith. When her experience is blank misery, she does
not deny it, or slur it over, or belie it by shamming that she is
happy. While her eyes turn upward with the agony that can find
no resting-place on earth, she indulges no Pagan or Atheistical
despair – she does not arraign God as cruel or unmindful of his
creatures – she still believes that the discipline of life is merciful;
but she does not pretend to solve God's providence – she rather
with a stern sincerity cries aloud that her soul is crushed, and
drinks the bitter cup with the full resolve not to sweeten the bitterness by delusion or fancy. She seems to think that the destiny of
some human beings is to drink deep of this cup, and that no
evasions, no attempts to make it out less bitter than it is, will turn
aside the hand of the avenging angel, or cause that cup to be taken
away one moment the sooner. We doubt the worldly philosophy of
this view, as much as we are sure that it is not in any high sense
Christian. It may, however, be a genuine effusion from an over-
strained endurance – a sort of introverted Stoicism, which gives to
the sufferer the strength of non-resistance and knowing the worst.

The characters that will most charm the readers of this book
must be those of Miss de Bassompierre and M. Paul Emanuel;
though the former is nearly as perfect as mortals ever can be; and

the latter one of the oddest but most real mixtures of the good and
disagreeable, of the generous and the little, that a hunter after
oddities could wish for his cabinet of curiosities. The relation
between this M. Paul and Lucy Snowe will recall both Rochester
and Jane Eyre and Louis and Shirley; though the differences are
striking, and the characters themselves have little resemblance.
But all three positions have those elements in common which show
them to be familiar to the writer, and favourable, in her opinion,
for drawing out the characteristic points of her heroes and
heroines. In all probability, they are three transcripts, varied by
imagination, of the same observed facts . . . [quotes from chapter
3, Paulina's childhood farewell to Graham Bretton and from
chapter 30 the opening description of Paul Emanuel].

The style of *Villette* has the same characteristics that distinguished Currer Bell's previous novels – that clearness and power
which are the result of mastery over the thoughts and feelings to be
expressed, over the persons and scenes to be described. When the
style becomes less pleasing, it is from an attempt to paint by highly
figurative language the violent emotions of the heart. This is sometimes done at such length, and with so much obscurity from strain-
ing after figure and allusion, as to become tedious and to induce
skipping.

SOURCE: *The Spectator,* 12 February 1853.

NOTE

Cp. the *Spectator's* review of *Jane Eyre,* p. 48 above, and see Introduction, p. 20.

Athenæum: 'Her talk is of duty, – her predilections lie with
passion'

So curious a novel as *Villette* seldom comes before us, – and rarely
one offering so much matter for remark. Its very outset exhibits

an indifference to certain precepts of Art, singular in one who by
artistic management alone interests us in an unpromising subject.
Villette is a narrative of the heart-affairs of the English instructress, and the Belgian professor of literature in a school at Brussels,
– containing no combinations so exciting as those that in its
author's memoirs of another teacher, *Jane Eyre*, riveted some
readers and shocked others. Yet, thrilling scenes there might have
been in it had our authoress pleased. The Benedick to whom Lucy
Snowe is Beatrice is a devout Roman Catholic educated by Jesuits.
During a considerable portion of the story we are led to expect
that the old well-thumbed case of conscience is going to be tried
again, – and that having dealt with a Calvinistic missionary in
Jane Eyre, Currer Bell is about to draw a full-length picture of a
disciple of Loyola in *Villette.* But the idea is suggested – not fulfilled. Our authoress is superior to the nonsense and narrowness
that call themselves religious controversy. She allows the peril of
the position to be felt, – without entering on the covert rancour,
the imperfect logic, and the inconclusive catastrophe which distinguish such polemics when they are made the theme of fiction. –
We fancied, again, from certain indications, that something of
supernatural awe and terror were to be evoked : – but as a sequel
to these, Currer Bell has fairly turned round upon herself with a
mockery little short of sarcasm. – The tale is merely one of the
affections. It may be found in some places tedious, in some of its
incidents trivial, – but it is remarkable as a picture of manners.
A burning heart glows throughout it, and one brilliantly distinct
character keeps it alive. – The oldest man, the sternest, and the
most scientific, who is a genuine novel-reader, will find it hard to
get out of Madame Beck's school when he has once entered there
with Lucy Snowe, and made acquaintance with the snappish,
choleric, vain, child-like, and noble-hearted arbiter of her destiny,
M. Paul Emanuel.

Thus far we have had to recognise the artist's hand which,
wherever it be met – whether in a De Hooghe or a Mantegna, a
Velasquez or a Gainsborough, a Watteau or a Dürer – is worthy of
respect. We must now return to the fault in *Villette* which we have

already mentioned as singularly provoking. To adopt a musical
phrase, the novel begins out of the key in which it is composed.
In its first chapters interest is excited for a character who disappears during a large part of the story, and who returns to it
merely as a second-rate figure. A character in truth, and not a
caricature, is the little Paulina. She is a variety among children,
but not an impossibility. We can accredit her quaintness, her
delicacy, her restlessness, her self-help and self-possession, her constancy and deep love, as a compound which has come within our
own observation, – and we hoped that Currer Bell was going to
trace out the girlhood, courtship, and matrimony of such a curious,
elvish mite. Instead of this, towards the middle of the first volume
the narrator steps into the part of heroine, with an inconsequence
and abruptness that suggest change of plan after the tale was
undertaken. From this point, we are once again invited to follow
the struggles and sufferings of a solitary woman, – to listen to the
confessions of a heart famishing for excitement and sympathy – at
last finding Love, not 'among the rocks', but in the midst of storm
and contradiction. Currer Bell will be surprised to be told, that
the burden of her Pindaric concerning 'Woman's mission' is vir-
tually identical with that sarcastic and depreciating proverb
(born among bachelor monks) which ranged Man's helpmate with
the ass and the walnut-tree, as 'three things that do nothing rightly
if not beaten'. But such is the case. – From the moment when
M. Paul Emanuel begins to insult Miss Lucy Snowe, we give up
her heart as gone. It is true, that it has shown signs of hanging
itself on another object less contradictory and fierce, – that it has
wisely and delicately rooted out such a fancy, owing to a perception of that other's serene worldliness; – but by the relish with
which, after such a fit of sickness, it sits up to scold in answer to the
scolding little Professor, – we know that the right man has only
now come, and that the match when made will be one after
Currer Bell's own heart. The recurrence of the same argument
(with unimportant variations) in this writer's three novels would
form a good thesis for a lecture in any court of Love where 'the
sex' is honoured, not with Arcadian phrases, but with grave and

simple truth. Fever, discontent, distress existing in a heart full of
tenderness and a head guided by conscientiousness – a longing for
adventure that finds its gratification in eccentric companionships,
in the keen encounter of passions and of wits, and its reward in
making 'meek and tame' the virtues that walk abroad in the guise
of *Orsons*[1] – of such material is composed the strange pathetic,
painful revelation of Woman's nature thrice offered by a woman.
Such a phase may – and possibly does – belong to our times. It
may be inevitable that the tendency of female authorship should
lean towards defence rather than deprecation : – but by per-
petually setting it forth, the chances of healing, calming, strength-
ening, setting free, and placing aright the sufferer are not
increased. There are such things as epidemic distemperatures, –
as moods of sorrow engendered by a too perpetual exposition of
sorrow. We do not suppose that Lucy Snowe is intended to figure
as an example, – but remembering Currer Bell's former novels,
we must protest against such perpetual expositions of grief dealt
with and care overcome. There are other ways for a woman of
squaring accounts with trial than that of rushing about the world
when the homeland becomes wearisome – of taking midnight
rambles through a city when the sense of agony drives off sleep –
of anticipating the chosen one in the disclosure of mutual affection
when intriguers try to set two hearts at variance. Currer Bell can
bring off her heroine in triumph, it is true, – can find her a respectable shelter, without the slightest previous prospect, the first day
that an unknown stranger sets foot in a foreign land, – can pilot
her home through illuminated Brussels on a gala night without a
rough word said to her, – can reward the frank declaration of her
breaking heart by as frank reply, 'with healing on its wings'. But
we fear that such sequences are to be found rather in the artist's
chambers of faëry imagery than on the pages of Reality's record.
Her books will drive many minds out among the breakers, – they
will guide few to sure havens. Her talk is of duty, – her predilections lie with passion.

Enough of this homily, – necessary as it has seemed at a juncture when every poetess seems bent on being a preacher and a

prophetess also. – Let us endeavour to justify our praise of *Villette* as a work of art and of power, by an extract or two. But good illustrative passages such as are susceptible of being detached are hard to find in this novel. The confidential and intimate minuteness of its imaginary writer's confessions – the fragmentary way in which they stop, to be resumed at some later period, or to be eked out by collateral disclosures, – while they give to *Villette* the semblance of a real record, render its scenes more than ordinarily unmanageable. – An episodical passage or two tempt us. Lucy Snowe's first experience of public amusements is gathered at a concert at Brussels. Her feelings on the occasion are described with capital truth. She sees great personages at the concert, and thus she paints them . . . [quotes from chapter 20, 'The Concert'].

By Lucy Snowe's own admission she has something of the blood of a born actress running in her veins, – and therefore on a subsequent evening she is strongly impressed by a great French tragic actress (who, the reader is assured, died many years ago)[2] . . . [quotes from chapter 23, 'Vashti'].

The formal entombment of such a Vashti as the above is as flimsy an attempt at mystification as the blue crape dress for a lady's morning wear in *Jane Eyre* – owing to which solecism in *costume* some so long maintained that Currer Bell wielded 'a male pen'.[3] – But the passages which have been given are only extra morsels of speculation. Since we have stated that M. Paul Emanuel is one of those 'beings of the mind' who are rarely to be found in fiction, we will exhibit him in one of his many appearances . . . [quotes from chapter 29, 'Monsieur's Fête'].

The scene quoted, however, is hardly a sketch so much as the scrap of one. By Lucy Snowe's notes of other experiences in which the irascibility, vanity, violence and childishness of this exigent little foreigner are relieved by traits of truth, simplicity, kindliness and self-sacrifice, her hero is brought before us with a vividness and a consistency rare even in male delineations of male characters so complex. Without precisely sympathising, we are made to understand how in her case curiosity brings on fear, – and fear, respect, – and respect, confidence, – and confidence, affection. But there are 'lions in the path,' – a he-jesuit and a she-jesuit. The latter is Madame Beck, the school-mistress, – whose character also is one of the truest portraitures of foreign humanity by an English writer with which we are acquainted. Little less excellent, in their secondary sphere, are Graham Bretton, with his benign, warm, honourable worldliness (on account of that worldliness alone falling short of perfection), and Miss De Bassompierre – the little Paulina of the first chapters, in whom (as we have said) and not in the ill-looking and impassioned imaginary narrator, we had hoped to find the heroine of this novel. – To conclude, *Villette* is a book which will please much those whom it pleases at all. Allowing for some superfluity of rhetoric used in a manner which reminds us of the elder Miss Jewsbury[4] – and for one or two rhapsodies, which might have been 'toned down' with advantage, – this tale is much better written than *Shirley,* the preceding one by its authoress.

SOURCE: *Athenæum,* 12 February 1853.

NOTES

1. Orson, the prince in the early French romance, *Valentine and Orson* (English version by Henry Watson *c.* 1550); he was captured by a bear in infancy, brought up as a wild man and underwent many adventures before returning to his inheritance.

2. 'Vashti' is a portrait of the celebrated French actress Rachel, otherwise Elisabeth Félix (1820–58).

3. One of many sarcastic allusions in reviews of Charlotte's work after 1848 to Elizabeth Rigby's remarks about 'Currer Bell's' ignorance of fashionable dress (p. 73 above).

4. Geraldine Endsor Jewsbury (1812–80), novelist and close friend of the Carlyles; her novels include *Zoe* (1846), *The Half-Sisters* (1848), *Marian Withers* (1851) and *Right and Wrong* (1859).

Eclectic Review: 'With all its talent as a composition it
fails to please as a fiction'

... The tale we have analysed requires from us some critical
observations, not only for its own sake, but also as a type of a
class. The observation of Horace upon poetry may be applied with
truth to fiction – that its great object is to charm and please, and
that if it fails of this it is to literature what discordant music is to
a convivial entertainment, which would be agreeable enough
without any music at all. Luxuries, as they are in political economy
the fittest subjects of taxation, so in the realm of letters they are
the most fastidiously read and the most freely criticised. In the
work before us there is so much to admire that it is not agreeable
to take exceptions, and yet the application of Horace's rule dis-
closes one cardinal shortcoming. With all its talent as a composition it fails to please as a fiction; and this for one or two reasons
which it is necessary candidly to specify.

In the first place, then, the characters are not such as are calculated to interest the sympathies and the heart of the reader. We
do not know that in making this remark it is necessary to take
more than a single exception. Dr John, in other words Dr John
Graham Bretton, is certainly intelligent, vivacious, humane, and
affectionate, but Mrs Bretton is too much a woman of the world.
She lacks tenderness even to her protégé, the heroine; indeed, her
whole nature seems absorbed in that pride in her son which looks
too much like a sort of secondary selfishness to awaken a deeper
feeling than complacency. Her recognition of Lucy, after years of
absence, under circumstances peculiarly startling and affecting,
is not only destitute of all enthusiasm or of natural surprise, but
even of that 'touch of nature' which 'makes the whole world kin'.
It is difficult to imagine a mother so apathetic in such a case. Yet
this does not appear to distress or even to chill the heroine, who
has long before recognised Dr John, when in medical attendance
at the school, as the companion of her childhood and the son of
her benefactress, without making herself known to him. Paulina

again, while she is most uninteresting as a child, excites no very impassioned interest at eighteen, owing to a strong-minded control of her affections, which contrasts a little with a fretful petulance that spoils both the dignity and the amiability of her character. Of Ginevra Fanshawe it is enough to say that she is a sort of Cleopatra in her way, selfish and sensuous, and equally destitute of faith and feeling. Nor can we, with every desire to do so, fall in love with the heroine herself. She is sensible, clever, and somewhat emotional, but she lacks enthusiasm and deep womanly love, with all those weaknesses and dangers which belong to it, and which irresistibly touch the heart and chain the interest of the reader. In perusing the pages of her autobiography we desiderate in vain those characteristics which have so often charmed us in the heroines of [Scott's] Waverley Novels, and which have made Flora Macdonald, Julia Mannering, and many others, as real personages, to our imaginations, as if they had been the living objects of an unsuccessful but unforgotten love... Professor Paul Emanuel, as the husband of the heroine, must, we suppose, on all the laws of fiction, be considered as the hero. But what a hero! A short, bustling, angry schoolmaster, between forty and fifty years of age; vain, passionate, and imperious, and who designates as his chief treasure the pair of spectacles that suits his defective eyesight; – a Jesuit, and of course a spy, whose highest glory is the most prominent exhibition of his person in a public assembly; a man who makes young ladies tremble before him in class, and seriously protests that he will hang the housemaid if she dares to venture into his class-room to announce that Mademoiselle Somebody is wanted for a music lesson in another apartment.

And this leads us to observe further that one great defect in this work is that it scarcely presents one instance of attractive virtue. We have said that the characters are uninteresting, but more than this, they present the worst features of our nature, and that too on a petty scale. There are some writers who invest even the bad with a sort of heroic sublimity, from the colossal pre-eminence of their wickedness. Milton's Satan, Shakespeare's Lady Macbeth, and a thousand others, will occur to the reader as illustrations of

our meaning. But even about the defects in the characters of our
author there is a tame negativeness which, as contrasted with their
unimpressive excellencies, suggests the idea of the mixture of acids
and alkalies, *minus* the effervescence.

And yet, after all, it is the plot alone that is defective; the
development of the characters, comparatively insipid as they are,
is achieved with a degree of talent, the triumph of which is ren
dered the more remarkable by comparison with the poverty and
scantiness of the material. The plot itself lacks incident, it contains few of what the dramatists call *situations,* and is chiefly
transacted in a girls' boarding school. Hence the work mainly
consists of dialogue, and although this is sustained with all the
vivacity of an unquestionably powerful pen, yet it tires by its same-
ness. The greatest master of fiction that ever wrote would have
fatigued his readers if he had dwelt upon crochet, guard-chains,
cookery, and dress, and all the vapid details of a girls' schoolroom. In a word, that Currer Bell possesses distinguished talents,
and that delicacy of touch which none but a female writer can
give, we most cheerfully concede; but the plan of her fictions is
not equal to their execution. If a bolder hand were to strike her
outline, and to develop the plot with her own admirable discrimi-
nation of light and shade, we think she would produce a work
far more worthy of her talents than any with which the public
has yet associated her fictitious name.

                    S O U R C E : *Eclectic Review,* March 1853.

NOTE

This Nonconformist periodical was founded in 1805 by the book-
seller and hymn writer Joseph Conder (died 1855). The uneasy mixture of praise and condemnation is fairly characteristic of its literary
reviews.

W . M . T H A C K E R A Y : 'Poor little woman of genius'

So you are all reading *Villette* to one another – a pretty amusement to be sure . . . The good of *Villette* in my opinion Miss is a
very fine style; and a remarkably happy way (which few female
authors possess) of carrying a metaphor logically through to its
conclusion. And it amuses me to read the author's naive confession of being in love with 2 men at the same time; and her
readiness to fall in love at any time. The poor little woman of
genius! The fiery little eager brave tremulous homely-faced
creature! I can read a great deal of her life as I fancy in her book,
and see that rather than have fame, rather than any other earthly
good or mayhap heavenly one she wants some Tomkins or another
to love and be in love with. But you see she is a little bit of a
creature without a penny worth of good looks, thirty years old I
should think, buried in the country, and eating up her own heart
there, and no Tomkins will come. You girls with pretty faces and
real boots (and what not) will get dozens of young fellows fluttering
about you – whereas here is one a genius, a noble heart longing to
mate itself and destined to wither away into old maidenhood
with no chance to fulfil the burning desire . . .

                S O U R C E : Letter to Lucy Baxter, 11 March 1853.

M A T T H E W A R N O L D : 'Hunger, rebellion and rage'

Why is *Villette* disagreeable? Because the writer's mind contains
nothing but hunger, rebellion and rage, and therefore that is
all that she can, in fact, put into her book. No fine writing can
hide this thoroughly, and it will be fatal to her in the long run . . .

                S O U R C E : Letter to Mrs Forster, 14 April 1853.

NOTE

Arnold met Charlotte Brontë in December 1850 while she was visit-
ing Ambleside as the guest of Harriet Martineau. His celebrated tribute to the Brontë sisters, 'Haworth Parsonage', appeared in *Fraser's
Magazine* for April 1855.

Putnam's Monthly Magazine : 'This *actuality* is the very genius
and spirit of modern English fiction'

The whole force of English romance-writing has been deployed
during the last six months. Dickens, Thackeray, and Bulwer, the
chiefs of that department of literature, have been in full play,
and Miss Brontë (*Jane Eyre*), Mrs Gaskell (*Mary Barton*), Mrs
Marsh, Mrs Gore, Miss Julia Kavanagh, and lesser ladies, have
advanced almost simultaneously, and platoon-wise, discharged
each a new novel. They have all, at least, achieved what Frenchmen, with their facile flattery, call a *succès d'estime*. A *succès*, by
the bye, with which no man nor woman was ever known to be content. We are not sure that Thackeray's *Henry Esmond* was more
ardently anticipated than Miss Brontë's *Villette*. *Jane Eyre* – a
novel with a heroine neither beautiful nor rich, an entirely abnor-
mal creation among the conventional heroines – came directly
upon *Vanity Fair, a Novel without a Hero*, and made friends as
warm, and foes as bitter, as that noted book. *Shirley* disappointed.
It is in fact entirely overshadowed by its predecessor. But now,
after six years, *Villette* appears, and takes rank at once with *Jane
Eyre*, displaying the same vigour – the same exuberant power –
the same bold outline – the same dramatic conception – and the
same invincible mastery and fusion of elements usually considered
repugnant to romance. The great success of *Jane Eyre* as a work
of art, and apart from the interest of the story, which is very great,

consists in its rejection of all the stage-appointments of novels – all the Adonis-Dukes and Lady Florimels in satin boudoirs, which puerile phantoms still haunt the pages of Bulwer (although he is rapidly laying them) and the remorseless [G.P.R.] James,[1] and are, of course, the staple of the swarm of 'the last new novels' which monthly inundate the circulating libraries in England. The author takes the reader among a crowd of ordinary human beings, and declares proudly, 'Here you shall find as much romance and thrilling interest, as in the perfumed purlieus of palaces.' And she keeps her word. It is as if we were dragged to a lonely common, jagged with sad trees, and confronted with the splendour of a sunset. Is it less gorgeous than when seen from your palace window streaming through the green-house? asks the bold painter who has drawn us thither, because he knew that the unutterable glories of nature needed no architectural nor upholstering setting.

This *actuality* is the very genius and spirit of modern English fiction, and this is its humane and prodigious triumph. The democratic principle has ordered romance to descend from thrones and evacuate the palace. Romance is one of the indefeasible 'rights of man'. Disraeli's *Young Duke* (1831) and Bulwer's Harley L'Estrange[2] and *Pelham* (1828) are tailor's blocks and fashion-plates. Give us *men,* scarred and seamed as you please, that we may feel the thrill of sympathy : and learn, if we may, from their thought and action, how we should think and act. Discrown the 'Lady Arabella' and the 'haughty Countess' sacred in satin from warm emotion, give us no 'impossible she', but,

> A creature not too bright and good
> For human nature's daily food.[3]

So cries the age, with stentorian lungs. And they come, thick-thronging poetry and prose, the women around whose heads glance the loveliest lights of human sympathy, in whose pictured forms we recognize the image of our sweet hopes – whose characters, fair and feminine, play amid the press of life like flowers in the wind. Or they come, as in Lucy Snowe and Jane Eyre, more brave than beautiful, but inspiring deeper reverence

for integrity, and strength, and devotion. We open our novels, and
there is our life mirrored, – dimly sometimes, and insufficiently –
but not impossibly nor incredibly.

This actuality we conceive to be the healthy principle of contemporary fiction. We will not now stop to say that it may very
easily run, on the right hand, into a want of that sufficient stimulus
which belongs to 'ideal' portraitures, and which, by the charm of
an almost fabulous virtue, allures us to excellence; and on the left,
into that sermonizing and romance of reform which is the quick
destruction of story-telling. No man bidden to a feast of fiction
expects to sit down to a sermon. Vinegar is good – under restric-
tions – but when you are smilingly turning a glass of supposed
Steinberger-Cabinet, suddenly to taste vinegar, is to be angry
with your host, to spoil your dinner, and to run the risk of an
indigestion. If the novelist do really hold the mirror up to nature,
he need not fear that any delicate reader will too finely scent a
moral. But if he attempt to pin the moral to the picture, – to say
that Johnny being good had a gooseberry tart and naughty
Tommy was put into a dark closet, – he simply assumes an accident as a consequent, and treats resolution . . .

Thackeray is the most ponderous protestant against this nursery
and primer view of human nature and human life, and close
upon him, comes Miss Brontë. Jane Eyre was a governess, and a
strongminded woman. She was by no means the lady with whom
Harley L'Estrange in or out of *My Novel* would ever fall in love.
There were great doubts whether she knew how to dress, and
none at all that she had no 'style'. She moved up and down the
novel totally regardless of nerves and the 'tea-table proprieties'.
She was a woman bullied by circumstances and coping bravely
with a hard lot, and finally proving her genuine force of character by winning the respect and love of a man who had exhausted
the world and been exhausted by it; a man in whom the noble
instincts were so deeply sunk, that they could only respond to a
ray so penetrant and pure that it would not be dispersed in fogs –
but which instinctively, when they *were* touched, would respond
and rule the life. Of course a novel of this kind, full of the truthful

and rapid play of character, and from which rustling silks and satins are rigorously excluded – except once, when they sweep, cloud-like, down the stairs, in one of the most picturesque passages of the book – has no interest for those who are snuffing in the air for perfumes. It wears an almost repulsive sternness to those who quiz it daintily through tortoise-shell eye-glasses.

Villette has the same virtues. It is a novel of absorbing interest as a story. It is somewhat less severe than *Jane Eyre*. Paulina is a strain of grace and tenderness that does not occur in the other book. Paul has many traits like Rochester. Lucy Snowe is a governess like Jane Eyre herself – neither very young, nor lovely, nor fascinating, as we can easily see from the impression she makes upon Graham Bretton. He is such a hero as daily experience supplies. We have all seen many Graham Brettons, free, joyous natures, bounding through life; and therefore we are the better for meeting him in *Villette*. Harley L'Estrange, on the contrary, is a boarding-school girl's 'Mortimer', and therefore of no use to us, though we do not meet him in *My Novel*. Graham Bretton loves Paulina, who loves him from her childhood. The opening pages of the book, depicting Paulina as a child, are remarkable. She is the 'creation' of the book. We have not met her in other stories, and her picture is like an alto-relievo, it is so strongly carved. Lucy Snowe fancies a little that she loves Graham; but Lucy Snowe, in her situation, would have loved any chivalrous man with whom she was intimately thrown. Certain flowers require a southern exposure; and it is no fault of Bretton's that his nature demanded in a mistress something more tropical than Lucy Snowe. He was always noble to her. She had doubted him sometimes; but unjustly, as the events always proved. When Paulina first saw Graham, she loved him although she was but six years old. He liked her as a child, but when he met the woman, he loved her. This part of the book is what is called 'natural'; and it is certainly very fascinating, for we all love beauty, and grace, and excellence. It is pleasanter to sit in the sun than in the rain. A beautiful queen is more lovely than a dirty beggar-girl. This we fully admit. But our quarrel with the novelists – to which we

D

have referred – is, that by making all their days sunny, they spoil
the nature in their pictures; and by making all queens beautiful,
they defy experience.

When Paul first comes upon the stage, the reader does not like
him. He has, however, like Rochester, the fascination of power,
and when, later in the book, that power is developed, not gro-
tesquely, but nobly, the reader smiles, and willingly puts Lucy's
hand in Paul's, with the same blessing he has invoked upon
Graham and Paulina. The skill of the treatment is shown in the
gradual melting of the dislike of Paul, until it is entirely replaced
by esteem; and this, by no means which seem forced, and which
are not quite naturally and easily evolved from character and
circumstance. The difficulty with the book as a work of art is that
the interest does not sufficiently concentrate upon the two chief
figures. Graham and Paulina are disproportionately interesting.
In fact, we are not sure that most readers are not more anxious
to marry Graham than to follow the destiny of Lucy Snowe.
There is a pause over his marriage, and a glance into the future,
which properly belong only to the close of the book, and which
materially affect the sequence of interest.

Yet it is a legitimate novel, a story told for the pleasure of telling
it, with only such a moral as is necessarily contained in the circumstances – a cheerful, inspiring confidence in integrity and valor.
The book overflows with exuberant power. Its scenery is vivid and
grim, like the pictures in *Jane Eyre*. But it is also more ambitious
in style, and more evidently so, which is a great fault. The per-
sonifications of passion are unnatural, and clumsily patched upon
the tale. They are the disagreeable rents in the scenery, making
you aware that it is a drama, and not a fact; that it is an author
writing a very fine book, and not scenes of life developing themselves before you. To be désillusioné in this manner is disagreeable. The finest passages in the book are the descriptions of the
dreary vacation. The portrait of Rachel is sketched in the lurid
gloom of the French melodramatic style. It partakes of the fault
of the personification to which we alluded. *Villette* has less variety,
but more grace than *Jane Eyre*. It is quite as bold, original, and

interesting, allowing always for the fact that we have had the type in the earlier book . . .[4]

SOURCE: *'Villette* and *Ruth'*, *Putnam's Monthly Magazine,* May 1853.

NOTES

1. See Introduction, p. 21 above.
2. In Bulwer Lytton's *My Novel* (1853), the most recent of his many stories; it was frequently reviewed alongside *Villette* together with other new novels of the season.
3. Wordsworth's 'She was a phantom of delight . . .' (1807), II 17–18.
4. The review continues with a discussion of Mrs Gaskell's *Ruth* as a 'sad and sweet story' which 'contrasts with the gusty tumult of *Villette*'; it concludes by finding that *'Villette* is written from a conscious study of character, *Ruth* from a profound sympathy with it [cp. Introduction, p. 21, above]. *Villette* is a joyful cry of conscious power from the heart of the struggle, *Ruth* is a tear, washing the eyes clear, so that they see the way out of it. They are both admirable and remarkable novels . . . '

Dublin University Magazine: 'Morbid sensibility' at variance with qualities of 'skill' and 'humour'

We were disposed to entertain some doubts whether the fame so justly acquired by the author of *Jane Eyre* and *Shirley,* would be sustained by the work we now proceed to notice : but the interest with which we opened these volumes increased as we went on, and however high the test by which the critic might be disposed to subject a new *brochure* by this distinguished author, we think there can hardly be a doubt, that in *Villette* her reputation will be amply sustained. The novel is not only constructed with great care, but there is displayed throughout so abundant a variety of resources, such a perfect mastery of the springs of character, and such graphic pictures of external life, which are all used with art admirably directed to the end in view, that whatever the casual reader may think of the degree of success with which the latter is worked out, he will not be likely to deem the canon of criticism applied by Goldsmith at all applicable, 'that the picture would have been better if the painter had taken more pains'.

The story takes its shape after the fashion of former models. It is in the form of an autobiography, a certain Lucy Snowe being the narrator. Than the outline of the plot nothing can be more simple. It may be told in a few words . . .

The characters are all new, at least they are new to us, and are worked out with a skill and a humour which cannot fail to give us a very high opinion of the author's powers. There is not an actor in the little drama, from Monsieur Paul to Doctor John Graham (for the friend of early days is found again in the shape of a flourishing medical practitioner) that is not a real creation of flesh and blood . . . In the delineation of the character of the heroine, we cannot help thinking there is displayed some inconsistency. The qualities with which she is endowed can scarcely be called natural, although, like Jane Eyre, she has that intense longing after affection, that strong devotion to the duties of her daily life, and those other qualities which would indicate a high moral tone of character; all these are in some degree marred and defaced by a species of morbid sensibility which seems strangely at variance with such attributes, while the aim of the book would seem to be the utterance of a further complaint against the destiny of such of the softer sex as are reduced by necessity to look for their living by the most irksome of all occupations – viz., that of teaching. The moral it would inculcate is that there can be no real happiness to a woman, at least independently of the exercise of those affections with which nature has endowed her.[1] We shall not stop to argue the metaphysical question which such an inquiry would necessarily involve. We shall only say that the doctrine is an unwise one, and likely to lead to most disastrous results, which would establish the necessity of indulgence in such feelings as indispensable to a calm enjoyment of life and an honourable and useful employment of it. We have each of us to bear our burden of sorrow; there is no house, however blessed with social advantages, which has not a skeleton hanging up in some quiet corner, and the philosophy which would inculcate the necessity of the indulgence of morbid feeling of any kind is obviously unsound in its conclusions. We will quote one passage of the book as illustrative of our observations [quotes from Chapter 22, 'I shudder at the thought . . . laughed at her, and she went by'].

In this passage is contained the point of the philosophy, upon the unsatisfactory nature of which we would most strenuously insist. If happiness be only a glory shining down out of Heaven, it is a blessing servile to the skiey influences, and as much out of our own control as the weather. To teaching such as this we object. In the sedulous performance of all life's daily duties; in the meek endurance of its cares and troubles; in the strength of will which it is necessary to call into exercise in order to subdue them; in all these, and in the exertion necessary to practise them, we believe true happiness will most frequently be found; it is, therefore, more or less within the reach of every man who prefers a life of active labour in whatever vocation it has pleased Providence to assign him, to a life of sluggish despondency. To forget sorrow is by no means necessary; all that we would insist upon is that it is wisest and safest to have it put aside, and kept carefully out of sight, that its remembrance should not be suffered to impede the more active operations of the mind; if this be done, all will go on well. We would incline to think that another rather prevailing defect in the book is the somewhat too elaborate analysis of characters with which we are occasionally presented, who have but little claim upon our sympathy or regard . . .

S O U R C E : *Dublin University Magazine,* November 1853.

NOTE

1. Cp. Harriet Martineau, p. 76 above.

G . H . L E W E S : 'An influence of truth as healthful as a mountain breeze'

Should a work of Art have a moral? In other words, must the
Artist, during creation, keep the wandering caprices of his fancy
within the limits of some didactic formula? The question has
been often, but somewhat confusedly, debated. It has been seen,
on the one hand, that the merely didactic tale frustrates, in a great
measure, its own objects : the reader resents having his pill gilded
– resents having the leaves of a religious tract slipped in between
the pages of a novel; and in the spirit of reaction, it has been
said that the Artist has nothing to do with morality. On the other
hand, there are people whose first question is, What is the moral?
What does this prove? Hegel has said very truly, that 'there is
a moral in every work of art, but it depends on him that draws it'.
George Sand . . . makes a decided stand against this moral requi-
sition, and both in her own person, and vicariously for all other
novelists, declares that 'art can prove nothing, nor should it be
expected to prove anything'. She says that readers have always
wished to see vice punished and virtue rewarded; and that, in
this respect, she is one of the public. But poetical justice proves
nothing either in a story or in a drama. When vice is not punished
on the stage or in a book – as it very often is not in life – this does
not prove that vice is unhateful and unworthy of punishment; for
a narrative can prove nothing. If the vessel which carried Paul
and Virginia had not been wrecked, would it have proved that
chaste love is always crowned with happiness? And because this
vessel goes to the bottom with the interesting heroine, what does
Paul and Virginia prove? It proves that youth, friendship, love,
and the tropics are beautiful things, when Bernardin de Saint
Pierre describes them. If Faust were not led away and vanquished by the devil, would it prove that the passions were weaker
than reason? And because the devil is stronger than the philosopher, does it prove that philosophy can never vanquish the passions? What does *Faust* prove? It proves that science, human life,

fantastic images, profound, graceful or terrible ideas, are wonderful things when Goethe makes out of them a sublime and moving
picture. So far George Sand; but this does not meet the question.
Although a narrative is not a demonstration, and cannot be made
one; although, therefore, in the strict sense of the word, Art proves
nothing; yet it is quite clear that the details of a narrative may be
so grouped as to satisfy the mind like a sermon. It is an exhorta-
tion, if you like, not a demonstration, but it does not the less
appeal to our moral sense . . . When the incidents of the story,
besides exciting our interest, run along moral lines, and call up
tableaux vivants of just retribution, and the happy terminations
of worthy lives, then not only is the faculty gratified to which
fiction more immediately appeals, but the moral sense is also
gratified . . .

Now, in the question of the moral as respects fiction, it is quite
clear, from French practice more than any other, that without
formally inculcating any immoral dogma, the writer may very
successfully produce an immoral effect. Who can mistake the
immoral moral which breathes through the pages of Eugène Sue?[1]
Who can mistake the foregone conclusion employed in his selection of main incidents and characters? . . . On the other hand,
there is no mistaking the moral influence of good novels; even
when no specific formula can be appended to the closing chapter.
The novel may carry its moral openly on its very title-page,
through all its conclusions; or, it may carry within it, not one but
many moral illustrations, naturally arising out of the way the
incidents are grouped, and the way the characters express themselves.

These two forms of moral are illustrated in *Ruth* and *Villette,*
two works by our most popular authoresses. *Ruth* has a moral
carried in the story; not preached, but manifested. It is a story
of seduction . . . Turning from *Ruth* to *Villette,* the contrasts meet
us on all sides. Never were two women's books more unlike each
other. There is a moral too in *Villette,* or rather many morals, but
not so distinctly a *morale en action.* It is a work of astonishing
power and passion. From its pages there issues an influence of

truth as healthful as a mountain breeze. Contempt of conventions in all things, in style, in thought, even in the art of story-telling, here visibly springs from the independent originality of a strong mind nurtured in solitude. As a novel, in the ordinary sense of the word, *Villette* has few claims; as a book, it is one which, having read, you will not easily forget. It is quite true that the episode of Miss Marchmont, early in the first volume, is unnecessary, having no obvious connexion with the plot or the characters; but with what wonderful imagination is it painted! Where shall we find such writing as in that description of her last night, wherein the memories of bygone years come trooping in upon her with a vividness partaking of the last energy of life? It is true also that the visit to London is unnecessary, and has many unreal details. Much of the book seems to be brought in merely that the writer may express something which is in her mind; but at any rate she has something in her mind, and expresses it as no other can . . .[2]

SOURCE: *'Ruth* and *Villette', Westminster Review*, April 1853.

NOTES

1. Marie-Joseph ('Eugène') Sue (1804–75), popular and prolific novelist; his best-known works in the 1840s and 1850s include *Les Mystères de Paris* (1842–3), *Le Juif Errant* (1844–5) and *Les Mystères du Peuple* (1849–56).
2. George Eliot, editor at the time of the *Westminster Review*, found this article 'unsatisfactory' (*The George Eliot Letters*, II 93, and see below, p. 112). Lewes repeats several points from his earlier review for the *Leader* (p. 78 above), but the comparison with Mrs Gaskell's *Ruth* (1853) – to which he devotes the greater part of his space – prompts these new reflections about art and morality, which are of interest as an index to contemporary opinion about this problem.

ANNE MOZLEY: 'We are not all proud of her as a
member of our reformed faith'

. . . After threading the maze of harrowing perplexities thus set
forth by Lady Georgina[1] . . . it is, we own, a relief to turn to the
work-day world of *Villette*. The rough winds of common life make
a better atmosphere for fiction than the stove heat of the 'higher
circles'. Currer Bell, by hardly earning her experience, has, at
least, won her knowledge in a field of action where more can
sympathise; though we cannot speak of sympathy, or of ourselves
as in any sense sharing in it, without a protest against the outrages
on decorum, the moral perversity, the toleration of, nay, indifference to vice which deform her first powerful picture of a desolate
woman's trials and sufferings – faults which make *Jane Eyre* a
dangerous book, and which must leave a permanent mistrust of
the author on all thoughtful and scrupulous minds. But however
alloyed with blame this sympathy has necessarily been, there are
indications of its having cheered her and done her good. Perhaps
. . . she has been the better for a little happiness and success, for
in many important moral points *Villette* is an improvement on
its predecessors. The author has gained both in amiability and
propriety since she first presented herself to the world, – soured,
coarse, and grumbling; an alien, it might seem, from society, and
amenable to none of its laws.

We have said that Currer Bell has found life not a home, but
a school . . . She may, indeed, be considered the novelist of the
schoolroom . . . because, as the scholastic world would seem to
have been the main theatre of her experience – as here have been
excited, in herself, many a vivid thought and keen interest – she
chooses that others shall enter it with her. She will not condescend
to shift the scene . . . what has interested her, she means shall
interest them : nor are we losers by the obligation. It cannot be
denied that hitherto the art of teaching has cast a suspicion of
coldness and dryness over its professors : it should not be so; it is
unfair to an honourable profession, which should at least be

cheered by sympathy in its irksome labours. In these days of educational enthusiasm the prejudice ought to be done away.[2] Currer Bell seems to regard it as the mission of her genius to effect this : her clear, forcible, picturesque style gives life to what our fancies thought but a vegetating existence. Not that she wishes to represent life in the schoolroom as happy; far from it; but she shows us that life does not stagnate there in an eternal round of grammar and dictionary – in a perpetual infusion of elementary knowledge; and wherever it can be shown to flow freely and vigorously, wherever the mind has scope and the heart and emotions free play, there we can find interest and excitement. *Villette* must be considered the most scholastic of the series. In *Jane Eyre* we have the melancholy experience of the Clergy-daughters' school, and her own subsequent position as governess; in *Shirley* we have the heart-enthralling tutor, and the heiress falling in love as she learns her French and writes her copy-books under the assumed austerity of his rule, – a wrong state of things, we need not say : but in *Villette* almost the whole corps of the drama is furnished for the Pensionnat de Demoiselles. The flirting beauty of a school-girl; the grave, thoughtful young English teacher, with her purely intellectual attractions; Madame, the directress, the presiding genius; the little French professor of Belleslettres, for the hero, and the classes and large school-garden for the scenes. Even the outer-world hero, Graham, comes in as the physician of the establishment, and is entangled by the school-girl beauty; though it is his business to introduce us sometimes to the world beyond the walls, which now and then affords a refreshing change.

Nor does she gain the point of interesting us by ignoring any professional peculiarity which belongs to the science of teaching. Even the writer (for it is an autobiography) is, we see clearly, in look and air the 'teacher' she describes herself : her manner affected and influenced by her position. The consciousness of being under-valued, the longings for some one to care for her leading to some undignified results, the necessary self-reliance, the demure air the intellect held in check, but indemnifying itself for the world's neglect and indifference by the secret indulgence of an arrow-

like penetration – all are portrayed; and for the hero – what can
be more like a professor and less like a standard hero than M.
Paul Emanuel? a character in the highest degree fresh and
original, but in no sense calculated to attract a lady's fancy except
in scenes where the world of male society is shut out as it is in large
female assemblies, – in schools, convents, and, according to the
satirist, old maid coteries, – in all of which a very small amount of
heroic qualities are often found enough to constitute a man a
hero . . .

. . . The defect of the plot is a want of continuity. In fact, the
style is rather that of an autobiography – and, perhaps, excusable
as adopting that form – than a novel. Persons are introduced in
the beginning who have no share in the conduct of the story; adventures are given, which begin and end in themselves. The whole
episode of Miss Marchmont is of this nature. At the end of it we
find our heroine – she would not give herself this ambitious title –
friendless and penniless, except for the £15 which remain from
her salary as Miss Marchmont's companion. The spirit of adventure rises with the need for exertion. She goes to London, and
from thence sails to Bouemarine, the sea-port of Labassecour, to
seek her fortune in a foreign land; and here commences the
scholastic part of the story, for on board she meets with Ginevra
Fanshawe, a girl of seventeen on her way to Madame Beck's
establishment at Villette . . .

Madame Beck's establishment is conducted on the system of
surveillance which some have thought necessary to good education, – a system of which she is complete mistress, being addicted
to arts which are usually supposed to be practised only by the
detective police of some tyrannical power, but which the present
writer traces to the influence of Roman Catholicism in the
countries where it prevails.

There is probably prejudice, but there may be also valuable
information, in her picture of even a good foreign school [quotes
from chapter 8, Madame Beck's disciplinary system and Lucy's
first introduction to her pupils] . . .

We believe that this peculiar aspect, these eyes, and hard unblushing brows, [i.e. of Lucy's pupils], are to be found in our island, under the same circumstances as foster them in Labasse-cour. Wherever girls and young women, for any purpose, are brought in great numbers together, and allowed to associate in wild unrestrained companionship, the same thing may be observed. Girls, we believe, are not suited to congregate in large numbers together : they lose their charm, the softness, and the bloom, and many of the precious things these flowery words typify, under such training. To such an exterior corresponds the following view of heart and principle. We give it with no means ourselves of verifying the truth of so awful a charge; nor are we told how the naive confession ever reached the author's Protestant ears :—

'To do all parties justice, the honest aboriginal Labassecourien-nes had an hypocrisy of their own too, but it was of coarse order, such as could deceive few. Whenever a lie was necessary for their occasions, they brought it out with a careless ease and breadth, altogether untroubled by the rebuke of conscience. Not a soul in Madame Beck's house, from the scullion to the directress herself, but was above being ashamed of a lie; they thought nothing of it; to invent might not be precisely a virtue, but it was the most venial of faults. "J'ai menti plusieurs fois," formed an item of every girl's and woman's monthly confession; the priest heard unshocked, and absolved unreluctant. If they had missed going to Mass, or read a chapter of a novel, that was another thing; these were crimes whereof rebuke and penance were the unfailing meed.' [Chapter 9]

Reflecting upon this extraordinary moral perversity, the English teacher once ventured to remonstrate, and to express her views of the relative depravity of the two sins – a lie, or an occa-sional omission in Church going . . . We are not at all proud of her as a representative of our reformed faith; and believe there might be much better reason for this than she would be willing to allow. We own we should be sorry to subject any child of ours to the teaching and insinuations of the mind here pictured; whose reli-gion is without awe, – who despises and sets down every form and distinction she cannot understand, – who rejects all guides but her Bible, and at the same time constantly quotes and plays with its sacred pages, as though they had been given to the world for no better purpose than to point a witticism or furnish an ingenious illustration ...

We have left the Professor for the duties of the story; it is fit now to return to him ... the following episode will give our reader a better notion of M. Emanuel than any further description. It could not be shortened without being spoiled, which must be our excuses for its length. Our authoress shines in such scenes. Her accuracy and truth of detail, the bright playful enjoyment of her own success, her power of seizing the point, of bringing minds in contact, of showing what vivid moments there are in scenes apparently trivial, if only a quick eye and graphic pen can catch the evanescent spirit, and give it consistency, are all delightful. Can our readers doubt that this scene is no invention, but in some modification or other has actually occurred [quotes the episode with Monsieur Paul from the opening of chapter 27] ...

We do not wonder, with such skill in turning this fiery little temper, that Miss Lucy found herself attracted towards the possessor of it ... With all his absurdities, M. Paul is a man of great ability, almost of genius. We are conscious of his real power while we laugh at him. It is a sort of simplicity and humility, an avowed contempt for his own dignity, which shows so prominently his vanity and other weak points. We are disposed in the end to adopt the writer's conclusion, that it is his nerves that are irritable, not his temper. His religion, too, after the fashion of his country, is a very real and genuine feature. We quite acquiesce in her content to have him as he is, without any attempt to make him like herself. He had been educated by a Jesuit, and is still most dutiful at confession, having to go through some tribulations on account of his predilection for the English heretic, whom he endeavours in vain to convert by laying persuasive brochures in her way, which she treats with true Protestant contempt. Childlike in his faith, he is also pure in life, and the soul of honour; in all these points being in happy contrast with his brother professors. Some romantic

acts of generosity and self-denial, which come out towards the
end of the story, have not truth enough about them to match
with his very true character; and in the same way the scenes of
love-making in the end, between him and Lucy, have a very
apocryphal air . . .

The moral purpose of this work seems to be to demand for a
certain class of minds a degree of sympathy not hitherto accorded
to them; a class of which Lucy Snowe is the type, who must be
supposed to embody much of the authoress's own feelings and
experience, all going one way to express a character which finds
itself unworthily represented by person and manner, conscious
of power, equally and painfully conscious of certain drawbacks,
which throw this superiority into shade and almost hopeless dis-
advantage. For such she demands room to expand, love, tenderness, and a place in happy domestic life. But in truth she draws a
character unfit for this home which she yearns for. We want a
woman at our hearth; and her impersonations are without the
feminine element, infringers of modest restraints, despisers of bash-
ful fears, self-reliant, contemptuous of prescriptive decorum; their
own unaided reason, their individual opinion of right and wrong,
discreet or imprudent, sole guides of conduct and rules of manners,
– the whole hedge of immemorial scruple and habit broken down
and trampled upon. We will sympathise with Lucy Snowe as
being fatherless and penniless, and are ready, if this were all, to
wish her a husband and a fire-side less trying than M. Paul's must
be, unless reformed out of all identity; but we cannot offer even
the affections of our fancy (right and due of every legitimate
heroine) to her unscrupulous, and self-dependent intellect – to
that whole habit of mind which, because it feels no reverence, can
never inspire for itself that one important, we may say, indispensable element of man's true love.

One suggestion we would make in parting with these two ladies
– a question applicable to other scrutinisers of the female bosom –
whether, indeed, they are consulting the interests of the sex, for
which they contend so earnestly, by betraying – what gallantry
is slow to credit – that women give away their hearts unsought as

often as they would have us believe? So long as men wrote
romance, that heart was described as an all-but-impregnable
fortress ... But now that our fair rivals wield the pen, the tables
are turned ... They show us the invader greeted from afar –
invited, indeed, within the walls. They betray the castle to have
been all the while wanting a commander, the heart an owner. If
it were indeed so, would the prize won on such easy terms be
thought so much worth the having? Would this 'more than wil-
lingness' satisfy the inherent love of difficulty and of achievement
in man's nature? But, happily, the question need not seriously
be asked. A restless heart and vagrant imagination, though owned
by woman, can have no sympathy or true insight into the really
feminine nature. Such cannot appreciate the hold which a daily
round of simple duties and pure pleasures has on those who are
content to practise and enjoy them. They do not know the power
of home over the heart – how it asserts its sway against new and
more enthralling interests. Those who own such influences will
still be difficult to win. Nor can we promise the aspirant to their
favour any such eloquent, unsought avowals as the maidens of
modern romance succeed so well in. He must be content to wait
for the genial influences of a new home, to unthaw reserve; for
trial, to prove constancy; and time and sorrow, to develop the full
force, the boundless resources, of a pure, unselfish affection.

S O U R C E : *Christian Remembrancer,* April 1853.

NOTES

On Anne Mozley and the attitude of this 'High Church periodical'
see Introduction, p. 20, above, and for its review of *Jane Eyre*, p. 57,
above.

1. Lady Georgina's *Ladybird* (1853) is the subject of the first
part of the review, see above, p. 57 n.

2. See R. A. Colby's essay, pp. 229–30, below.

GEORGE ELIOT: 'Almost preternatural in its power'

I am only just returned to a sense of the real world about me for I have been reading *Villette*, a still more wonderful book than *Jane Eyre*. There is something almost preternatural in its power.

SOURCE: Letter to Mrs Charles Bray, 15 February 1853.

NOTE

For her earlier opinion of *Jane Eyre*, see above, p. 61. George Lewes may have infected her with something of his own enthusiasm after they had met in 1852.

PART TWO

Later Victorian Assessments
1850-1899

SYDNEY DOBELL: 'The authoress of *Jane Eyre* is the novelist of the coming time'

... whatever absolute superiority we may discover in *Jane Eyre,* we find in it only further evidence of the same producing qualities to which *Wuthering Heights* bears testimony. Those qualities, indurated by time, armed by experience, and harmonised by the natural growth of a maturing brain, have here exhibited, in a more favourable field, and under stronger guidance, the same virtues and the same faults . . . In *Shirley* we see the qualities of the author of *Jane Eyre* labouring in an exhausted soil . . . *Jane Eyre* is the real spar – the slow deposit which the heart of genius filters from the daily stream of time and circumstance. Open the later work where you will, this crystal sparkles in your eyes; break it up piecemeal, and every fragment glitters. Turn over the first chapter, and pause at hazard. There is no apparent consciousness of wisdom – no parading of truths or setting forth of paradoxes – no dealing in aphorisms, axioms, or generals of any kind. Yet one could preach a sermon from every sentence. Who that remembers early childhood, can read without emotion the little Jane Eyre's night journey to Lowood? How finely . . . are those peculiar aspects of things which cease with childhood developed in this simple history; – that feeling of unlimited vastness in the world around – that absence of all habitual expectations, which make even a new room a field of discovery, wherein the infant perceptions go, slowly struggling and enlightening, like a faint candle in a dark night. There is something intensely, almost fearfully, inter-

esting in the diary of a child's feelings ... But pass over the striking passages in these chapters; take some sentence which the
circulating library will skip. It is full of the moralities of nature.
Little, ill-used Jane Eyre does not hush her doll, but we are the
better for it. 'I was happy', says she, 'believing it to be happy likewise' ... Take this little sentence reverently, for it contains a great
psychological truth ... how few of us recognise ... that the best
abiding happiness must arise from the happiness of others ...
Those few words are a masterstroke of genius. Only let Jane Eyre
give you her nursery confessions and they shall help you to read
the heart of three-score and ten. 'When thus gentle', writes she,
'Bessie ... seemed to me the BEST, *prettiest,* kindest being in the
world.' Alas! for the guilt of those everyday sinners, and the
wrongs of those hourly sufferers, of whom Aunt Read and Jane
Eyre are the types ... To how many young nursery slaves ... has
some vulgar Bessie grown to be 'the *prettiest, best,* kindest being in
the world'? ... But we might multiply extracts as easily as turn
the page ... We sat down to this paper with no intention of what
is ordinarily expected in a review. We look on it as a morning
walk with that accomplished young writer, with whose name we
have graced it ... We rise to take leave in the conviction with
which we entered – that the authoress of *Jane Eyre* is the novelist
of the coming time ... [she] combines all the natural and acci-
dental attributes of the novelist of her day. In the ecclesiastical
tendencies of her education and habits – in the youthful ambiguity of her politics – in a certain old-world air, which hangs about
her pictures, we see her passing into circles which otherwise she
would never reach. Into them she is carrying, unperceived, the
elements of infallible disruption and revolution. In the specialities
of her religious belief ... in the keen satiric faculty she has shown
... in her unmistakeable hatred of oppression and determination
to be free ... we acknowledge the best pledge that that passport,
already torn, will one day be scattered to the winds. The pecu-
liarities of her local position – evidently Lancashire or Yorkshire –
give her opportunity for investigating a class of character out of
the latitude of the London *littérateur* ... ; and in the strange

combination of factory and moorland, the complexities of civilisa-
tion and the simple majesty of nature, she has before her at one
glance, the highest materials for the philosopher and the poet –
the most magnificent emblem of the inner heart of the time. One
day, with freer hands, more practised eye, an ampler horizon, an
enlarged experience, she must give us such revelations of that
heart – of its joys, woes, hopes, beliefs, duties and destinies – as
shall make it leap like a dumb man healed . . .

S O U R C E : from 'Currer Bell', *Palladium,* September 1850.

N O T E

Sydney Dobell (1824–74), one of the poets associated with the so-
called 'Spasmodic School', had recently published his dramatic poem
'The Roman'. Notwithstanding Charlotte's disclaimer in the second
edition of *Jane Eyre* (Introduction, p. 19), he was convinced that
'Currer Bell' was the author of all the 'Bell' novels and his essay for
the *Palladium* is in effect a celebration of the remarkable talent which
produced *Wuthering Heights,* to which he devoted the greater part
of his space (Introduction, p. 31). Charlotte was especially touched
by his recognition of Emily's imaginative power and sent him a copy
of the 1850 edition of *Wuthering Heights* and *Agnes Grey* as soon
as it was ready; for his response to the new information about Emily
and Anne and his subsequent correspondence with Charlotte see *LL*
III 186, 217–19, 226, 229, 235–6, 238, 253.

M A R G A R E T   O L I P H A N T : The 'new Bellona' in *Jane Eyre*
and *Villette*

. . . Ten years ago we professed an orthodox system of novel-
making. Our lovers were humble and devoted – our ladies were
beautiful, and might be capricious if it pleased them; and we
held it a very proper and most laudable arrangement that Jacob

should serve seven years for Rachel, and recorded it as one of the articles of our creed; and that the only true-love worth having was that reverent, knightly, chivalrous true-love which consecrated all womankind, and served one with fervour and enthusiasm. Such was our ideal, and such our system, in the old halcyon days of novel writing; when suddenly there stole upon the scene, without either flourish of trumpets or public proclamation, a little fierce incendiary, doomed to turn the world of fancy upside down. She stole upon the scene – pale, small, by no means beautiful – something of a genius, something of a vixen – a dangerous little person, inimical to the peace of society. After we became acquainted with herself, we were introduced to her lover. Such a lover! – a vast, burly, sensual Englishman, one of those Hogarth men, whose power consists in some singular animal force of life and character, which it is impossible to describe or analyse. Such a wooing! – the lover is rude, brutal, cruel. The little woman fights against him with courage and spirit – begins to find the excitement and relish of a new life in this struggle – begins to think of her antagonist all day long – falls into fierce love and jealousy – betrays herself – is tantalised and slighted, to prove her devotion – and then suddenly seized upon and taken possession of, with love several degrees fiercer than her own. Then comes the catastrophe which prevents this extraordinary love from running smooth. Our heroine runs away to save herself – falls in with another man almost as singular as her first love – and very nearly suffers herself to be reduced to marry this unloved and unloving wooer; but, escaping that risk, finally discovers that the obstacle is removed which stood between her and her former tyrant, and rushes back straightway to be graciously accepted by the blind and weakened Rochester. Such was the impetuous little spirit which dashed into our well-ordered world, broke its boundaries, and defied its principles – and the most alarming revolution of modern times has followed the invasion of *Jane Eyre*.

It is not to be wondered at that speculation should run wild about this remarkable production. Sober people, with a sober respect for womankind, and not sufficient penetration to perceive that the grossness of the book was such grossness as only could be perpetrated by a woman, contested indignantly the sex of the writer. The established authorities brought forth proofs in the form of incorrect costume, and errors in dress. Nobody perceived that it was the new generation nailing its colours to its mast. No one would understand that this furious love-making was but a wild declaration of the 'Rights of Woman' in a new aspect. The old-fashioned deference and respect – the old-fashioned wooing – what were they but so many proofs of the inferior position of the woman, to whom the man condescended with the gracious court-liness of his loftier elevation! The honours paid to her in society – the pretty fictions of politeness, they were all degrading tokens of her subjection, if she were but sufficiently enlightened to see their true meaning. The man who presumed to treat her with reverence was one who insulted her pretensions; while the lover who struggled with her, as he would have struggled with another man, only adding a certain amount of contemptuous brutality, which no man would tolerate, was the only one who truly recognised her claims of equality. 'A fair field and no favour', screams the repre-sentative of womanhood. 'Let him take me captive, seize upon me, overpower me if he is the better man – let us fight it out, my weapons against his weapons, and see which is the strongest. You poor fellow, do you not see how you are insulting and humiliating that Rachel, for whom you serve seven years? Let her feel she is your equal – make her your lawful spoil by your bow and by your spear. The cause of the strong hand for ever – and let us fight it out!' Whereupon our heroine rushes into the field, makes desperate sorties out of her Sebastopol,[1] blazes abroad her ammu-nition into the skies, commits herself beyond redemption, and finally permits herself to be ignominiously captured, and seized upon with a ferocious appropriation which is very much unlike the noble and grand sentiment which we used to call love.

Yes, it is but a mere vulgar boiling over of the political cauldron, which tosses your French monarch into chaos, and makes a new one in his stead. Here is your true revolution. France is but one of the Western Powers; woman is the half of the world. Talk of a balance of power which may be adjusted by taking a Crimea, or fighting a dozen battles – here is a battle which must always be going forward – a balance of power only to be decided by single combat, deadly and uncompromising, where the combatants, so far from being guided by the old punctilios of the duello, make no secret of their ferocity, but throw sly javelins at each other, instead of shaking hands before they begin. Do you think that young lady is an angelic being, young gentleman? Do you compare her to roses and lilies, and stars and sunbeams, in your deluded imagination? . . . Unhappy youth! She is a fair gladiator – she is not an angel. In her secret heart she longs to rush upon you, and try a grapple with you, to prove her strength and her equality . . . And this new Bellona steps forth in armour, throws down her glove and defies you – to conquer her if you can. Do you like it, gentle lover? – would you rather break her head and win, or leave her alone and love her? The alternative is quite distinct and unmistakable – only do not insult her with your respect and humility, for this is something more than she can bear.

These are the doctrines, startling and original, propounded by Jane Eyre; and they are not Jane Eyre's opinions only, as we may guess from the host of followers or imitators who have copied them. There is a degree of refined indelicacy possible to a woman, which no man can reach. Her very ignorance of evil seems to give a certain piquancy and relish to her attempts to realise it. She gives a runaway, far-off glimpse – a strange improper situation, and whenever she has succeeded in raising a sufficient amount of excitement to make it possible that something very wrong might follow, she prevents the wrong by a bold *coup,* and runs off in delight. There are some conversations between Rochester and Jane Eyre which no *man* could have dared to give – which only could have been given by the overboldness of innocence and ignorance trying to imagine what it never could understand, and which are as womanish as they are unwomanly.

When all this is said, *Jane Eyre* remains one of the most remarkable works of modern times – as remarkable as *Villette,* and more perfect. We know no one else who has such a grasp of persons and places, and a perfect command of the changes of the atmosphere, and the looks of a country under rain or wind. There is no fiction in these wonderful scenes of hers. The Yorkshire dales, the north-country moor, the streets of Brussels, are illusions equally complete. Who does not know Madame Beck's house, white and square and lofty, with its level rows of windows, its green shutters, and the sun that beams upon its blinds, and on the sultry pavement before the door? How French is Paul Emanuel and all his accessories! How English is Lucy Snowe! We feel no art in these remarkable books. What we feel is a force which makes everything real – a motion which is irresistible. We are swept on in the current, and never draw breath till the tale is ended. Afterwards we may disapprove at our leisure, but it is certain that we have not a moment's pause to be critical till we come to the end.

The effect of a great literary success, especially in fiction, is a strange thing to observe, – the direct influence it has on some one or two similar minds, and the indirect bias which it gives to a great many others. There is at least one other writer of considerable gifts, whose books are all so many reflections of *Jane Eyre*. We mean no disparagement to Miss Kavanagh; but, from *Nathalie* to *Grace Lee*,[2] she has done little else than repeat the attractive story of this conflict and combat of love or war – for either name will do... The story of *Grace Lee* is a story of mutual 'aggravation', in which the lady first persecutes the gentleman with attentions, kindnesses, scorn, and love; and the gentleman afterwards persecutes the lady in the self-same way... We might perhaps trace the origin of this passion for *strength* further back than *Jane Eyre*; as far back, perhaps, as Mr Carlyle's idolatry of the 'Canning' – the king, man, and hero.[3] But it is a sad thing, with all our cultivation and refinement, to be thrown back upon sheer blind force as our universal conqueror...

Mrs Gaskell, a sensible and considerate woman, and herself ranking high in her sphere, has just fallen subject to the same delusion. *North and South* is extremely clever, as a story;[4] and, without taking any secondary qualification to build its merits upon, it is perhaps better and livelier than any of Mrs Gaskell's previous works; yet here are still the wide circles in the water, showing that not far off is the identical spot where Jane Eyre and Lucy Snowe, in their wild sport, have been casting stones; here is again the desperate, bitter quarrel out of which love is to come; here is love itself, always in a fury, often looking exceedingly like hatred, and by no means distinguished for its good manners, or its graces of speech . . .

SOURCE : from 'Modern Novelists – Great and Small', *Blackwood's Magazine*, May 1855.

NOTES

Margaret Oliphant (1828–97), voluminous novelist and regular contributor to *Blackwood's Magazine*, published her *Annals* of Blackwood's publishing house in 1897 and her *Autobiography* in 1899. Her best known stories include *Chronicles of Carlingford* (1863–76), containing, notably, *Salem Chapel* and *Miss Marjoribanks; Passages in the Life of Mrs Maitland* (1849); and the supernatural tales 'A Beleaguered City' (1830) and 'A Little Pilgrim of the Unseen' (1862). This extract is taken from one of her many literary surveys written for *Blackwood's* over a period of some forty years and was prepared before she received the news of Charlotte's death in March. She adds a farewell tribute at the end of the article. For other of her comments on Charlotte see Introduction, pp. 29–30.

1. The war in the Crimean peninsula (1853–56), which centred on Sebastopol, still had another year to run.

2. Julia Kavanagh (1824–77) wrote, among other novels, *Madeleine* (1848), *Nathalie* (1850), *Daisy Burns* (1853) and *Grace Lee* (1855). Charlotte liked this unassuming younger writer, whose admiration for herself had been conveyed by W. S. Williams; she sent her a copy of the second edition of *Jane Eyre* in 1848 and visited her in London in 1850. For their correspondence and Charlotte's comments on her work see *LL* II 182, 185, 270, 287–8; II 118, 159, 203; IV 51. Cf. pp. 235–6, below R. A. Colby's essay on *Villette*.

3. Carlyle's *On Heroes, Hero-Worship and the Heroic in History* was published 1841.

4. Mrs Gaskell returned in *North and South* (1855) to the industrial themes of her first novel, *Mary Barton* (1848). She had published in the interval *Cranford* (1851–3), *Ruth* (1853) and many other stories and sketches.

J O H N   S K E L T O N : *Jane Eyre, Villette* and 'the realities of life'

Jane Eyre has been austerely condemned by austere critics. It is said that in it the interest depends on the terrible and the immoral, – two elements of interest which cannot be rightly appropriated by fiction. Admitting that the charge is true, we inquire – why not?

The old dramatists, at least, did not judge so; and the result was that they evoked 'high passions and high actions' which stir our hearts to the core. Where in modern tragedy, with its guarded touch and surface propriety, shall we find such an appeal to our deepest feelings, as – leaving Shakespeare altogether out of the question – in Hieronimo's madness:

> In truth it is a thing of nothing,
> The murder of a son or so;
> A thing of nothing, my lord;

in Annabella's –

> Forgive him, Heaven, and me, my sins.
> Farewell
> Brother unkind, unkind;

in Calantha's –

> Oh my lords!
> I but deceived your eyes with antick gesture.
> When one news straight came huddling on another –
> Of death, and death, and death; still I danced forward.
> But it struck home, and here, and in an instant.
> They are the silent griefs which cut the heartstrings.
> Let me die smiling.
> One kiss on these cold lips – my last; crack, crack,
> Argos now's Sparta's king.[1]

They looked terror and death, the momentous issues of life, fear-
lessly in the face; wherever the true tragic came out, there we find
them. And they succeeded in impressing on us a sense of its greatness, its reality, its infinite capacities for grief or gladness, such as
we now seldom obtain. Seldom, because we have become afraid of
its sternness, and gloss it over; because very few of our poets dare
to gauge boldly the perilous pains of the spirit, the great majority
contenting themselves with saying pretty things at their fastidious
leisure about sorrows which are as genuine as a pasteboard doll's;
because when a woman like Charlotte Brontë does try to evoke
that mighty spirit of tragedy which lurks in the heart of every man,
she is told that she is creating the horrible, and breaking artistic
statutes more immutable than those of the Medes and Persians.

The charge of immorality is one easily made – still more easily
repeated. According to certain scrupulous zealots, everything is
immoral in our present art – from *Marie* and *La Traviata,* to
Ruth, Jane Eyre, and *Aurora Leigh*[2] – which presumes to assert
that society is not a mass of respectabilities . . . But if *Aurora Leigh*
is such a book, then *Jane Eyre* may be included in the class. For it
speaks freely of many questionable matters on which our sancti-
monious society closes its eyes or passes by on the other side; and
it exhibits a freedom and latitude in discussing difficult questions
which have struck many pious souls with consternation. Wiser
critics there are, however, who may judge more leniently. They
may hold that rudeness, indelicacy, masculine directness, are
words that have been somewhat loosely applied to describe a fine
and peculiar insight into the heart of man. They may even go the
length of inquiring, as we do – Why should not holy hypocrisy be
unmasked and scarified? Why should not the struggle between
virtue and vice be chronicled? Why should it not be said – She
was tempted, and she overcame; nay, even – She was tempted,
and fell? . . . But while we aver without hesitation that *Jane Eyre*
is not an immoral book, we are bound to admit that those parts
which have been censured are by no means blameless, when considered artistically. The confidence between Jane Eyre and
Rochester is much too sudden and excessive. There is too little

attractiveness in the heroine to account for a violent passion in such a man. The explanation is inadequate. Why should so much fondness be lavished upon this demure, keen-eyed little woman? Why should it be? we ask; and the reply is, It would not be so with us; and a feeling of contempt for the infatuation of this otherwise astute and daring man of the world is the result.

The characters, also, though drawn with mastery, are too strongly marked. Rochester is the type of one order of mind; St John Rivers of another; and the features in each case are exaggerated to produce an effective contrast. Still, both are of the grand order of men. The broad-chested, grim-mouthed Rochester, sweeping past us on his black horse Mesrour, and followed by his Gytrash-like sleuth hound, is a modern apparition of Black Bothwell . . . St John is the warrior-priest, cool and inflexible as death. His integrity is austere, his conscientiousness implacable. It is impossible to love him; nay, even Rochester, in his devilish madness, is preferable to this inexorable priest. Yet the man is not tranquil; there is a passionate unrest at the bottom of his heart. A statue of snow, and fire burns underneath! But the fire will not thaw the ice . . .

Shirley presents a notable contrast to Miss Brontë's other novels . . . The world of toil and suffering lies behind, but ever so far away. True, it must be again encountered, its problems resolved, its sores probed; the hard and obstinate war again waged manfully; but in the mean time the burn foams and sparkles through the glen; there is sunshine among the purple harebells; and the leaves in the birken glade dance merrily in the summer wind.

In *Villette* Miss Brontë returns to the realities of life; but with power more conscious and sustained. She is less absorbed, and more comprehensive. There is the same passionate force; but the horizon is wider.

Villette is by no means a cheerful book; on the contrary, it is often very painful, especially where the central figure – the heroine – is involved. *Her* pain – her tearless pain – is intense and protracted. And in this connexion *Villette* may be regarded as an

elaborate psychological examination – the anatomy of a powerful
but pained intellect – of exuberant emotions watchfully and vigil-
antly curbed. The character of this woman is peculiar, but drawn
with a masterly hand. She *endures* much in a certain Pagan
strength, not defiantly, but coldly and without submission. Over
her heart and her intellect she exercises an incessant restraint – a
restraint whose vigilant activity curbs every feeling, controls every
speculation, becomes as it were engrained into her very nature.
She, at least, will by all means look at the world as it is – a hard,
dry, practical world, not wholly devoid of certain compensating
elements – and she will not be cajoled into seeing it, or making
others see it, under any other light. For herself, she will live
honestly upon the earth, and invite or suffer no delusions; strong,
composed, self-reliant, sedate in the sustaining sense of independence. But cold and reserved as she may appear, she is not without imagination – rich, even, and affluent as a poet's. This is in a
measure, however, the root of her peculiar misery. The dull and
cheerless routine of homely life is not in her case relieved and
penetrated by the creative intellect, but on the contrary, acquires
through its aid a subtle and sensitive energy to hurt, to afflict, and
to annoy. Thus she is not always strong; her imagination sometimes becomes loaded and surcharged; but she is always passionately ashamed of weakness. And through all this torture she is
very solitary : her heart is very empty; she bears her own burden.
There are cheerful hearths, and the pleasant firelight plays on the
purple drapery that shuts out the inhospitable night; but none are
here who can convey to her the profound sympathy her heart
needs pitifully; and so she passes on, pale and unrelenting, into the
night. Undoubtedly there is a very subtle, some may say obnox-
ious, charm in this pale, watchful, lynx-like woman – a charm,
certainly, but for our own part we have an ancient prejudice in
behalf of 'Shirley's' piquant and charming ferocity.

Miss Brontë always wrote earnestly, and in *Villette* she is per-
emptorily honest. In it she shows no mercy for any of the engaging *ruses* and artifices of life : with her it is something too real,
earnest, and even tragic, to be wantonly trifled with or foolishly

disguised. She will therefore tolerate no hypocrisy, however decent
or fastidious; and her subdued and direct insight goes at once to
the root of the matter. She carries this perhaps too far – it may be
she lacks a measure of charity and toleration, not for what is bad
– for *that* there must be no toleration – but for what is humanly
weak and insufficient. Graham Bretton, for instance, with his light
hair and kind heart and pleasant sensitiveness, is ultimately treated
with a certain implied contempt; and this solely because he hap-
pens to be what God made him, and not something deeper and
more devout, the incarnation of another and more vivid kind of
goodness, which it is not in his nature to be, and to which he makes
no claim. It is the patience, the fortitude, the endurance, the strong
love that has been consecrated by Death and the Grave, the spirit
that has been tried in fire and mortal pain and temptation, – it is
these alone she can utterly admire. We believe she is wrong. But
as we recall the lone woman sitting by the desolate hearthstone,
and remember all that she lost and suffered, we cannot blame very
gravely the occasional harshness and impatience of her language
when dealing with men who have been cast in a different mould.

Villette excels Miss Brontë's other fictions in the artistic skill
with which the characters are – I use the word advisedly –
developed. She brings us into contact with certain men and women
with whom she wishes to make us acquainted. She writes no formal
biography; there is no elaborate introduction; the characters
appear incidently during the course of the narrative, and by
degrees are worked into the heart of the every-day life with which
the story is concerned. But the dissection goes on patiently all the
time – so leisurely and yet so ruthlessly – one homely trait accumulated upon another with such steady, untiring pertinacity, that the
man grows upon us line by line, feature by feature, until his idiosyncrasy is stamped and branded upon the brain. Probably the
most genuine power is manifested in the mode in which the interest
is shifted from Graham Bretton to the ill-favoured little despot
– Paul Emanuel. No essential change takes place in *their* characters, *they* remain the same, the colours in which they were originally painted were quite faithful, perfectly accurate – not by any

means exaggerated for subsequent effect and contrast. It is only that a deeper insight has been gained by *us,* and if our original judgment undergoes modification, it is not because any new or inconsistent element has been introduced, but because, the conditions remaining the same, *we* see further. Leaf after leaf has been unfolded with a cold and impartial hand, until we have been let down into the innermost hearts of the men, and taught by the scrutiny a new sense of their relative value and worthiness. And Paul Emanuel is surely a very rich and genuine conception. 'The Professor' will ever be associated in our memory with a certain soft and breezy laughter; for though the love he inspires in the heroine is very deep and even pathetic after its kind, yet the whole idea of the man is wrought and worked out in a spirit of joyous and mellow ridicule, that is full of affection, however, and perhaps at times closely akin to tears.

M. Heger, of the Brussels *Pension,* was probably the original of Paul Emanuel; but we cannot help believing that the author of *Vanity Fair* was in Miss Brontë's thoughts when she wrote. Thackeray was, as we have said, after 'the Great Duke', her peculiar hero; *their* portraits hung in the parsonage parlour side by side . . .

To ourselves, one of the most surprising gifts of the authoress of these volumes is the racy and inimitable English she writes. No other Englishwoman ever commanded such language – terse and compact, and yet fiercely eloquent. We have already had occasion to notice the absence of comparison or metaphor in her poetry; the same is true of her prose. The lava is at white heat; it pours down clear, silent, pitiless; there are no bright bubbles nor gleaming foam. A mind of this order – tempered, and which cuts like steel – uses none of the pretty dexterities of the imagination; for to use these infers a pause of satisfied reflection and conscious enjoyment which it seldom or never experiences. Its rigorous intellect seeks no trappings of pearl or gold. It is content to abide in its white veil of marble – naked and chaste, like 'Death' in the Vatican. Yet, the still severity is more effective than any paint could make it. The chisel has been held by a Greek, the marble hewed from Pentelicus.

Compare, side by side, these pictures of the Winter and Summer twilight [quotes from *Jane Eyre* chapter 12, 'The ground was hard, the air was chill . . . sough of the most remote' and chapter 23, 'A splendid midsummer shone over England . . . beneath the horizon'] . . .

S O U R C E : *Fraser's Magazine,* May 1857.

N O T E S

Sir John Skelton (1831–97), author and essayist, was an assiduous reviewer, especially for *Blackwood's Magazine*. His review of Mrs Gaskell's *Life*, from which this extract is taken, appeared over his customary nom de plume, 'Shirley'.

1. The quotations are from, respectively, Kyd's *Spanish Tragedy* and Ford's *'Tis Pity She's a Whore* and *The Broken Heart*.

2. Verdi's *La Traviata,* opera based on *La Dame aux Camélias* (1848) by Dumas fils (described in Brewer's *Dictionary of Phrase and Fable*, 14th ed., as 'the most immoral work in existence'); Mrs Gaskell's *Ruth* (1853; see pp. 99, 103–4), Mrs Browning's *Aurora Leigh* (1856), romance in blank verse. *Marie* may be Gustave-Auguste de Beaumont de la Bonninière's *Marie, ou l'Esclavage aux Etats-Unis* (1835).

3. Skelton devotes considerable space to an account of Charlotte's attitude to Thackeray and her spirited exchanges with him.

W . C . R O S C O E : 'She . . . never paints development of character'

. . . It is this power of 'making out' – the intense vividness with which she summoned up her creations before her own eyes – that gives their enthralling air of actual fact to her narrations. The events *were* so and so to her; she seemed to herself to be discovering rather than inventing. She could not fancy and build up at her leisure; she must wait till she could *see* how it really was. Her father was most anxious *Villette* should end happily; but how

E

could it? Monsieur Paul Emanuel really *did* die at sea. There was no help for it; all she could do was to conceal his fate in ambiguous phrases . . .

In her novels, it is not so much the whole story as the separate scenes and detached incidents that delight us; and it is not the characters themselves so much as the mode in which they display themselves under particular circumstances. She is perfectly master of the art of narration; her events are linked in so easy and continuous a succession, that the reader loses the sense of the exquisite art by which it is done; and the wonderful thing is that there are no dull places. Long she is sometimes, but never dull. A certain sinewy vigour gives interest to every paragraph. Character is her favourite study; but, like most people who deliberately study character, she never thoroughly comprehends it. True perception of character seems to be something intuitive. It requires, at any rate, a nature of very extended though not necessarily deep sympathies, which finds something in itself answering to all hints, and ready to gather up all clues. Miss Brontë had nothing of this. She studies the manifestations, the workings of character; and it is these alone, for the most part, that she is enabled to reproduce . . .

In her love for the study of character, she is apt to be led too far. Her sketches, in which observation alone worked, are admirable. Her Mrs Reeds, her Miss Temple, her Miss Marchmont, her M. Pelet, are sharp and characteristic; but in her more elaborate efforts she attempts too much. No artist can delineate the whole of the character of a human being; the most successful have been those who, having taken up their creations from a certain point of view, always look at them steadily from thence, throw the light on some side they wish to be prominent, and let the rest fade off into an obscurity, which the eye of the reader rounds dimly off, partly by the aid of his own imagination. They indicate a character, and dwell on one side of it. This gives the reader peace; he has time to gather a distinct image, which gains new clearness as he gazes at it. But Miss Brontë gives him no peace, she must always see the reverse side, she is anxious if possible to see both sides at once; she is always making new discoveries in her characters, we never know when we have them. Yet she never represents them in course of change, never paints development of character; and she is so absorbed with what is before her, so much taken up with the scene immediately in hand, that she is apt insensibly to mould her personages so as to suit it, and give it the highest effect. She forgets what they are in thinking of what they are doing, and hence they are sometimes different people at different times. Jane Eyre is one person as a child, another with Mr Rochester, and a third with the St Johns. In *Villette,* Graham is one person, Dr John a second, Dr Bretton a third. Perhaps he affords the most marked instance of discontinuity of general character in all these novels ...

s o u r c e : from the review of Mrs Gaskell's *Life of Charlotte Brontë* in *National Review,* July 1857; reprinted in W. C. Roscoe, *Poems and Essays,* vol. ii (1860).

NOTE

William Caldwell Roscoe (1823 60), poet and essayist, was the grandson of the historian William Roscoe (1753–1831) and the friend of Walter Bagehot and R. H. Hutton.

E . S . D A L L A S : *Villette* and *The Professor*

... *The Professor* is a picture of school-life at Brussels; and although it is very remarkable as a literary curiosity, it is in itself the poorest of all Charlotte Brontë's productions. It seems indeed to be a natural product of the Low Countries, in which the transactions that are recorded occur. Afterwards, when she became more accustomed to the expression of impassioned thought, she rewrote the tale, and as by some volcanic agency interminable plains are elevated into mountains and sink into gloomy ravines, the story ceases to be flat, and becomes vigorous and lifelike as a land of hill and heather. The novel thus rewritten is known to the public under the name of *Villette*; and in the history of its origin, now revealed,[1] we have some explanation of the fact that, if not the most powerful, it is the most finished of Currer Bell's performances. *The Professor,* too, while certainly deficient in dramatic interest, is, when read in connection with *Villette,* one of the most curious works that have ever been printed. It is strange to compare the two novels – alike, and yet so different; displaying in every page how conscientiously the writer laboured, as in the general design, which, in the later novel is quite revolutionised, she proves how perfectly her art had been matured. In *Villette,* it will be remembered that the story is told by Lucy Snowe, and that the most important personage in the volume is the Professor, M. Paul Emanuel. In the earlier tale the Professor tells the story; he is himself rather commonplace, and the interest is centred in a sort of feminine Paul – a Mademoiselle Henri. In the first half of *Villette,* while she has only made up her mind to work out the idea of *The Professor,* the story is dull, and moves on but slowly. It is not till she seizes a new idea, and begins to work out the character of Paul in accordance with it, that she at length rises to the full height of her powers.

SOURCE: from the review of Mrs Gaskell's *Life of Charlotte Brontë* in *Blackwood's Magazine,* July 1857.

NOTES

Eneas Sweetland Dallas (1828–79), lively journalist and aesthetic theorist, whose published works include *Poetics* (1852), an abridgment of Richardson's *Clarissa* (1856) and *The Gay Science* (1866). He is the 'friend' referred to by John Blackwood in his letter to G. H. Lewes of 28 April 1857, 'I am greatly disposed to have a walk into the biographer of poor Charlotte Brontë, and a friend has proposed a paper to me. There is execrable taste in the book, and I detest this bookmaking out of the remains of the dead which must be so grating to the feelings of all whom the dead cared for' (*The George Eliot Letters* (1954) II 322–3). This distaste for biography – which was

common among Victorian readers – does not noticeably influence
Dallas's review.
1. See Introduction, pp. 19–20.

É M I L E   M O N T É G U T :   *'Jane Eyre* is the "Poetic Life" and
Villette is the "True Life" of Charlotte Brontë'

The life of Charlotte Brontë is the very substance of her novels;
three times she summarised what she had imagined, seen or felt. In
Jane Eyre she depicted her imaginative life; in *Villette*, her true
moral life; in *Shirley,* coming out of herself a little – though very
little in fact – and standing as it were at the window of her soul, she
depicted the corner of Yorkshire where she lived and what little
she had seen of human society.

Each of her books has therefore a very marked character. In the
first, *Jane Eyre*, the author – as stated – put the whole of her imaginative life and nothing but her imaginative life. Hence the extraordinary attraction, the overwhelming fascination of this strange
work. *Jane Eyre* has been reproached with being an immoral book
and although no good reason for the accusation has ever been
given, it is not entirely unfounded. The author has struck only one
chord of the human heart, the most powerful it is true, and has set
it vibrating alone, to the exclusion of all the rest. In *Jane Eyre,* the
imagination alone speaks and when imagination is sole master one
can be sure that it will run to strange, fiery passions, difficult of
interpretation. If men's purest dreams were discernible, it would
generally be found that there was something equivocal about
them. Now, *Jane Eyre* is a passionate dream, a perfect castle in
Spain. In this book the soul of Charlotte Brontë, leaving reality
and forgetting the vicissitudes of ordinary life, dreams and imagines for us the life she might have had and the characters she would
have liked to meet; she tells us how she would have liked to love
and who she could have loved and what treasures of eloquence she
would have had always ready to bestow on her heart's dearest one.
   . . . *Jane Eyre* refers, therefore, to Charlotte's imaginative life

and only to her imaginative life. Here is the romance; does reality correspond to it? Charlotte Brontë has depicted reality in her novel *Villette*. Of course, Lucy Snowe is still Jane Eyre, and yet they form a complete contrast. Jane Eyre is the ideal and poetic Charlotte; Lucy Snowe is the prosaic, living Charlotte; they are sisters but there lies between them all the distance that separates reality from illusion. The great Goethe, who knew that man does not live on reality alone and that even the most accurate memories are transformed by the imagination and by the passage of time, gave to his memoirs the profound title: *Poetry and Truth* (Dichtung und Wahrheit). Charlotte's two novels could be considered as autobiography and could bear the same title; *Jane Eyre* would be entitled the *Poetic Life*, and *Villette* the *True Life* of Charlotte Brontë. This time Charlotte makes no imaginative excursions. Lucy Snowe has not, and cannot have, a romance. She is plain, poor and abandoned. No hope for her of an Edward Rochester, or even a St John Rivers. But she is a woman; despised or not, she has a heart and will suffer, and – supreme cruelty of fate – she will suffer in silence. Confidences are denied her; out of self-respect and fear of ridicule, she is obliged to keep her torments to herself. What confidant, hearing the confessions of the teacher and seeing her face, would not think her a crazed monomaniac? Give up these illusions, he would tell her, happiness and love are not for you; fate has condemned you to solitude and abandonment; resign yourself and cease to suffer.

But Lucy, the silent Lucy, does not resign herself any more than Jane Eyre; only, unlike Jane Eyre, she has not the strength to fight. She gives in, but out of lassitude . . .

. . . It is the nature of *Villette* to arouse quite the opposite feeling to that of *Jane Eyre*. In *Jane Eyre*, where imagination triumphs, the reader finally emerges, in spite of all, with an impression of happiness and joy. After reading *Villette*, one is as weary and defeated as the heroine and one has a sad, harsh, feverish impression; one is tempted to cry: Oh! for a little attractiveness; for pity's sake, cruel poetess, give Lucy Snowe some of the brilliant gifts that graced the piquant, rebellious, eloquent sorceress, Jane

Eyre. Don't you see, the suffering is too great, so great that the heroine no longer feels it; but this prayer ... is absolutely resisted by the pitiless Charlotte ...

... The characters in *Jane Eyre* can be painted full-length, with their full breadth and stature, since their natures are so powerful that there is no fear of exceeding them. Very great characters and very great passions have the advantage for the artist that it is not possible to set any definite limits to them or say where they end. Ordinary characters do not give the artist the same freedom. If the characters in *Shirley* are drawn half-size, it is because they are themselves small; they belong to the middle-classes. In this environment, their natural powers have not atrophied, they have shrunk and hardened; their characters all have something twisted, something crooked about them. Their natures have been arrested by the circumstances of their semi-developed condition; they display oddities rather than originality, callousness rather than real hardness, absurdities and faults rather than vices ...

... of the three books, undoubtedly the finest is that which belongs solely to the author's imagination – *Jane Eyre*. In spite of the immense success of this book, I venture to say that it is not esteemed at its true value. I attach little importance to certain glaringly artificial details, certain melodramatic inventions, certain over-romantic combinations. The sentimental tales with which Cervantes and Le Sage sprinkle their masterpieces are not very excellent inventions either; there are in certain comedies of Molière, of Molière in reasonable mood, notably in *l'Avare*, certain miraculous changes of fortune, certain dénouements which exceed in romantic improbability the worst improbabilities with which the author of *Jane Eyre* has been reproached. Moreover, these improbabilities are in my opinion much better motivated than has generally been acknowledged. Thus, the burning down of the house and Rochester's blindness have perfectly good cause. Again, it is said that melodramatic effects abound. This is true, but are these effects powerful, do they denote a vigorous and sound imagination? Imagine the mystery of the madwoman and her nocturnal visits as a dramatic tool in the hands of any ordinary

writer; one side of *Jane Eyre* touches on the novels of Mrs Radcliffe.[1] And who would dare to say so? Who would dare to say
that he has not felt the shiver of apprehension felt by Jane Eyre
when she hears for the first time that sinister and mysterious laugh
echoing through the lofty rooms of Thornfield manor? Who has
not, like her, listened anxiously when, sitting up in bed, she hears
an unknown hand fumbling at the door of her room? In a letter
to Lewes, who had reproached her with excessive use of melodramatic devices, Miss Brontë replied, quite rightly in our view,
that imagination had its rights as well as experience.[2] These
methods are therefore legitimate : everything depends on how
they are employed and one of the great aspects of Miss Brontë's
talent is precisely this, that she had the art of employing them.

She excels in the natural depiction of the feelings born of
spiritual terrors, the superstitions of solitude and the hallucinations
of despair; she brings infinite art to the rendering of these intense
and irresistible emotions...

...When, in the episode of the red room, Jane Eyre as a child
sees a ghost, we do not find her terror exaggerated and we do not
for a moment doubt the reality of the apparition. The soul has risen
to such heights, has suffered so formidable a strain, that it needs,
– so to speak – to seek oblivion in swooning. Unconsciousness is
salutary; without it, the soul would shatter in death or plunge into
the abyss of madness. In *Villette,* there is an admirable chapter
entitled 'The Long Vacation'. Harassed by the visions of fever and
the demons of solitude, Lucy Snowe goes out one evening from the
deserted pensionnat which is haunted only by the bad dreams that
trouble her nights and the hideous depression that clings to her
like a shadow all day long. She walks at random, urged on by an
involuntary impulse : she enters a church bathed in the shadows
of twilight and sees a priest seated in a confessional; she goes up to
the confessional and kneels – she, a protestant and a determined
heretic... What surprises us is that she should have had the
courage to reply to the priest's first words: 'Mon père, je suis
protestante...' After the varied emotions we have been through
with her, it would be no surprise to see her rush off and enter a

Carmelite convent or seek sympathy from the first passer-by. And it is not only in the representation of powerful and dramatic effects that Miss Brontë excels. All intense emotions, violent or delicate, fall within her province : the fleeting caprices of an original temperament, strange smiles, magnetic glances, the passionate working of facial muscles, sudden shivers – harbingers of momentary happiness or transitory sadness – . . . *Jane Eyre* is full of these subtle and delicate impressions; but the author's masterpiece in this line is the first fifty pages of *Villette* which describe Paulina Mary's childhood. These pages are as strange as certain impressions on the face of an invalid, as painful as the notes of the harmonica.

Miss Brontë is extremely eloquent and critics have almost made a fault of this virtue. She has been blamed for the length of the conversations between Jane Eyre and Rochester, these conversations are interminable : well, I confess that I would not have them a syllable shorter . . .

. . . The more one re-reads these singular conversations, the less one is surprised that *Jane Eyre* should so have shocked English moral susceptibilities; they are as stifling as a hot summer day, as intoxicating as the exhalations of nature; they possess the mind like a contagion. They have another strangely original feature, which distinguishes them from all the love-scenes I have read, and that is a mixture of the irresistible eloquence of nature and the artificial charms of a cunning and resourceful passion. Rochester, for all his passion, is at the same time highly astute. Jane, reserved as she is, is singularly provocative. These two lovers know all the manoeuvers, all the passes in the dangerous fencing match in which they are engaged. That Rochester should be past-master in the art of simulating anger or delivering a passionate tirade at the required moment : this one has no difficulty in understanding. But Jane? She does, in truth, divine a great many things. This little sorceress with the inquisitive eye, the alert mind, the ambitious heart, knows how a word spoken in season and with just the right inflection will calm the fury of the worst storm; she knows the power of the touch of a woman's hand on a lover's brow to heal wounded pride. Oh, what an amazing pair of lovers! ...

... But the great merit of *Jane Eyre* does not consist in powerful effects of terror nor even in the eloquence and originality of the passions; it consists in the conception of the three characters. They are three extraordinary creations, three characters invented, *discovered,* which have no precedents in literature. No hero in any novel, old or new, resembles them; they have a physiognomy peculiar to themselves, vigorously eccentric, the features of which remain indelibly engraved on the memory. They spring fully armed from the novelist's brain, they are born of the author's communion with nature, they have no literary relatives, near or distant ...

... Jane Eyre, Rochester and St John Rivers are three characters drawn from *human nature at its grandest*; they belong to the most interesting families of the broad and complex human race. They are not pale shadows, distinguished one from the other only by imperceptible shades of difference, they are three distinct types. Edward Rochester belongs quite simply to the great family of Mirabeau, stormy, equivocal, powerful and attractive ...

... In Jane, he meets a character capable of loving him. Superior to her sorry outward appearance, superior to her humiliating situation, superior to the blows of fate, Jane is one of those women who are equal to all the vicissitudes of life. She loves only strength, energy and freedom. In the face of this redoubtable monster, she feels calm and secure. From the first moment she loves him and looks on him without fear; from the first moment, she is sure of him. The abyss into which he almost dragged her, the involuntary betrayal of which she was almost a victim, drew neither complaint nor reproach from her. Mr Rochester, even were he criminal, would remain for ever in her memory for, guilty or not, her whole life began and ended with him ...

... But the most extraordinary of the three characters in my opinion is St John Rivers. If Edward Rochester belongs to the family of Mirabeau,[3] St John Rivers belongs to that of Calvin and Knox, hard and austere men, without tenderness, without love for creatures of flesh and blood. His are purely spiritual passions. It brings tears to the eyes to see his sad, dry look resting on the beautiful young girl whose love he disdains. A calm heart and an unquiet spirit, he dreams only of martyrdom, of the pursuit of the ideal goal and the conquest of eternal salvation. He is ambitious for moral truth as a conqueror is ambitious for kingdoms and empires . . .

. . . The energetic Jane, so quiet and sure of herself in the face of Rochester's violent passions, turns in fear from this calm despot whose movements are all so measured and whose speech is so quiet. She feels that this man, who is so virtuous and who believes he loves only the truth, in fact loves only himself . . .

Such are these three characters . . . We are so unused to natures of this kind that at first they seem like spirits from a lost world; but they belong to the family of those original souls, truly worth depicting, which always have presented and always will present a challenge to artists and poets worthy of the name; they personify some of the great aspects of human life : fanaticism, liberty, defiance of the world and of fate. Add to this that these characters in *Jane Eyre* are English, completely English, so that it takes some time to penetrate their hard exterior and to recognise in them elements common to all humanity . . .

Jane Eyre is not only Miss Brontë's finest novel, it is perhaps the finest novel of our time. In no other modern novel does one encounter three characters so worthy of attention or which grip the imagination so powerfully as those of the little governess, the erring aristocrat and the despotic clergyman. The book will live and succeeding generations will no more notice its romantic improbabilities than we today notice the crudities of Fielding or the long sermons of Richardson. We remark on these defects and having done so place *Tom Jones* and *Clarissa* among the masterpieces of the imagination . . .

s o u r c e : translated from 'Charlotte Brontë, IV : Les Œuvres', *Review des deux Mondes*, August 1857, reprinted in *Ecrivains modernes de l'Angleterre*, Première série, 1885.

NOTES

Émile Montégut (1825–95), critic and essayist, was associated from 1847 with the *Revue des deux Mondes,* for which he wrote many of his best articles on English, American and French writers. His books include *Libres Opnions: morales et historiques* (1858), *Essais sur la littérature anglaise* (1883) and *Ecrivains modernes de l'Angleterre* (1885–92).

1. There was still a readership in England and France for Mrs Radcliffe's 'Gothick' novels, even if not of the ardent kind which had followed their first appearance in the 1790s. On Charlotte and the 'Gothick' see Introduction, p. 16.

2. See Introduction, p. 22.

3. See above, p. 81 n.

QUEEN VICTORIA: 'That melancholy, interesting book, *Jane Eyre*'

1858

March 7. Began reading *Jane Eyre* to my dear Albert, having finished *Northanger Abbey,* one of Miss Austen's admirable novels.

March 21. Read to Albert out of that melancholy, interesting book, *Jane Eyre.*

May 13. We dined alone and talked and read, going on reading till past 11 in that intensely interesting novel *Jane Eyre.*

May 19. We dined alone with Mama and read afterwards in *Jane Eyre,* in which we are so deeply interested.

May 21. We remained up reading in *Jane Eyre* till ½ p. 11 – quite creepy from the awful account of what happened the night before the marriage, which was interrupted in the church.

August 2. We read in *Jane Eyre,* which proved so interesting that we went on till quite late. It was the part in which comes the moment of her finding Rochester again, blind, and with the loss of a hand!

August 4. (On board the *Victoria & Albert*). At near 10 we went below and nearly finished reading that most interesting book *Jane Eyre*. A peaceful, happy evening.

S O U R C E : from the unpublished portion of Queen Victoria's diary, as copied out by Princess Beatrice.[1]

N O T E

Queen Victoria read *Jane Eyre* again in 1880; her interest in the story then, as recorded in her journals, suggests that she had forgotten all about her earlier reading (which had extended over a period of five months!). See the entry for 23 November 1880, *The Letters and Journals of Queen Victoria*, edited by G. E. Buckle and A. C. Benson (1926–7), III 259.

1. Reproduced in *Brontë Society Transactions* (1968), XIII (no. 3) 296, the information 'kindly provided by Sir Owen Morshead, K.C.M.G., D.S.O., M.C., by the gracious permission of H.M. the Queen'.

G E O R G E   S M I T H : '*Jane Eyre* fascinating, *Villette* uninteresting'

The reading world has very seldom been startled by such a genuine and powerful piece of originality as *Jane Eyre*. One can almost gauge the feeling, after reading it, which caused Charlotte Brontë to be such an enthusiastic admirer of Thackeray. He, at any rate, she knew, would appreciate her efforts, for was he not also engaged (with even more splendid talents) in the crusade against conventionality? He, at least, understood her burning words, when she affirmed that 'conventionality is not morality, self-righteousness is not religion. To attack the first is not to assail the last. To pluck the

mask from the face of the Pharisee, is not to lift an impious hand
to the Crown of Thorns.' These words will sufficiently show how
she endeavoured to tread in the steps of 'the first social regenerator
of the day', and to whom she inscribed the second edition of her
most widely known book. *Jane Eyre* is an autobiography, and its
intention is to present a plain, unbiassed narrative of a woman's
life from its commencement to a period when it is supposed to
have ceased to possess interest to mankind generally. It is told fear-
lessly, and with a burning pen. But there is no *suppressio veri*; that,
its author would have scorned : perhaps it would have been better
for its reception in some quarters – limited in range we are happy
to think – if the narrator of the story had glossed over some por-
tions of her heroine's history. She has chosen, however, to adhere
to stern reality, and there it is finally for us, unpleasant and rough
though it be in some of its recorded experiences. The book shows
the most opposite qualities – light, darkness; beauty, deformity;
strength, tenderness. Its pathos is of the finest quality, stirring most
deeply because it is simple and unforced. The situations are very
vivid; several scenes being depicted which it would be impossible
to eradicate from the memory after the most extensive reading of
serial literature. Even those who regard it as coarse must admit
its strange fascination. It was a book that could afford to be independent of criticism, and accordingly we find that, before the
reviews appeared, anxious and continuous inquiries respecting
it began to be made at the libraries. There was not much fiction
being written which fixed the public eye, and the issue of this novel
almost created an era. Forgotten now is the savage criticism of the
reviewer who said of the author of *Jane Eyre,* 'She must be one
who for some sufficient reason has long forfeited the society of her
sex,' whilst the work which baffled his judgment but earned his
vituperation, still remains, a memento of real genius which could
not be suppressed. Although chiefly remarkable for its prominent
delineation of the passion of love in strong and impulsive natures,
there are many other points which are noticeable about it, and
should therefore be mentioned. The keen observation of the writer
is manifest on almost every page. Intense realism is its chief charac-

teristic. The pictures are as vivid and bold as though etched by a Rembrandt, or drawn by a Salvator Rosa. Dickens has been almost equalled by the description of the school at Lowood, to which Miss Eyre was sent, and which might well be described as Dothegirls' Hall...

If the sisters Brontë had early in life been accustomed to mingle in society, and had not been imprisoned within the walls of Haworth parsonage, there can be little question that we should have had more masterly and more general works from their hands. The skill they exhibit in delineating life should not have been confined to the inhabitants of those northern moors, but should have been employed in other haunts and other scenes likewise. Their field has been necessarily restricted, though their genius had full play on the subjects within their reach. But to demonstrate the capacity to turn experience to account wherever it might be obtained, we only need to direct the reader's attention to Charlotte Brontë's latest work, *Villette*. It is redolent of the flavour of Brussels, where the author and her sister spent some years of their lives. To the ordinary English reader it is probably the most uninteresting of all the works of Miss Brontë, as page after page is composed mostly of French, and that sometimes difficult and idiomatic. This doubtless operated to some extent against its popularity with the mass of novel-readers, though the book seems to have earned the most lavish encomiums from the critics. It exhibits, however, the genius neither of *Jane Eyre* nor of *Shirley*: it is, in truth, superior to the fiction of ninety per cent of novelists, but it scarcely warranted the extravagant terms of praise which were showered upon it by the reviewers. These valuable individuals, however, were, as is too often the case unfortunately, wise after the event – that is, they found it tolerably safe to eulogise a new work from the hand of one who had already established her position as amongst the most original writers of the age. One or two of the *dramatis personae* evoke sentiments of approval on account of their originality, conspicuous amongst them being Mr Paul Emanuel and Miss de Bassompierre; but on the whole, the book is disappointing, for there is no one character whose fortunes we are anxious to follow; and a novel which fails to beget a personal interest must be said to have lost its chief charm . . .

SOURCE: from 'The Brontës', *Cornhill Magazine*, July 1873, reprinted in *Poets and Novelists*, 1875.

NOTE

George Smith, of Smith, Elder, Charlotte's publishers, was a tall, active young man in his early twenties when Charlotte first sent her work to him, and he had recently assumed responsibility for the firm's business (his father, who had founded the firm with his fellow-Scott, Alexander Elder, in 1816, died in 1846; Elder retired in 1845). Charlotte's portraits of Graham Bretton and Mrs Bretton owe something to her acquaintance with George Smith and his mother. The firm later added many celebrated names to its lists – including those of Matthew Arnold, Mrs Gaskell and Thackeray, the last two being largely owed to their success with Charlotte – and also founded the *Cornhill Magazine* in 1860, with Thackeray as the first editor (see George Smith : *A Memoir by his Widow*, 1902, and Leonard Huxley's *The House of Smith Elder, 1816–1916*, privately printed 1923). The essay from which this extract is taken is somewhat conventionally written though obviously of considerable interest because of its source. More lively are Smith's personal reminiscences for the *Cornhill* in 1900, which record his first encounters with Charlotte and her work.

A. C. SWINBURNE: 'A great and absolute genius for the painting and handling of human characters in mutual relation . . .'

. . . Perhaps we may reasonably divide all imaginative work into three classes; the lowest, which leaves us in a complacent mood of acquiescence with the graceful or natural inventions and fancies of an honest and ingenious workman, and in no mind to question or dispute the accuracy of his transcript from life . . . ; the second, of high enough quality to engage our judgment in its service, and make direct demand on our grave attention for deliberate assentor dissent; the third, which in the exercise of its faculties at their best neither solicits nor seduces nor provokes us to acquiescence or demur, but compels us without question to positive acceptance and belief. Of the first class it would be superfluous to cite instances from among writers of our own day, nor undeserving of serious respect and of genuine gratitude for much honest work done and honest pleasure conferred on us. Of the second order our literature has no more apt and brilliant examples than George Eliot and George Meredith. Of the third . . . there is no clearer and more positive instance in the whole world of letters than that supplied by the genius of Charlotte Brontë.

I do not mean that such an instance is to be found in the treatment of each figure in each of her three great books. If this could accurately be said, it could not reasonably be denied that she might justly claim . . . that seat by the side of Shakespeare which certain critics of the hour are prompt alike to assign alternatively to the author of *Adam Bede* and the author of *Queen Mary*[1] . . . But, without putting in a claim for the author of *Jane Eyre* as qualified to ascend the height on which a minority of not overwise admirers would fain enthrone a demigoddess of more dubious divinity than hers, I must take leave to reiterate my conviction that no living English or female writer can rationally be held her equal in what I cannot but regard as the highest and rarest quality which supplies the hardest and surest proof of a great and absolute genius for the painting and handling of human characters in mutual relation and reaction. Even the glorious mistress of all forms and powers of imaginative prose, who has lately left France afresh in mourning – even George Sand herself had not this gift in like measure[2] . . . The gift of which I speak is that of a power to make us feel in every nerve, at every step forward which our imagination is compelled to take under the guidance of another's, that thus and not otherwise . . . it was and it must have been with the human figures set before us in their action and their suffering; that thus and not otherwise they absolutely must and would have felt and thought and spoken under the proposed conditions. It is something for a writer to have achieved if he has made it worth our fancy's while to consider by the light of imaginative reason whether the creatures of his own fancy would in actual fact and life have done as he made them do or not ... But no definite terms of comparison will suffice to express how much more than this it is to have done what the youngest of capable readers must feel on first opening *Jane Eyre* that the writer of its very first pages has shown herself competent to do. In ... almost all the sovereign masterpieces even of Fielding, of Thackeray, ... of Sir Walter Scott himself ... we do not find this faculty so innate ... as in hers ... When Jane Eyre answers Edward Rochester's question, whether she feels in him the absolute fitness and correspondence to herself which he feels to himself in her, with the words ... – 'To the finest fibre of my nature, sir' – we feel to the finest fibre of our own being that these are no mere words ... In knowledge, in culture, perhaps in capacity for knowledge and for culture, Charlotte was no more comparable to George Eliot than George Eliot is comparable to Charlotte Brontë in purity of passion, in depth and ardour of feeling, in spiritual force and fervour of forthright inspiration. It would be rather a rough and sweeping than a loose or inaccurate division which should define the one as a type of genius distinguished from intellect, the other of intellect as opposed to genius. But it would ... be little or nothing more or less than accurate to recognise in George Eliot a type of intelligence vivified and coloured by a vein of genius, in Charlotte Brontë a type of genius directed and moulded by the touch of intelligence ...

Paul Emanuel and Lucy Snowe

Supreme as is the spiritual triumph of Cervantes in the person of his perfect knight over all insult and mockery ... it is hardly a more marvellous or a completer example of imaginative and moral mastery than the triumph of Charlotte Brontë in the quaint person of her grim little professor over his own eccentric infirmities of habit and temper, more hazardous to our sense of respect than any outward risk or infliction of alien violence or mockery from duchesses or muleteers; a triumph so naturally drawn out and delicately displayed in the swift steady gradations of change and development, now ludicrous and now attractive, and well-nigh adorable at last, through which the figure of M. Paul seems to pass as under summer lights and shadows, till it gradually opens upon us in human fullness of self-unconscious charm and almost sacred beauty – yet always with the sense of some latent infusion, some tender native admixture of a quality at once loveable and laughable; with something indeed of that quaint sweet kind of earnest affection and half-smiling veneration which all men fit to read him feel . . . for the person even more than for the writings of Charles Lamb. That our smile should in no wise impair for one instant our reverence, that our reverence should in no wise make us abashed or ashamed for one moment at the recollection of our smile – this is the final test and triumph of a genius to which we find no likeness outside the very highest rank of creators in the sphere of spiritual invention or of moral imagination . . .

Those who would understand Charlotte . . . should study the difference of tenderness between the touch that drew Shirley Keeldar and the touch that drew Lucy Snowe. This later figure, as Mr Wemyss Reid has observed[3]. . . , if never meant to win liking or made to find favour in the general reader's eyes, is yet none the less evidently on that account the faithful likeness of Charlotte Brontë, studied from the life, and painted by her own hand with the sharp austere precision of a photograph rather than a portrait. But it is herself with the consolation and support of her genius wit drawn, with the strength of her spiritual arm immeasurably shortened, the cunning of her right hand comparatively cancelled; and it is this that makes the main undertone and ultimate result of the book somewhat mournfuller even than the literal record of her mournful and glorious life. In the house where I now write this there is a . . . landscape by Crome; showing just such a wild track of shoreward brushwood and chill fen, blasted and wasted by the bitter breath of the east wind blowing off the eastward sea, shrivelled and subdued and resigned as it were with a sort of grim

submission to the dark dumb tyranny of a full-charged thunder-
cloud ... As with all this it is yet always a pleasure to look upon
so beautiful and noble a study of so sad and harsh-featured an
outlying byway through the weariest waste places of the world,
so is it in its kind a perpetual pleasure to revisit the well-nigh
sunless landscape of Lucy Snowe's sad, passionate, and valiant
life ...

SOURCE: *A Note on Charlotte Brontë*, 1877.

NOTES

See Introduction, pp. 27, 30–1, on Swinburne's admiration for
Charlotte Brontë's writings.

1. George Eliot's *Adam Bede* was published in 1859, Tennyson's
historical drama, *Queen Mary*, in 1875.

2. See Introduction, p. 17, and p. 78 above.

3. Reid has a brief discussion of *Villette* as a reflection of its
author's tragic personal experience in his *Charlotte Brontë* (1877),
pp. 222–4; for his main concern in the book, see Introduction, p. 30.

LESLIE STEPHEN: Paul Emanuel and Mr Rochester: 'a
pervading flaw'

When we measure M. Paul Emanuel by this test,[1] we feel instinctively that there is something wanting. The most obvious contrast
is that M. Emanuel is no humourist himself, nor even a product
of humour. The imperfections, the lovable absurdities, of Uncle
Toby are imbedded in the structure of character. His whims and
oddities always leave us in the appropriate mood of blended smiles
and tears. Many people, especially 'earnest' young ladies, will
prefer M. Paul Emanuel, who, like his creator, is always in deadly
earnest. At bottom he is always (like all ladies' heroes) a true

woman, simple, pure, heroic, and loving – a real Joan of Arc, as Mr Thackeray said of his creator, in the beard and blouse of a French professor. He attaches extravagant importance to trifles, indeed, for his irascible and impetuous temperament is always converting him into an Æolus of the duck-pond. So far there is, we may admit, a kind of pseudo-humorous element in his composition; but the humour, such as it is, lies entirely on the surface. He is perfectly sane and sensible, though a trifle choleric. Give him a larger sphere of action, and his impetuosity will be imposing instead of absurd. It is the mere accident of situation which gives, even for a moment, a ludicrous tinge to his proceedings.

Uncle Toby, on the contrary, would be even more of a humourist as a general on the battle-field than in his mimic sieges on the bowling green. The humour is in his very marrow, not in his surroundings; and the reason is that Sterne feels what every genuine humourist feels, and what, indeed, it is his main function to express – a strong sense of the irony of fate, of the queer mixture of good and bad, of the heroic and the ludicrous, of this world of ours, and of what we may call the perversity of things in general. Whether such a treatment is altogether right and healthy is another question; and most certainly Sterne's view of life is in many respects not only unworthy, but positively base. But it remains true that the deep humourist is finding a voice for one of the most pervading and profound of the sentiments raised in a philosophical observer who is struck by the discords of the universe. Sensitiveness to such discords is one of the marks of a truly reflective intellect, though a humourist suggests one mode of escape from the pain which they cause, whilst a philosophic and religious mind may find another and perhaps a more profound solution.

Now M. Paul Emanuel, admirable and amiable as he is, never carries us into the higher regions of thought. We are told, even ostentatiously, of the narrow prejudices which he shares, though they do not make him harsh and uncharitable. The prejudices were obvious in this case to the creator, because her own happened to be of a different kind. The 'Tory and clergyman's daughter' was rather puzzled by finding that a bigoted Papist with a Jesuit

education might still be a good man, and points out conscientiously
the defects which she ascribes to his early training. But the mere
fact of the narrowness, the want of familiarity with a wider sphere
of thought, the acceptance of a narrow code of belief and morality,
does not strike here as in itself having either a comic or a melancholy side. M. Paul has the wrong set of prejudices, but is not as
wrong as prejudiced, and therefore we feel that a Sterne, or, say,
a George Sand, whilst doing equal justice to M. Emanuel's excellent qualities, would have had a feeling (which in her was altogether wanting) of his limitation and his incongruity with the great
system of the world. Seen from an intellectual point of view,
placed in his due relation to the great currents of thought and
feeling of the time, we should have been made to feel the pathetic
and humorous aspects of M. Emanuel's character, and he might
have been equally a living individual and yet a type of some more
general idea. The philosopher might ask, for example, what is the
exact value of unselfish heroism guided by narrow theories or
employed on unworthy tasks; and the philosophic humourist or
artist might embody the answer in a portrait of M. Emanuel considered from a cosmic or a cosmopolitan point of view. From the
lower standpoint accessible to Miss Brontë he is still most attractive; but we see only his relations to the little scholastic circle, and
have no such perception as the greatest writers would give us of
his relations to the universe, or, as the next order would give, of his
relations to the great world without.

Although the secret of Miss Brontë's power lies, to a great
extent, in the singular force with which she can reproduce acute
observations of character from without, her most esoteric teaching,
the most accurate reflex from her familiar idiosyncrasy, is of
course to be found in the characters painted from within. We may
infer her personality more or less accurately from the mode in
which she contemplates her neighbours, but it is directly manifested in various avatars of her own spirit. Among the characters
who are more or less mouthpieces of her peculiar sentiment we
may reckon not only Lucy Snowe and Jane Eyre, but, to some
extent, Shirley, and, even more decidedly, Rochester. When they

speak we are really listening to her own voice, though it is more or less disguised in conformity to dramatic necessity. There are great differences between them; but they are such differences as would exist between members of the same family, or might be explained by change of health or internal circumstances. Jane Eyre has not had such bitter experience as Lucy Snowe; Shirley is generally Jane Eyre in high spirits, and freed from harassing anxiety; and Rochester is really a spirited sister of Shirley's, though he does his very best to be a man, and even an unusually masculine specimen of his sex.

Mr Rochester, indeed, has imposed upon a good many people; and he is probably responsible in part for some of the muscular heroes who have appeared since his time in the world of fiction. I must, however, admit that, in spite of some opposing authority, he does not appear to me to be a real character at all, except as a reflection of a certain side of his creator. He is in reality the personification of a true woman's longing (may one say it now?) for a strong master. But the knowledge is wanting. He is a very bold but necessarily unsuccessful attempt at an impossibility. The parson's daughter did not really know anything about the class of which he is supposed to be a type, and he remains vague and inconsistent in spite of all his vigour. He is intended to be a person who has surfeited from the fruit of the tree of knowledge, and addresses the inexperienced governess from the height – or depth – of his worldly wisdom. And he really knows just as little of the world as she does. He has to impose upon her by giving an account of his adventures taken from the first novel at hand of the early Bulwer school, or a diluted recollection of Byron. There is not a trace of real cynicism – of the strong nature turned sour by experience – in his whole conversation. He is supposed to be specially simple and masculine, and yet he is as self-conscious as a young lady on her first appearance in society, and can do nothing but discourse about his feelings, and his looks, and his phrenological symptoms, to his admiring hearer. Set him beside any man's character of a man, and one feels at once that he has no real solidity or vitality in him. He has, of course, strong nerves and muscles, but they are articles which can be supplied in unlimited quantities with little expense to the imagination. Nor can one deny that his conduct to Miss Eyre is abominable. If he had proposed to her to ignore the existence of the mad Mrs Rochester, he would have acted like a rake, but not like a sneak. But the attempt to entrap Jane into a bigamous connection by concealing the wife's existence, is a piece of treachery for which it is hard to forgive him. When he challenges the lawyer and the clergyman to condemn him after putting themselves in his place, their answer is surely obvious. One may take a lenient view of a man who chooses by his own will to annul his marriage to a filthy lunatic; but he was a knave for trying to entrap a defenceless girl by a mock ceremony. He puts himself in a position in which the contemptible Mr Mason has a moral advantage.

This is by far the worst blot in Miss Brontë's work, and may partly explain, though it cannot justify, the harsh criticisms made at the time. It is easy now to win a cheap reputation for generosity by trampling upon the dead bodies of the luckless critics who blundered so hopelessly. The time for anger is past; and mere oblivion is the fittest doom for such offenders. Inexperience, and consequently inadequate appreciation of the demands of the situation, was Miss Brontë's chief fault in this matter, and most certainly not any want of true purity and moral elevation. But the fact that she, in whom an instinctive nobility of spirit is, perhaps, the most marked characteristic, should have given scandal to the respectable, is suggestive of another inference. What, in fact, is the true significance of this singular strain of thought and feeling, which puts on various and yet closely allied forms in the three remarkable novels we have been considering? It displays itself at one moment in some vivid description – for 'description' seems too faint a word – some forcible presentation to our mind's eye of a fragment of moorland scenery; at another, it appears as an ardently sympathetic portrayal of some trait of character at once vigorous and tender; then it utters itself in a passionate soliloquy, which establishes the fact that its author possessed the proverbial claim to knowledge of the heavenly powers; or again, it produces

one of those singular little prose-poems – such as Shirley's description of Eve – which, with all their force, have just enough flavour
of the 'devoirs' at M. Heger's establishment to suggest that they
are the work of an inspired school-girl. To gather up into a single
formula the meaning of such a character as Lucy Snowe, or in
other words, of Charlotte Brontë, is, of course, impossible. But at
least such utterances always give us the impression of a fiery soul
imprisoned in too narrow and too frail a tenement. The fire is
pure and intense. It is kindled in a nature intensely emotional, and
yet aided by a heroic sense of duty. The imprisonment is not merely
that of a feeble body in uncongenial regions, but that of a narrow
circle of thought, and consequently of a mind which has never
worked itself clear by reflection, or developed a harmonious and
consistent view of life. There is a certain feverish disquiet which is
marked by the peculiar mannerism of the style. At its best, we
have admirable flashes of vivid expression, where the material
of language is the incarnation of keen intuitive thought. At its
worst, it is strangely contorted, crowded by rather awkward per-
sonifications, and degenerates towards a rather unpleasant
Ossianesque.[2] More severity of taste would increase the power by
restraining the abuse. We feel an aspiration after more than can
be accomplished, an unsatisfied yearning for potent excitement,
which is sometimes more fretful than forcible.

The symptoms are significant of the pervading flaw in otherwise
most effective workmanship. They imply what, in a scientific sense,
would be an inconsistent theory, and, in an æsthetic sense, an in-
harmonious representation of life. One great aim of the writing,
explained in the preface to the second edition of *Jane Eyre,* is a
protest against conventionality. But the protest is combined with
a most unflinching adherence to the proper conventions of society;
and we are left in great doubt as to where the line ought to be
drawn. Where does the unlawful pressure of society upon the
individual begin, and what are the demands which it may right-
fully make upon our respect? At one moment in *Jane Eyre* we
seem to be drifting towards the solution that strong passion is the
one really good thing in the world, and that all human conventions

which oppose it should be disregarded. This was the tendency which shocked the respectable reviewers of the time. Of course they should have seen that the strongest sympathy of the author goes with the heroic self-conquest of the heroine under temptation. She triumphs at the cost of a determined self-sacrifice, and undoubtedly we are meant to sympathise with the martyr. Yet it is also true that we are left with the sense of an unsolved discord. Sheer stoical regard for duty is represented as something repulsive, however imposing, in the figure of St John Rivers and virtue is rewarded by the arbitrary removal of the obstacles which made it unpleasant. What would Jane Eyre have done and what would our sympathies have been, had she found that Mrs Rochester had not been burnt in the fire at Thornfield? That is rather an awkward question. Duty is supreme, seems to be the moral of the story; but duty sometimes involves a strain almost too hard for mortal faculties.

If in the conflict between duty and passion, the good so often borders upon the impracticable, the greatest blessing in the world should be a will powerful enough to be an inflexible law for itself under all pressure of circumstances. Even a will directed to evil purposes has a kind of royal prerogative, and we may rightly do it homage. That seems to be the seminal thought in *Wuthering Heights,* that strange book to which we can hardly find a parallel in our literature, unless in such works as the *Revenger's Tragedy,* and some other crude but startling productions of the Elizabethan dramatists. But Emily Brontë's feeble grasp of external facts makes her book a kind of baseless nightmare, which we read with wonder and with distressing curiosity, but with far more pain than pleasure or profit. Charlotte's mode of conceiving the problem is given most fully in *Villette,* the book of which one can hardly say, with a recent critic, that it represents her 'ripest wisdom', but which seems to give her best solution of the great problem of life. Wisdom, in fact, is not the word to apply to a state of mind which seems to be radically inconsistent and tentative. The spontaneous and intense affection of kindred and noble natures is the one really precious thing in life, it seems to say; and, so far, the thought is true or a partial aspect of the truth, and the high feeling undeniable. But then, the author seems to add, such happiness is all but chimerical. It falls to the lot only of a few exceptional people, upon whom fortune or Providence has delighted to shower its gifts. To all others life is either a wretched grovelling business, an affair of making money and gratifying sensuality, or else it is a prolonged martyrdom. Yield to your feelings, and the chances are enormously great that you are trampled upon by the selfish, or that you come into collision with some of those conventions which must be venerated, for they are the only barriers against moral degradation, and which yet somehow seem to make in favour of the cruel and the self-seeking. The only safe plan is that of the lady in the ballad, to 'lock your heart in a case of gold, and pin it with a silver pin'. Mortify your affections, scourge yourself with rods, and sit in sackcloth and ashes; stamp vigorously upon the cruel thorns that strew your pathway, and learn not to shrink when they lacerate the most tender flesh. Be an ascetic, in brief, and yet without the true aim of the ascetic. For, unlike him, you must admit that these affections are precisely the best part of you, and that the offers of the Church, which proposes to wean you from the world, and reward you by a loftier prize, are a delusion and a snare. They are the lessons of a designing priesthood, and imply a blasphemy against the most divine instincts of human nature.

This is the unhappy discord which runs through Miss Brontë's conceptions of life, and, whilst it gives an indescribable pathos to many pages, leaves us with a sense of something morbid and unsatisfactory. She seems to be turning for relief alternately to different teachers, to the promptings of her own heart, to the precepts of those whom she has been taught to revere, and occasionally, though timidly and tentatively, to alien schools of thought. The attitude of mind is, indeed, best indicated by the story (a true story, like most of her incidents) of her visit to the confessional in Brussels. Had she been a Catholic, or a Positivist, or a rebel against all the creeds, she might have reached some consistency of doctrine, and therefore some harmony of design. As it is, she seems to be under a desire which makes her restless and unhappy, because her best impulses are continually warring against each other. She is between the opposite poles of duty and happiness, and cannot see how to reconcile their claims – for perhaps no one can solve that, or any other great problem exhaustively – how distinctly to state the question at issue. She pursues one path energetically, till she feels her self to be in danger, and then shrinks with a kind of instinctive dread, and resolves not only that life is a mystery, but that happiness must be sought by courting misery. Undoubtedly such a position speaks of a mind diseased, and a more powerful intellect would even under her conditions have worked out some more comprehensible and harmonious solution.

For us, however, it is allowable to interpret her complaints in our own fashion, whatever it may be. We may give our own answer to the dark problem, or at least indicate the path by which an answer must be reached. For a poor soul so grievously beset within and without by troubles in which we all have a share, we can but feel the strongest sympathy. We cannot sit at her feet as a great teacher, nor admit that her view of life is satisfactory or even intelligible. But we feel for her as for a fellow-sufferer who has at least felt with extraordinary keenness the sorrows and disappointments which torture most cruelly the most noble virtues, and has clung throughout her troubles to beliefs which must in some form or other be the guiding lights of all worthy actions. She is not in the highest rank amongst those who have fought their way to a clearer atmosphere, and can help us to clearer conceptions; but she is amongst the first of those who have felt the necessity of consolation, and therefore stimulated to more successful efforts.

SOURCE: 'Hours in a Library' in *Cornhill Magazine,* December 1877; reprinted in *Hours in a Library,* third series, 1879.

NOTES

Sir Leslie Stephen (1832–1904), philosopher, historian, literary critic and father of Virginia Woolf, edited the *Cornhill Magazine* (see above, p. 144 n.) during 1871–82; his 'Hours in a Library', the series of critical essays which he contributed to the magazine, were published in three volumes, with additions, 1874–9, 1892; and, with further additions, in four volumes, 1907.

1. That is, the breadth of comic invention informing the character of Uncle Toby in Sterne's *Tristram Shandy* (1759–67). Stephen is taking issue with Swinburne (pp. 146–7 above) over his view that Paul Emanuel must be regarded as one of literature's major serio-comic characterisations.

2. Alluding to the strongly romantic rhythms and effects associated with Ossian (or Osin), the legendary Gaelic bard and warrior; such 'Ossianesque' qualities had been popularised in the eighteenth century by James Macpherson (1736–96) in his 'Ossianic' poems *Fingal* (1762) and *Temora* (1763).

ANTHONY TROLLOPE : 'A marvellous woman'

Charlotte Brontë was surely a marvellous woman.[1] If it could be right to judge the work of a novelist from one small portion of one novel, and to say of an author that he is to be accounted as strong as he shows himself to be in his strongest morsel of work, I should be inclined to put Miss Brontë very high indeed. I know no interest more thrilling than that which she has been able to throw into the characters of Rochester and the governess, in the second volume of *Jane Eyre*. She lived with those characters, and felt with every fibre of her heart, the longings of the one and the sufferings of the other. And therefore, though the end of the book is weak, and the beginning not very good, I venture to predict that *Jane Eyre* will be read among English novels when many whose names are now better known shall have been forgotten. *Jane Eyre*, and *Esmond*, and *Adam Bede* will be in he hands of our grandchildren, when Pickwick, and *Pelham* and *Harry Lorrequer*[2] are forgotten; because the men and women depicted are human in their aspirations, human in their sympathies, and human in their actions.

In *Villette,* too, and in *Shirley,* there is to be found human life as natural and as real, though in circumstances not so full of interest as those told in *Jane Eyre.* The character of Paul in the former of the two is a wonderful study. She must herself have been in love with some Paul when she wrote the book, and have been determined to prove to herself that she was capable of loving one whose exterior circumstances were mean and in every way unprepossessing.

SOURCE: 'On English Novelists of the Present Day' in *Autobiography,* 1883.

NOTES

1. Trollope places Charlotte Brontë fourth in order after Thackeray, George Eliot and Dickens.
2. Bulwer Lytton's *Pelham* (1828); Charles Lever's *Harry Lorrequer* (1837).

MARY WARD: 'This mixture of Celtic dreaming with English realism and self-control'

From Introduction to Jane Eyre

... Now certainly there never was a plot, which pretended to be a plot, of looser texture than that of *Jane Eyre.* It abounds with absurdities and inconsistencies. The critics of Charlotte Brontë's time had no difficulty in pointing them out; they lie, indeed, on the surface for all to see. That such incidents should have happened to Jane Eyre in Mr Rochester's house as did happen, without awakening her suspicions; that the existence of a lunatic should have been commonly known to all the servants of the house, yet wholly concealed from the governess; that Mr Rochester should have been a man of honour and generosity, a man with whom not only Jane Eyre, but clearly the writer herself, is in love, and yet capable of deliberately betraying and deceiving a girl of twenty placed in a singularly helpless position; – these are the fundamental puzzles of the story. Mrs Fairfax is a mystery throughout. How, knowing what she did, did she not inevitably know more? – what was her real relation to Rochester? – to Jane Eyre? These are questions that no one can answer out of the four corners of the book. The country-house party is a tissue of extravagance throughout; the sarcasms and brutalities of the beautiful Miss Ingram are no more credible than the manners assumed by the aristocratic Rochester from the beginning towards his ward's governess, or the amazing freedom with which he pours into the ears of the same governess – a virtuous girl of twenty, who has been no more than a few weeks under his roof – the story of his relations with Adèle's mother ...

As to the other weaknesses of plot and conception, they are very obvious and very simple. The 'arrangements' by which Jane Eyre is led to find a home in the Rivers household, and becomes at once her uncle's heiress, and the good angel of her newly discovered cousins; the device of the phantom voice that recalls her to Rochester's side; the fire that destroys the mad wife, and delivers into Jane's hands a subdued and helpless Rochester; – all these belong to that more mechanical and external sort of plot-making, which the modern novelist of feeling and passion – as distinguished from the novelist of adventure – prides himself on renouncing ... The true subject of *Jane Eyre* is the courage with which a friendless and loving girl confronts her own passion, and, in the interest of some strange social instinct which she knows as 'duty', which she cannot explain and can only obey, tramples her love underfoot, and goes out miserable into the world. Beside this wrestle of the human will, everything else is trivial or vulgar. The various expedients – legacies, uncles, fires, and coincidences – by which Jane Eyre is ultimately brought to happiness, cheapen and degrade the book without convincing the reader. In fact – to return to our *advocatus diaboli* – *Jane Eyre* is on the one side a rather poor novel of incident, planned on the conventional pat-

tern, and full of clumsy execution; on another side it is a picture
of passion and of ideas, for which in truth the writer had no sufficient equipment; she moves imprisoned, to quote Mr Leslie Stephen, in 'a narrow circle of thoughts'; if you press it, the psychology of the book is really childish; Rochester is absurd, Jane Eyre,
in spite of the stir that she makes, is only half-realised and half-
conscious ...

So far the objector; yet in spite of it all, *Jane Eyre* persists, and
Charlotte Brontë is with the immortals. What is it a critic of this
type forgets – what item does he drop out of the reckoning yet,
in the addition, decides the sum?

Simply, one might say, Charlotte Brontë herself[1] ... The main
secret of the charm that clings to Charlotte Brontë's books is, and
always will be, the contact which they give us with her own fresh,
indomitable, surprising personality ... Personality then – strong,
free, passionate personality – is the sole but the sufficient spell of
these books. Can we analyse some of its elements? ... has it ever
been sufficiently recognised that Charlotte Brontë is first and
foremost *an Irishwoman,* that her genius is at bottom a Celtic
genius? ... The main characteristics indeed of the Celt are all
hers – disinterestedness, melancholy, wildness, a wayward force
and passion, for ever wooed by sounds and sights to which other
natures are insensible – by murmurs from the earth, by colours in
the sky, by tones and accents of the soul, that speak to the Celtic
sense as to no other ... Then, as to the Celtic pride, the Celtic
shyness, the Celtic endurance, – Charlotte Brontë was rich in them
all ... And all three qualities – pride, shrinking, endurance – are
writ large in her books. With passion added they *are* Jane Eyre
and Lucy Snowe ... And one other Celtic quality there is in Charlotte Brontë and her books, which is responsible perhaps for half
their defects. It is a quality of exuberance, of extravagance, of
what her contemporaries called 'bad taste' ... there was in Miss
Brontë a curious vein of recklessness, roughness, one might say
hoydenism – that exists side by side with an exquisite delicacy and
a true dignity,[2] and is none the less Irish and Celtic for that ...

The Irish and Celtic element . . . however, is not all . . . Crossing, controlling the wild impetuous temper of the Irishwoman is an influence from another world, an influence of habit and long association breathed from Yorkshire and the hard, frugal persistent North . . . it is this mixture of Celtic dreaming with English realism and self-control which gives value and originality to all they (the Brontës) do . . . As to the outer and material history of *Jane Eyre,* it is written to some extent in Mrs Gaskell's *Life,* and has employed the pens of many a critic and local antiquary since. We all know that Lowood is Cowan Bridge, that Helen Burns stands for Maria Brontë, that 'Miss Temple' and 'Miss Scatcherd' were drawn from real people; we are told that Thornfield Hall was suggested by one old Yorkshire house and Ferndean Manor by another; that St John Rivers had an original : we may take for granted that Charlotte's own experiences as a governess have passed into the bitterness with which the rich and 'society' are described . . . Such identifications and researches will always have their interest, though the artist never sees as the critic sees, and is often filled with secret amusement when he or she is led back to the scene or the person which . . . furnished . . . the germ and the clay . . . The literary affiliations and connections of the book would be far more important and significant if one could trace them . . . There were no children's books in Haworth Parsonage. The children were nourished upon . . . the Bible, Shakespeare, Addison, Johnson, Sheridan, Cowper for the past; Scott, Byron, Southey, Wordsworth, Coleridge, *Blackwood's Magazine, Fraser's Magazine* and Leigh Hunt for the moderns . . . Thus strongly were the foundations laid, deep in the rich main soil of English life and letters . . . Later on . . . certain foreign influences come in . . . Charlotte probably owed much – more, I am inclined to believe, than has yet been recognised[3] – to the books of French Romanticism, that great movement starting from Chateaubriand at the beginning of the century, and already at its height before *Jane Eyre* was written . . . In 1840 . . . Charlotte writes that she has received 'another bale of French books . . . containing upwards of forty volumes . . .'[4] Victor Hugo . . . , Alfred de Musset . . . , were

F

they in the packet that reached Charlotte . . . ? . . . We know . . .
that . . . she did read George Sand . . . and the influence of that
great romantic artist . . . was of some true importance in the development of Charlotte Brontë's genius . . . The differences . . . are
great and fundamental. Charlotte Brontë's main *stuff* is English,
Protestant, law-respecting, conventional, even . . . No judgment
was ever more foolish than that which detected a social rebel in the
writer of *Jane Eyre*.[5] She thought French books . . . 'clever, wicked,
sophistical, and immoral'. But she read them and for all her revolt
from them, they quickened and fertilised her genius . . . The influence which she absorbed from them has given her a special
place in our literature of imagination . . . One may say of it, indeed, that it belongs more to the European than to the special
English tradition. For all its strongly marked national and provincial elements, it was very early understood and raised in France;
and it was of a French critic and a French critic only, that Charlotte said with gratitude . . . 'he follows Currer Bell through every
winding, discerns every point, discriminates every shade . . . '[6]

From Introduction to Villette
'*Villette*', says Mrs Gaskell, 'was received with one burst of accla-
mation'. There was no question then among 'the judicious', and
there can be still less question now, that it is the writer's masterpiece. It has never been so widely read as *Jane Eyre*; and probably
the majority of English readers prefer *Shirley*.[7] The narrowness
of the stage on which the action passes, the foreign setting, the very
fulness of poetry, of visualising force, that runs through it, like
a fiery stream bathing and kindling all it touches . . . are repellent
or tiring to a mind that has no energy of its own responsive to the
energy of the writer. But not seldom the qualities which give a
book immortality are the qualities that for a time guard it from
the crowd – till its bloom of fame has grown to a safe maturity
beyond injury or doubt . . . From beginning to end it seems to be
written in flame . . . The story is, as it were, upborne by something
lambent and rushing . . . And the detail is as a rule much more
assured and masterly than in the two earlier books. Here and

there are a few absurdities that recall the drawing-room scenes of *Jane Eyre* – a few unfortunate or irrelevant disgressions like the chapter 'Cleopatra' ... But they are very few; they spoil no pleasure. And as a rule the book has not only imagination and romance, it has knowledge of life, and accuracy of social vision, in addition to all the native shrewdness, the incisive force of the early chapters of *Jane Eyre*.

Of all the characters, Dr John no doubt is the least tangible, the least alive ... As to Paul Emanuel ... we need not try to question ... his place among the immortals ... what variety, what invention, what truth, have been lavished upon him! and what a triumph to have evolved from such materials, – a schoolroom, a garden, a professor, a few lessons, conversations, walks, – so rich and sparkling a whole! Madame Beck and Ginevra Fanshawe are in their way equally admirable ... And Lucy Snowe? Well – Lucy Snowe is Jane Eyre again, the friendless girl, fighting the word as best she may, her only weapon a strong and chainless will, her constant hindrances, the passionate nature that makes her the slave of sympathy, of the first kind look or word, and the wild poetic imagination that forbids her all reconciliation with her own lot, the lot of the unbeautiful and obscure. But ... there are differences, and all, it seems to me, to Lucy's advantage. She is far more intelligible – truer to life and feeling ... There are some touches that displease, indeed, because it is impossible to believe in them. Lucy Snowe could never have broken down, never appealed for mercy, never have cried 'My heart will break!' before her treacherous rival, Madame Beck, in Paul Emanuel's presence ... But Charlotte has given to her more of her own rich inner life, more of her own poetry and fiery distinction than to Jane Eyre ... Miss Martineau's criticism of *Villette* ... shows a singular, yet not surprising blindness[8]. . . pointing to the gulf between Miss Martineau's type of culture – which alike in its strength and its weakness is that of English provincial Puritanism – and that more European and cosmopolitan type, to which, for all her strong English and Yorkshire qualities ..., Charlotte, as an artist, really belonged. The truth, of course, that it is precisely in and through her treatment of passion – mainly, no doubt, as it affects the woman's heart and life – that she has earned and still maintains her fame . . .

SOURCE: from the Introductions to *Jane Eyre* and *Villette*, *The Life and Works or Charlotte Brontë and her Sisters* (Haworth Edition), edited by Mrs Humphry Ward and C. K. Shorter, 7 vols (1899–1900).

NOTES

Mary Augusta Ward, better known as Mrs Humphry Ward (1851–1920), was the wife of T. H. Ward and niece of Matthew Arnold. She was herself a novelist, her best-known novels including *Robert Elsmere* (1885) and *Helbeck of Bannisdale* (1898). Her comprehensive and sensible introductions for the Haworth Edition (Introduction, p. 32) are indispensable for anyone interested in the Brontës and include, besides the more general impressions represented here, illuminating and lively commentaries on narrative, theme, structure and style in each of the Brontë novels.

1. Cp. David Cecil, pp. 167–8 below.

2. A shrewd addition to the various early diagnoses of the Brontës' so-called 'coarseness'.

3. See Introduction, pp. 16–17.

4. Letter to Ellen Nussey, 20 August 1840, *LL* I 215.

5. See Introduction, pp. 23–4.

6. Eugène Forçade; see above, pp. 66–7.

7. There is little evidence to support this view.

8. See above, p. 75.

PART THREE

Some Twentieth-Century Views

David Cecil

CHARLOTTE BRONTË AS A 'FREAK GENIUS' (1934)

... Charlotte Brontë's imagination is stimulated to create by certain aspects of man's inner life as that of Dickens or Thackeray by certain aspects of his external life. As Thackeray was the first English writer to make the novel a vehicle of a conscious criticism of life, so she is the first to make it the vehicle of personal revelation. She is our first subjective novelist, the ancestor of Proust and Mr James Joyce and all the rest of the historians of the private consciousness. And like theirs her range is limited to those aspects of experience which stimulate to significance and activity the private consciousness of their various heroes and heroines.

Even of these she does not give us a complete picture. Her range is, further, limited as that of Proust and Mr Joyce is not. They, however subjective in their matter, are objective in their manner of treating it. They take intellectual interest in the inner life, they seek to analyse it, to discover and exhibit the laws by which it is governed. Charlotte Brontë had no such interest : nor the detachment necessary to pursue it if she had. Her heroines do not try to disentangle the chaos of their consciousness, they do not analyse their emotions or motives. Indeed, they do not analyse anything. They only feel very strongly about everything. And the sole purpose of their torrential autobiographies is to express their feelings. *Jane Eyre*, *Villette*, *The Professor*, the best parts of *Shirley*, are not exercises of the mind, but cries of the heart; not a deliberate self-diagnosis, but an involuntary self-revelation.

Further, they are all revelations of the same self ... Fundamentally, her principal characters are all the same person; and that is

Charlotte Brontë. Her range is confined, not only to a direct expression of an individual's emotions and impressions, but to a direct expression of Charlotte Brontë's emotions and impressions. In this, her final limitation, we come indeed to the distinguishing fact of her character as a novelist. The world she creates is the world of her own inner life; she is her own subject.

This does not mean, of course, that she never writes about anything but her own character. She is a story-teller, and a story shows character in action, character, that is, as it appears in contact with the world of external event and personality . . . Charlotte Brontë's picture of the external world is a picture of her own reactions to the external world. Her account of Vashti's acting in *Villette* does not go into its aesthetic merits like Proust's description of Berma's acting, but only into the impression it made on Lucy Snowe. And similarly her secondary characters are presented only as they appear to Jane Eyre or Lucy Snowe. We see as much of them as they saw of them : and what we do see is coloured by the intervening painted glass of Lucy Snowe's or Jane Eyre's temperament. At the best they are the barest sketches compared with the elaborately-finished portrait of the character through whose eyes we look at them. We see Lucy Snowe and Jane Eyre full-length, life-size; of Dr John, St John Rivers, and the rest, only the hostile or friendly expression of face, the hand outstretched in welcome, the shoulder turned in contempt, which chances to cross Jane Eyre's or Lucy Snowe's line of vision . . .

Her books – and this is true of no other English novelist of comparable merit – are, but for the continued presence of certain figures, incoherent. Nor is this because they are like *Pickwick,* a succession of adventures only connected by a hero. No, each is a drama : but not one drama. Charlotte Brontë will embark on a dramatic action and then, when it is half finished, without warning abandon it for another, equally dramatic, but without bearing on what has come before will follow after. The first quarter of *Jane Eyre* is about Jane's life as a child; the next half is devoted to her relation with Rochester : in the last quarter of the book, St John Rivers appears, and the rest of the book, except for the final chapters, is concerned with her relation to him. However, *Jane Eyre* does maintain a continuous interest in one central figure. *Villette* and *Shirley* do not even possess this frail principle of unity. The first three chapters of *Villette* are concerned wholly with the child Polly, Lucy Snowe is merely a narrator. In Chapter Four she suddenly takes the centre of the stage; but only to follow the same capricious career as Jane Eyre. After a brief interlude describing her association with Miss Marchmont, she is whisked off to the continent, where for several hundred pages the book is wholly concerned in describing her dawning intimacy with Dr John. But just when this seems likely to reach a culmination the centre of the interest again changes. Poor Dr John is cavalierly dismissed to the position of a minor figure; and his place is taken by Paul Emanuel . . . She does not pause to consider probability either . . . Her plots are not dull; but they have every other defect that a plot could have; they are at once conventional, confusing and unlikely. *The Professor,* indeed, save in the affair of Mr Vandenhuten, palpably introduced to establish Crimsworth in the comfortable circumstances necessary to give the book a happy ending, is credible enough; while *Shirley,* though its plot is mildly unconvincing all through, is marred only by one gross improbability, the conduct of Mrs Pryor. But the stories of her masterpieces, *Jane Eyre* and *Villette,* are, if regarded in a rational aspect, unbelievable from start to finish. *Jane Eyre,* and here too Charlotte Brontë shows herself like Dickens, is a roaring melodrama. But the melodrama of *Bleak House* itself seems sober compared with that of *Jane Eyre.* Not one of the main incidents on which its action turns but is incredible. It is incredible that Rochester should hide a mad wife on the top floor of Thornfield Hall, and hide her so imperfectly that she constantly gets loose and roams yelling about the house, without any of his numerous servants and guests suspecting anything: it is incredible that Mrs Reed, a conventional if disagreeable woman, should conspire to cheat Jane Eyre out of a fortune because she had been rude to her as a child of ten: it is supremely incredible that when Jane Eyre collapses on an unknown doorstep after her flight from Rochester it should turn out to be the doorstep of her only surviving amiable relations. *Villette* has not a melodramatic plot. But by a majestic feat of literary perversity Charlotte Brontë manages to make this quiet chronicle of a school teacher as bristling with improbability as *Jane Eyre*. She stretches the long arm of coincidence till it becomes positively dislocated. It is possible to believe that the only man who happened to be on the spot to assist Lucy Snowe's arrival in Belgium was her long-lost cousin, Graham Bretton. It is harder to believe that he should again be the only man on the spot to help her when she faints in the street six months later. It is altogether impossible to believe that he and his mother should nurse her through an illness without recognising her, though she had stayed for months in their house only a few years before; and that finally he should rescue another girl and that she should turn out to be his only other female friend of childhood. In a world of artificial intrigue, like that of Wilkie Collins, say, we can accept a certain amount of improbability as part of the convention within which the story is built; but in a living human document like *Villette,* it stares out at us as crudely unconvincing as a bit of stage scenery in the open air.

Nor are her faults of form her only faults . . . Charlotte Brontë was about as well-equipped to be a satirist as she was to be a ballet-dancer. Satire demands acute observation and a light touch. Charlotte Brontë, indifferent to the outside world and generally in a state of tension, observes little, and never speaks lightly of anything. In consequence her satirical darts fall wide of the mark and as ponderous as lead. Painstakingly she tunes her throbbing accents to a facetious tone, conscientiously she contorts her austere countenance to a humorous grimace. Lady Ingram and Mr Sweeting remain as obstinately, as embarrassingly, unamusing as the patter of a conjuror.

But though her lack of humour prevents her amusing us when she means to, it often amuses us very much when she does not. Her crudeness, her lack of restraint, and the extreme seriousness with which she envisages life, combine to deprive her of any sense of ironic proportion. What could be more comic, if considered in the

clear daylight of commonsense, than the scene in *Villette* where
Lucy Snowe is called upon to play the part of a young man in
some amateur theatricals : her horrified determination not to wear
male costume, Mlle Zélie's determination that she shall, and the
compromise, a purple crêpe skirt surmounted by a tail-coat and
top-hat, attired in which she finally appears before the footlights?
Not less absurd are the Byronic wooings of Rochester, dressed up
in the shawl and bonnet of an old gypsy woman. Yet Charlotte
Brontë describes both scenes with the same agitated earnestness
with which she describes Mrs Reed's death; and as a result they
seem even more ridiculous than before. Her dialogue, too, is often
preposterous, especially when she leaves that territory of the heart
which is her native country to reproduce the chit-chat of conventional life. Listen to the fashionable Miss Blanche Ingram, reprov-
ing with appropriate sternness a servant : ' "Cease that chatter,
blockhead, and do my bidding" '; or coquetting with an admirer
at the piano . . .

All the same, unconscious humour is not her worst fault; if it is
a fault at all. It springs from the very nature of her work, from the
fact that she presents life from an individual point of view : to
remove the absurdity would be to remove the individuality at the
same time. Moreover, it is possible to describe a scene vividly without seeing its funny side : a man may express himself fantastically
and yet express himself well. The play in *Villette*, Rochester's proposal, are among the most memorable scenes in Charlotte Brontë's
books; and we enjoy them whole-heartedly. Only, our enjoyment
is enriched by an ironic amusement which it could hardly have
been her intention to stimulate.

But her chief defect cannot be so lightly dismissed. Charlotte
Brontë fails, and fails often, over the most important part of a
novelist's work – over character. Even at her best she is not among
the greatest drawers of character. Her secondary figures do not
move before us with the solid reality of Jane Austen's : seen as
they are through the narrow lens of her heroine's temperament, it
is impossible that they should. And the heroines themselves are
presented too subjectively for us to see them in the round as we see

Maggie Tulliver or Emma Bovary. Nor is her failure solely due to
the limitations imposed by her angle of approach. Since she feels
rather than understands, she cannot penetrate to the inner structure of a character to discover its basic elements. Most of her
characters are only presented fragmentarily as they happen to
catch the eye of her heroine[1] . . . And sometimes they are not only
fragmentary, they are lifeless. Her satirical, realistic figures, of
course, are especially lifeless. The curates in *Shirley,* the house-
party in *Jane Eyre,* these are as garishly unreal as the cardboard
puppets in a toy theatre. It is not just that they are unlike human
beings in actual life : Mr Micawber is very unlike actual life. But
he is alive with the compelling vitality of Dickens' original imagination. Lady Ingram is not original : she is extremely conventional,
the conventional silly grande dame of third-rate farce. Charlotte
Brontë, unacquainted with such a character herself, has just copied
it from the crude type which she found in the commonplace fiction
of the time. And her lack of technical skill has made her copy even
cruder than its model.

She can fail over serious character too : particularly male
character. Serious male characters are always a problem for a
woman novelist. And for Charlotte Brontë, exclusively concentrated as she was on the reactions of her highly feminine temperament, they were especially a problem. Nor did she solve it . . .
Ignorant what men are like, but convinced that at any rate they
must be unlike women, she endows them only with those characteristics she looks on as particularly male : and accentuates these
to such a degree that they cease to be human at all. No flesh-and-
blood man could be so exclusively composed of violence and
virility and masculine vanity as Mr Rochester. As a matter of fact
Mr Rochester and Robert Moore were the wild savage type that
stimulated Charlotte Brontë's imagination : so that, unlike Lady
Ingram, they have a certain vitality . . . Rochester is a straightforward portrait of a man for whom we are intended to feel admiration and sympathy. And the fact that he is unreal, makes that
impossible. On the other hand, Charlotte Brontë's more orthodox
heroes like Dr John have not even got imaginative life ; they are

mere tedious aggregations of good qualities, painted figureheads of virtue like the heroes of Scott. Only in Paul Emanuel has Charlotte Brontë drawn a hero who is also a living man. And he is deliberately presented on unheroic lines. For more than two-thirds of the story in which he appears, we are unaware that he is meant to be anything but a grotesque 'character part'.

Charlotte Brontë's hand does not only falter over her heroes. In Caroline and Shirley, her two objectively-conceived heroines, it is equally uncertain. Both are departures from her usual type. Caroline is described as gentle, sweet and charming, Shirley as charming, brilliant and high-spirited. In company they sustain their rôles convincingly enough. But the moment they are alone they change, they become like each other and unlike either of the characters in which they first appear; in fact . . . they reveal themselves as two more portraits of that single woman whose other names are Jane Eyre, Lucy Snowe and Charlotte Brontë.

Formless, improbable, humourless, exaggerated, uncertain in their handling of character – there is assuredly a great deal to be said against Charlotte Brontë's novels. So much, indeed, that one may well wonder if she is a good novelist at all. All the same she is; she is even great. Her books are as living today as those of Dickens; and for the same reason. They have creative imagination; and creative imagination of the most powerful kind, able to assimilate to its purpose the strongest feelings, the most momentous experiences. Nor is it intermittent in its action. Charlotte Brontë, and here again she is like Dickens, is, even at her worst, imaginative. Miss Ingram herself, though she may be a lifeless dummy, is described by Jane Eyre in tones that are far from lifeless. So that the scenes in which she appears, preposterous though they may be, are not lifeless either. Every page of Charlotte Brontë's novels burns and breathes vitality. Out of her improbabilities and her absurdities, she constructed an original vision of life; from the scattered, distorted fragments of experience which managed to penetrate her huge self-absorption, she created a world.

But her limitations make it very unlike the life of any other novelists' world. For, unhelped as she is by any great power of observation and analysis, her world is almost exclusively an imaginary world. Its character and energy derive nothing important from the character and energy of the world she purports to describe; they are the character and energy of her own personality . . .

S O U R C E : from *Early Victorian Novelists*, 1934.[2]

NOTES

1. Cp. W. C. Roscoe's comments and see Introduction (pp. 130–1, 28, 30).

2. The essay continues with a detailed analysis taking its direction from the statement, 'Any description of her achievement, therefore, resolves itself into a description of her personality', which is 'a compound of the most incongruous elements'. These are, notably, 'Childish naiveté, rigid Puritanism, fiery passion', qualities which are the true source of her originality and power. In the end they make 'her achievement almost impossible finally to estimate. To the conscientious Court Chamberlains of criticism intent to range the motley mob of English writers in their correct order of precedence, she always will present a problem. She cannot be placed with the great painters of human character, the Shakespeares, the Scotts, the Jane Austens; her faults are too glaring, her inspiration too eccentric. But equally she cannot be dismissed to a minor rank, to the Fanny Burneys, the Charles Reades : for unlike them she rises at times to the greatest heights. She is . . . among the unplaceable anomalies, the freak geniuses; along with Ford and Tourneur [cp. John Skelton, pp. 123–4] and Herman Melville and D. H. Lawrence . . . their strange flame, lit as it is at the central white hot fire of creative inspiration, will in every age find them followers. And on these they exercise a unique, a thrilling, a perennial fascination.'

M. H. Scargill

POETIC SYMBOLISM IN
JANE EYRE (1950)

From the day of its first appearance *Jane Eyre* has been accredited
with adding something new to the tradition of the English novel,
though just what this is, and whether it is desirable, continues to
puzzle the critics. To some the new quality is the voice of a woman
who speaks with perfect frankness about herself; to others it is
'passion', though the nature of this 'passion' is left undefined.[1] To
all, *Jane Eyre* is remarkable for its intensity, and this intensity is
usually taken as sufficient to counteract what critics regard as a
sensational and poorly constructed plot.[2] The cause of this intensity remains uncertain. Some have suggested that it is love;[3] some
even go so far as to suggest that it is the memory of a real love
which Charlotte Brontë herself had experienced, that is that the
novel is some kind of autobiography[4] and, if we take this view to
its logical conclusion, not a novel at all.

If we trace the development of the English novel up to the
middle of the nineteenth century, we see that it had concerned itself mainly with the external and had tried to secure belief by a
faithful representation of that external through probability of
events and convincing characters. The art, if it be an art, of imposing belief (instead of securing it) in those things which are not the
product of facsimile of external life, had been confined to the poets
and to those dramatists who are also poets. No one can call *King
Lear* probable : no one can deny that it imposes upon us the necessity of belief by its intensity, expressed in language and in imagery
that is far from normal.

With the publication of *Jane Eyre,* the English novel, which had already absorbed elements from the essay, the 'character', and the drama, turned away from the external towards the expression of an experience exclusively personal. This experience is not necessarily factual, but it is none the less real, and it is important, as much poetry is important, for the intensity of its feeling and the adequacy of its expression. It is intensity of feeling which has attracted readers to *Jane Eyre*; it is the origin and nature of this feeling and its means of expression, adequate or inadequate, that have puzzled them.

To many readers passion is synonymous with love, and to these it is as a love story that *Jane Eyre* appeals, a love story told with great frankness by a woman who, as Cross would put it, is 'a realist of the feelings'.[5] To others passion is an admirable but indescribable feeling, which appeals simply because it is a feeling – by no means a foolish value to attract one to a book and infinitely superior to that which leads to admiration of *Jane Eyre* as a kind of real 'confession'. Intensity of feeling *Jane Eyre* has, but it is not centred exclusively upon love; in fact, in total impact of *Jane Eyre* religious ecstasy plays a part as important as love for a person.

The greatness of a work of art is commensurate with the greatness of its inspiration and the adequacy of its means of communication. Now, the story of a woman in love would be interesting but not necessarily great; the story of a woman's fight to express her own personality in love would be even more interesting but yet not necessarily great. *Jane Eyre* is great because it is these things and also something more. It is a love story; it is a fight for the free expression of personality in love; but it is also a record of the eternal conflict between the flesh and the spirit, a conflict which is solved satisfactorily when all passion is spent. *Jane Eyre* may speak for many women, but it speaks also for all humanity, and it speaks in unmistakable terms. *Jane Eyre* is the record of an intense spiritual experience, as powerful in its way as King Lear's ordeal of purgation, and it ends nobly on a note of calm . . .

We make no demands of probability on the poet. All we ask is that he shall symbolise his experience, recreate it for us, by whatever means he thinks best. But of the novelist we seem inclined to demand probability, a reproduction of life, regardless of the novelist's purpose. Charlotte Brontë had experienced an emotion which one would expect her to express through the medium of poetry. But she used the conventional elements of the novel, the medium she understood best. It seems logical to suppose that such a use, conscious or unconscious, of the elements of fiction would produce a new type of novel. And this is precisely the case with *Jane Eyre*. The conventions have become symbols : the fictional lover has become The Lover; the mad woman of the Gothic novel has been put to an allegorical use. *Jane Eyre* contains the elements of fiction used as a poet employs language and imagery – to impose belief, even though it be by irrational means.

When Jane Eyre leaves Lowood School, she is but a novice in the world, in spite of her contact with the spiritual in the saintly Helen Burns and with the fleshly in Mrs Reed and Mr Brockle-hurst. Indeed, to Jane the greatest thing in life is to be loved by a person. And we need not be surprised, for love of any kind has been so far denied to the child throughout her short life. But, as Helen Burns says, love of a person is not all . 'Hush, Jane! You think too much of the love of human beings; you are too impulsive, too vehement : the sovereign Hand that created your frame, and put life into it, has provided you with other resources than your feeble self, or than creatures feeble as you' (chapter 8).

Before such a novice, to whom the yearnings of the flesh and the spirit are at best indistinguishable, is placed the specious tempta-tion of love, love imagined in its most stirring form, impetuous and violent – Mr Rochester. To such a love Jane Eyre responds, and she responds in the manner we expect of the girl described by Helen Burns : 'My future husband was becoming to me my whole world; and more than the world; almost my hope of heaven. He stood between me and every thought of religion, as an eclipse intervenes between man and the broad sun. I could not, in those days, see God for His creature, of whom I had made an idol' (chapter 14).

But behind Mr Rochester, nay, a very part of him, is Bertha Mason, the mad wife. Rochester symbolises uncontrolled physical passion, and with uncontrolled passion there is always the menacing figure of complete degeneracy and madness. For what is madness but loss of control?

At first Jane Eyre is unaware of the presence of this danger. How was she to know about it? But as she yields more and more to Rochester's importuning, the danger that comes from loss of control begins to threaten her, as it threatens Rochester all the time. Bertha Mason tears Jane's wedding veil in two, and after the broken marriage ceremony the mad woman and all she represents stand as a barrier between the lovers.

Jane's struggle is a hard one; she is unwilling to leave Rochester, although she has seen the danger : 'I wrestled with my own resolution : I wanted to be weak that I might avoid the awful passage of further suffering I saw laid out for me; and Conscience, turned tyrant, held Passion by the throat, told her tauntingly she had yet but dipped her dainty feet in the slough, and swore that with an arm of iron he would thrust her down to unsounded depths of agony' (chapter 27).

But at last Jane flies from unrestrained physical passion with all its grossness, as many another has fled before and since, and she is guided in her resolve by a vision [quotes from chapter 27, 'That night I never thought to sleep . . . flee temptation']

To Jane, now, is offered another choice – the rejection of life, the journey into asceticism with St John Rivers. It is an episode surrounded with improbabilities; it is as unlikely as King Lear's division of his kingdom, but like that it serves its purpose. The symbol is the thing, no matter how it be achieved. And was there ever a more powerful symbol of the ascetic than St John Rivers? Tennyson's Simeon Stylites pales into insignificance beside him. Shall Jane Eyre, bewildered and hurt by her experience with Rochester, deny the world and all that it has to offer? Shall she leave the physical completely, without trying to control it, and enter a loveless marriage? . . .

The struggle is long and hard, and it is no less intense than that symbolised by her life at Thornfield. St John Rivers prays for Jane that she may be guided into the right way, and the exaltation

which accompanies his prayer communicates itself in no uncertain manner to her. She feels that here is the answer – to die to life
and to live again in God : 'I stood motionless under my hiero-
phant's touch. My refusals were forgotten – my fears overcome –
my wrestlings paralysed. . . . Religion called – angels beckoned –
God commanded – life rolled together like a scroll – death's gates
opening showed eternity beyond : it seemed that for safety and
bliss there, all here might be sacrificed in a second' (chapter 35).

But, in an oft-criticised passage, guidance comes, and it comes
in the voice of Rochester. The world and the flesh have to be
reckoned with, their defeat cannot come through a plain denial of
their existence. The probability of this voice has often been denied,
but its effectiveness is certain. How else should Jane Eyre be called
back to the world she was rejecting if not by its own voice and the
voice of its Creator? 'I broke from St John who had followed, and
would have detained me. It was my time to assume ascen-
dancy. . . . I mounted to my chamber; locked myself in; and fell
on my knees; and prayed in my way – a different way to St John's,
but effective in its own fashion. I seemed to penetrate very near a
Mighty Spirit; and my soul rushed out in gratitude at His feet'
(chapter 35).

Jane returns to Mr Rochester and finds that he has passed
through his ordeal by fire, both spiritual and physical. It is a new
Rochester who can speak these words : 'I thank my Maker, that,
in the midst of judgment, He has remembered mercy. I humbly
entreat my Redeemer to give me strength to lead henceforth a
purer life than I have done hitherto' (chapter 37).

This whole episode of the fire has also been criticised as trite and
improbable, and the criticism would be valid if the novel were to
be regarded as a realistic record of events. But there is a distinction
between a factual truth and poetic truth, and when we read *Jane
Eyre* as a poetic work, the episode is artistically appropriate.
Bertha Mason has destroyed herself, the madness that can accom-
pany unrestrained passion has burned itself out, though it has left
Rochester, who gave way to it, disfigured and blinded.

They marry, not in that first violent, physical anguish in which we saw them, but in a calmer, nobler mood, 'all passion spent'. Neither the flesh, nor the spirit, will tear Jane Eyre again, for from her double ordeal she has emerged unscathed, neither a profligate nor an ascetic, but a woman who has found an equable solution to the age-old problem which troubled others besides the Victorians but which troubled them intensely,

> Ah love, could thou and I with Him conspire
> To grasp this sorry scheme of things entire,
> Would we not shatter it to bits – and then
> Remould it nearer to the Heart's Desire!

That is *Jane Eyre* as it appears to me, a new contribution to English fiction, a novel which must not be criticised in the spirit in which we criticise *Vanity Fair* or *Tom Jones*.

The Ingram episode – a further example of wrongful criticism – is decried as 'artificial'. People never spoke as Blanche Ingram speaks, say the critics. But the episode is not meant to be a faithful picture of a drawing-room; it is worldliness, pride, stripped of all pretensions, and it appears as an ugly symbol. But then, what shall we say of Lear's curse? [I iv 285–8]. Neither passage is very polite, but each one is very clear.

If *Jane Eyre* is to be blamed, because it doesn't do what *Tom Jones* and *Vanity Fair* do, then literary criticism is at fault. We must be willing to accept *Jane Eyre* as a profound, spiritual experience, expressed in the most adequate symbolism, a symbolism which, if divorced from its emotion, is as improbable as all poetic symbols. That way lies a truer appreciation of *Jane Eyre*. We have felt its greatness: we have often excused its means of expression. Let us now admit that in *Jane Eyre* fiction has become poetry,[6] and let us enlarge our idea of fiction accordingly.

S O U R C E : from 'All Passion Spent : a revaluation of *Jane Eyre*' in *University of Toronto Quarterly*, 19, 1950.

NOTES

[The following notes are the author's. For the critical context of the essay see Introduction, p. 34.]

1. 'The Brontës had fire and passion . . . but were limited in range to the exceptional, the eccentric, the outrageous. . . .' Gerald Bullet in *George Eliot* (London, 1947) 161.

2. 'Clumsiness and glaring improbabilities in the plot, blunders and absurdities in the picturing of a society to which Charlotte Brontë was a complete stranger, were as nothing beside the fierce sincerity with which she depicted life as it had imprinted itself upon her quivering sensibilities, from childhood to womanhood.' E. A. Baker, *The History of the Novel* (London, 1937) VIII, 36.

3. 'It is in the depiction of the growth of love . . . that *Jane Eyre* is perhaps most notably different from earlier English fiction.' B. Mc-Cullough, *Representative English Novelists* (New York, 1946) p. 183.

4. 'With all its faults, its narrowness of range, its occasional extravagances, *Jane Eyre* will long be remembered . . . among the most vivid masterpieces in the rare order of literary "confessions." ' F. Harrison, *Studies in Early Victorian Literature* (London, 1906) p. 162.

5. 'We have in Charlotte Brontë a realist of the feelings, trailing, however, the bright colours of romanticism.' W. L. Cross, *The Development of the English Novel* (London, 1919) p. 233. E. A. Baker also has a further reference to the effect of the intense feeling in *Jane Eyre*. He says : ' . . . it is a rendering, not of life as it is observed, but life as it is felt, as it is known in its elements' (*The History of the Novel*, VIII, 37).

6. Similar recognition has been granted to *Wuthering Heights* by such critics as E. A. Baker (*The History of the Novel*, VIII, 37).

Kathleen Tillotson

JANE EYRE AND THE TRIUMPH
OVER ANGRIA (1954)

... the whole tone of *The Professor* [shows] the completeness of [Charlotte's] moral emancipation from the world of Angria, where 'romantic domestic treachery' was the norm ... It remained to discover the structure, the unity, which a whole novel demands; and, now safely anchored upon those shores, to rediscover the realm of dream. *The Professor* was a necessary stage; it set up a bare framework of 'working one's way through life' with a 'rational mind', a framework unknown to Angria, and from which none of her later narratives seriously departs; but it perhaps sacrificed too much to down-to-earth truthfulness in its conscientious avoidance of sudden turns of fortune and extremes of feeling ...

Jane Eyre is the completion of her victory; writing it, she was able to accept and keep in due subordination material from her fantasy world. There, Angria has become a positive value; for she has asserted her dominion, and the reader of this novel has never any doubt that she, and not any of her creatures, is in control. Like Lamb's true poet, she 'dreams, *being awake*', and 'treads the burning marl without dismay'.[1]

When the Angrian plot-material in *Jane Eyre* is recognised,[2] its subordination is seen to be a triumph of structure and emphasis. Had the story begun with the nodal situation, we should have been on a distant island (Spanish Town standing for Glass Town or Verdopolis) and have seen Rochester's father and elder brother entrapping him into marriage with a vicious lunatic. Instead, this situation is embedded in the main story, revealed retrospectively only at its climax; it is there not for its sensational sake, but as precisely that situation which will make Rochester's deception most nearly excusable, and Jane's resistance most difficult, producing the maximum of conflict between conscience and compassion and holding the reader's sympathies in true balance. By holding its revelation in reserve the author keeps the two rising lines of suspense in the middle chapters ironically parallel; Jane draws nearer and nearer to the mystery of Thornfield, unaware that it holds the destruction of her growing love. More incidental Angrian material is usually distanced in time or space, even as Spanish Town, Madeira, and India lie out on the edges of the novel's world. It is disinfected of feverish emotion : Rochester's mistresses are recollected with moderate tranquillity, and Adèle, the dancer's illegitimate child, is almost visibly stripped of glamour. Only in Blanche Ingram and Rochester's deliberate use of her as a means of tormenting Jane is there any approximation to the Angrian tone. Elsewhere, radical differences belie a superficial similarity; a girl's arrival at a strange house, with an absent and mysterious master, is recurrent in Angria (as in all romance), but is not there accompanied by a solidly reassuring Mrs Fairfax, nor by the heroine's rationality and courage and her concern to earn an honest competence. Mr Rochester looms up at first like Zamorna; but, unlike him, he can be mocked, has wit, intellect, and a conscience dormant, not dead. He is at worst an outlaw, where Zamorna was despot of a lawless world. Jane, the steady centre of the narrative, represents what no Angrian heroine ever had : an incorruptible heart. Angria storms behind locked doors; the walls between chaos and the world are thin, but they will stand.

'The first duty of an author is, I conceive, a faithful allegiance to Truth and Nature.' The statement, coming from Charlotte Brontë in 1848, [*LL* II 243] is no truism; for her, that allegiance was hard-won. And it was natural also for her to place second to it the duty of a 'conscientious study of Art'; that came second in order for her, and *Jane Eyre* is her first work to show it. *The Professor* contains art, but is not a total work of art; in design and control, thanks to the backward drag of Angria, it is a broken-backed whole. Its inferiority to *Agnes Grey* as well as to *Wuthering Heights,* and the startling advance in *Jane Eyre* suggest that she may have learnt from her sisters' novels, in this as in other ways.[3] Different as they are, both had the power to teach her an economy of construction which *The Professor* lacks and *Jane Eyre* has.

Anne's unassuming but forcible narrative may have shown Charlotte the possibilities of a first-person angle of vision approximating to the author's experience : that of the solitary governess, observant and stoical in the strange and uncongenial world of other people's houses . . .

Wuthering Heights, on the other hand, could contribute the courage of its passion[4] and some part of its elaboration of structure.[5] Perhaps its most useful lesson was that it employed a device of exposition, not used before by Charlotte, which makes for a satisfying complexity : a present mystery is gradually illuminated by the unfolding of the past. In *Jane Eyre* this is done mainly by retrospection; whereas Emily displays two or three levels of time, bridged by a common observer. But both novels must have been planned backwards, and with a close regard for chronology; and that is the prosaic kind of planning which one might suppose very likely to be discussed. Further, one of Emily's larger purposes is reflected though differently achieved, in *Jane Eyre* : that is, to show the pressures of childhood experience in the full-grown character, with artfully contrived recurrences and contrasts. The conflicts of character in the two novels are not comparable; for Emily, the visionary, by-passes the moral world, rising straight from the jungle of childhood love-and-hate to the spiritual world and seeing them as one. Nor are the settings, the sense of place and season, alike; but there is the same 'exaltation of the senses'[6] whose absence has been remarked in *The Professor. Wuthering Heights* may have shown Charlotte that she need not deny her poetic imagination for the sake of allegiance to Truth . . . 'An Autobiography' : the choice of this form is of vital importance to the structure of the novel. Not, however, because the author is ever transcribing experience . . . it is an *illusion* of identification that is produced by the use of feminine first-person narrative.

She had not attempted it before[7] and its novelty for her was no doubt an advantage; it imparts a warmth and confidence to the passages of self-analysis lacking in *The Professor*. The way it is used may be influenced by her sister's example, in *Agnes Grey*, and in parts of *Wuthering Heights*; and also perhaps by *Pamela*, whose central situation *Jane Eyre* reproduces with a difference. It was the method of narrative that suited her best; her unease without it is manifest in *Shirley*, which lacks a single centre of interest, and disposes its much greater masses of material without informing them with unity.[8]

For the peculiar unity of *Jane Eyre*, the use of the heroine as narrator is mainly responsible.

All is seen from the vantage-ground of the single experience of the central character, with which experience the author has imaginatively identified herself, and invited the engagement, again even to the point of imaginative identification, of every reader. For both author and reader the threads of actual common experience are unbreakable, if slender; and they lead into the realms not of daydream, but of art. Only ingenuousness or assured mastery would choose such a method; to charge its limitations with the utmost significance, to avoid all its pitfalls, is the fortunate achievement of very few. The single point of view may be easily held at the circumference of the narrative and the emotional interest; but Jane continually, quietly, triumphantly occupies the centre, never receding into the role of mere reflector or observer – as does David Copperfield for several chapters at a time. Nor is she ever seen ironically, with the author hovering just visibly beyond her, hinting at her obtuseness and self-deception; an effect well-contrived, for example, by Dickens, notably in the Steerforth scenes of *David Copperfield*, and almost pervasively in *Great Expectations*; by Mrs Gaskell in *Cousin Phillis*; and by Stevenson in *Kidnapped*. These are masterpieces of first-person narrative, but they all sacrifice something that *Jane Eyre* retains; the ironic hovering sets the reader at a further distance from the central character – invited to understand it better than it does itself, he admires it, and identifies himself with it, a shade the less. But the reader of *Jane Eyre* at best

keeps pace with the heroine, with her understanding of events
(it would be a safe assumption that every reader shares her suspicions of Grace Poole) and of character, including her own. A
special difficulty of presenting a central character in first-person
narration (and one more incident to heroines, since custom allows
women less latitude here) is that of combining enough self-descrip-
tion and self-analysis to define, with enough self-forgetfulness to
attract. This difficulty also Charlotte Brontë circumvents; Jane is
not tediously egotistical like Pamela, nor so transparently useful to
the author as Esther Summerson, uncomprehendingly recording
the compliments paid to her. Jane is self-critical, but also self-
respecting; her modesty attracts while never making the reader
take her at her own initial valuation. We watch a personality discovering itself not by long introspection but by a habit of keeping
pace with her own experience. It is from her own explicit record
that we are convinced both of her plainness and her charm, her
delicacy and her endurance, her humility and her pride. Contriv-
ance is never obtrusive and on a first reading probably unnoticed as
such; in the rapid current of the narrative the deliberate contribu
tion of others' views of her is accepted unconsciously as part of our
picture of Jane. 'If she were a nice, pretty child, one might compas-
sionate her forlornness; but one really cannot care for such a little
toad as that.' The speaker (Abbot, the commonplace heartless servant, deflecting Bessie's first stirrings of pity) is just enough defined
for the testimony to be given due but not excessive weight. Five
chapters and a few weeks later, in the sweep of Helen Burns's impassioned sermon, comes this, 'I read a sincere nature in your ardent eyes and on your clear front' (chapter 8); again, we know the
witness and can weigh the testimony. At Thornfield, Mr Rochester's half-irritated speculations on Jane's appearance and nature
build up a still clearer definition; but we are so much occupied in
discovering his own still more mysterious character and attitude
that we hardly notice *how* we are being helped to see Jane . . . Even
when, disguised as the gipsy fortune-teller, he describes and inter-
prets her character at length (chapter 19), the situation justifies it;
as the gipsy's testimony, it is accepted as the oracular revelation

of the true Jane; as Mr Rochester's, it is evidence alike of his love and understanding, and of the 'finest fibre of [her] nature'; as yet not consciously realised by him. All that has gone before and follows in the novel is embedded in his concluding words [quotes frrom chapter 19, 'The forehead declares . . . dictates of conscience'] . . .

The consistency and flexibility of the first person method is unusual, and its use in a narrative of childhood perhaps an absolute novelty in fiction. The novel would have lost incalculably had it started later in Jane's life – say, at her setting out for Thornfield . . . *Jane Eyre* arrests attention in its opening chapters by disclosing an individual character enmeshed in, yet independent of, unusual circumstances . . .

The deliberate dryness of tone and accompanying self-criticism make the early chapters less harrowing than they could have been – and than the Murdstone chapters of *David Copperfield* are. The facts are terrible enough . . . But they are counterbalanced by our sense of a character growing from its own inward strength, like grass pushing up between stones. This growth is reflected in the clear shallow pool of Bessie's 'You little sharp thing! You've got quite a new way of talking. What makes you so venturesome and hardy?' (chapter 4).

The impact of Mr Brocklehurst is the more terrifying from the precise use of the physical child's-eye view ('I looked up at – a black pillar'); but under moral and theological bullying the animal again fights back [quotes from chapter 4, ' "And what is hell? . . . I must keep in good health, and not die" '] . . .

Figures in the pattern recur; Lady Ingram will remind Jane of Mrs Reed, as a worldly cold-hearted mother of conventionally attractive daughters, who personifies the same threat to her happiness. The two sisters are indeed three times repeated, as the Brocklehursts, Ingrams, and Riverses. Most significantly, the image used for Mr Brocklehurst is repeated for St John Rivers – 'at the fireside, . . . a cold cumbrous column, gloomy and out of place'.[9] He gathers into himself the cousinship of John Reed, the formidable religious sanctions of Mr Brocklehurst, and the desire for possession of Mr Rochester : it takes more than Jane's mature powers of resistance for her to fight back at this final enemy; supernatural aid is hers.

Above all, in these early chapters there is gradually disengaged from the generic impression of a child robbed of its birthright the individual figure of a heart hungering for affection. Save for a few unconsciously dropped crumbs from Bessie, at Gateshead her bread is stones; in the choric words of Bessie's song 'Men are hardhearted', and the assurance that 'Kind angels only Watch o'er the steps of the poor orphan child' is as yet barren of comfort; there are no angels in Mr Brocklehurst's religion. Lowood opens inauspiciously, with still harsher physical discomfort – not merely piercingly actual (the taste of the burnt porridge, the starved arms wrapped in pinafores) but symbolic of a loveless order of things.[10] In Helen Burns and Miss Temple appear the first shadowings of hope; the warm fire and the cake from the cupboard in Miss Temple's room are assertions of individual loving-kindness, though also of its limited power; and Helen's comfort in injustice reaches her as from another world ...

The vehement, impulsive hunger of her nature is not satisfied at Lowood; it is only assuaged ...

The next twelve chapters, the longest stretch of the novel, belong to Thornfield; with one significant exception – the visit to Gateshead at Mrs Reed's death, where the return to the theme of the first movement marks the passage of time and Jane's own progress, as well as satisfying poetic justice. At Thornfield, saturation in the present is at its most intense; a whole year passes, each season marked, from autumn to summer. Through vicissitudes of doubt, jealousy, unsolved mystery, we are brought with Jane to the verge of satisfaction of her long heart's-hunger, on Midsummer Eve. Then, at her marriage, in the very church, the existence of Bertha Rochester is revealed : 'a Christmas frost had come at midsummer'.

The longer chapter that follows (chapter 10), in which 'conscience, turned tyrant, held passion by the throat', is the true centre of the novel, to and from which all else leads; the crisis of event,

character, and spirit, culminating in Jane's final resistance and her
flight from Thornfield. She resists not only her love and Mr
Rochester's, but her compassion and the human sense of justice
aroused by his history; and resists, not through any sense of social
convention, or shocked morality [quotes from chapter 10, 'Is it
better to drive a fellow-creature to despair ... I will keep the law
given by God; sanctioned by man ...']

Her resistance belongs to a world beyond that of human love; a
world whose presence has lain across the whole novel, if only half-
perceived. Helen Burns is its spokesman [quotes from chapter 8,
'Hush, Jane ... commissioned to guard us']. It is hinted in the
terrors of the Red Room (recalled at this very crisis), in Bessie's
song, in Jane's 'look of another world'. To that world indeed
belong incidents which would be unacceptable in an ordinary
domestic novel: the seeming coincidence of Jane's meeting with
the Rivers family, who prove to be her cousins; and to that world
belongs the miraculous voice which recalls her to Mr Rochester.
Part of the novel's inclusiveness and unity comes from Jane's
spiritual growth: her individual religion – sharply distinguished
from the loveless creeds of Mr Brocklehurst, Eliza Reed, and St
John Rivers – is fully discovered only in this crisis; but it has been
prepared for, even as early as the first long conversation with Mr
Rochester [quotes from chapter 14, 'I know what my aim is ...
"Let it be right" ']. There is a warning a few weeks before the
marriage-day, emphasised by its placing at the end of a chapter
[14] :

My future husband was becoming to me my whole world; and, more
than the world : almost my hope of heaven. He stood between me
and every thought of religion, as an eclipse intervenes between man
and the broad sun. I could not, in those days, see God for his creature:
of whom I had made an idol.

When therefore in her deepest despair 'One idea only still throbbed
life-like within me – a remembrance of God' and 'begot an
unuttered prayer' [chaper 26], it is no merely rhetorical gesture.

This is not to counter the attacks of the *Quarterly Review* by claiming *Jane Eyre* as a Christian novel; though it expresses, more directly than any other novel, the convictions of many creedless Christians in the eighteen-forties;[11] the conviction that 'not a May-game is this man's life, but a battle and a march, a warfare with principalities and powers'.[12] The master-influence of the decade is audible when Jane asserts to Rochester, 'We are born to strive and to endure'.

That the reader is aware of the 'other world', into whatever formulae he may choose to translate it, and that Jane's progress is one of spiritual growth as well as emotional adventure, is perhaps made most evident if one imagines the alternative issue. If Jane had yielded,[13] the novel would still be 'serious'; a novel with a purpose indeed, striking a blow for insurgent feminism, the anarchy of passion, and the reform of the divorce laws. But it would have been smaller and narrower, and would have violated its own moral pattern.

It would also have lost had it ended with renunciation. The phase which ends with Jane's resistance and flight is in fact the third Act; there are ten chapters – nearly a third of the novel – before we reach harbour with, 'Reader, I married him'. They are the least appreciated part of the novel : but an essential part of its unity, knitted alike to the Thornfield and the Lowood chapters. For they show Jane becoming calm after suffering, again giving 'allegiance to duty and order', again studying, again teaching in a school, submitting to Miss Temple. They also show her tempted by and withstanding the opposite temptation to Mr Rochester – that of duty and virtue which take no account of passion, personified in St John Rivers, in appearance and manner Rochester's anti-thesis, with his 'Greek face, very pure in outline' and his 'firmness and self control' – 'the material from which Nature hews her heroes . . . a steadfast bulwark . . . but at the fireside, too often a cold, cumbrous column, gloomy and out of place'. His religion seems more noble than any Jane has yet encountered; but some-thing is wanting; there is 'an absence of consolatory gentleness'; St John 'pure-lived, conscientious, zealous as he was', has, she

thinks, not yet found 'that peace of God that passeth all understanding'.

Nearly another year elapses at Marsh End and Morton; the
seasons are marked as before. But instead of progress there is
quiescence; what St John at first appeared, so he remains. Reason,
duty, cousinly affection lead to his proposal – of marriage and a
life of devoted service as missionaries in India. The service she
would accept, but not the marriage . . . She waits only for a sign
from Heaven; it comes, and it is the voice of Mr Rochester, borne
by the wind. The invisible world has spoken.

She makes her last journey – 'like the messenger-pigeon flying
home'; first to Thornfield, the burnt-out shell of the past, and at
last to Ferndean and Mr Rochester, blind and desolate, a 'caged
eagle'. The stage is set for the conventional happy ending; but the
'needle of repartee' still keeps us from the 'gulf of sentiment'. The
uses of St John Rivers are not exhausted; the tables must be turned,
and she mocks her one-time tormentor, in a long, provocative,
teasing dialogue. It is the most artful reconciliation possible – not
only of Jane and Rochester, but of the different kinds of love
threaded through the novel; and the appropriate assurance of
future happiness to these so articulate lovers – after ten years'
marriage she can still say, 'We talk, I believe, all day long'. The
spiritual pattern is also resolved; not only by his new dependence
on her, but the disclosure that at the moment of the miraculous
voice, he was calling to her, in penitence and prayer. 'I kept these
things, then, and pondered them in my heart.' But the true climax,
the justified superlative, is the last proposal :

'Jane suits me : do I suit her?'
'To the finest fibre of my nature, sir.'

with the typically practical consequence :

'The case being so, we have nothing in the world to wait for; we
must be married instantly.'

The discovery and revelation of that fineness of fibre is this
novel's triumph. There is no character in any novel of the eighteen-

forties whom the reader knows as intimately as Jane Eyre : and it is an intimacy at all levels – alike with the fiery spirit and the shivering child.

S O U R C E : From *Novels of the Eighteen-Forties,* 1954.

N O T E S

[The following notes are the author's.]
1. 'Sanity of True Genius,' in *Last Essays of Elia.* The whole essay is deeply relevant to Charlotte Brontë's progress.
2. See Ratchford (Bibliography, p. 244 below), pp. 200–14. I do not find all her parallels convincing, but there is certainly a reminiscence of Zamorna's wooing of Zenobia and her mad jealousy in Rochester's marriage to Bertha Mason, and also of the menacing hag Bertha in the deserted castle of 'The Green Dwarf'. Adèle Varens' parentage and past history recalls Caroline Vernon's, the Reed sisters recall Eliza and Georgiana Seymour, 'tall haughty blondes, proud of their accomplishments'.
3. The writing of *Jane Eyre* was wholly subsequent to that of *Wuthering Heights* and *Agnes Grey,* a fact of which critics have made too little.
4. 'It is not possible that Charlotte, of all people, should have read *Wuthering Heights* without a shock of enlightenment; that she should not have compared it with her own bloodless work; that she should not have felt the wrong done to her genius by her self-repression' (May Sinclair, *The Three Brontës,* 1912, 1914 (rev.), p. 125. Miss Sinclair was writing before the Angrian writings were known, so that the contrast between the first two novels seemed still more inexplicable).
5. Though not, of course, its most remarkable feature, and the one most alien to the narrative modes of the time : the presentation of the narrative from the points of view of two onlookers, Lockwood and Nelly, and therefore the invisibility of the author herself.
6. May Sinclair, *The Three Brontës* (1914), pp. 121–2.
7. The first-person narratives in the Angrian cycle are all masculine, as in *The Professor.*

G

8. The unity she was groping after there was perhaps that of a social microcosm, seen in *The Newcomes* and *Middlemarch*.

9. Ch. xxxiv. This image was probably in Swinburne's mind when he called St John 'this white marble clergyman (counterpart, as it were, of the "black marble" Brocklehurst)'. *A Note on Charlotte Brontë* (1877), p. 69.

10. Compare the emphasis on hunger in her flight from Thornfield (ch. xxviii).

11. Sydney Dobell commends Charlotte Brontë's 'unshaken faith' – a faith 'positive and energetic . . . united with a vigour of private judgment, without which there is nothing for it but famine in these days' (*Palladium,* September 1850).

12. Thomas Carlyle, *Past and Present* iv 7.

13. As George Eliot seems to have wished [quotes her letter, p. 61 above].

Robert Heilman

CHARLOTTE BRONTË'S 'NEW' GOTHIC IN *JANE EYRE* AND *VILLETTE* (1958)

From childhood terrors to all those mysteriously threatening sights, sounds, and injurious acts that reveal the presence of some male-volent force and that anticipate the holocaust at Thornfield, the traditional Gothic in *Jane Eyre* has often been noted, and as often disparaged. It need not be argued that Charlotte Brontë did not reach the heights while using hand-me-down devices, though a tendency to work through the conventions of fictional art was a strong element in her make-up. This is true of all her novels, but it is no more true than her counter-tendency to modify, most inter-estingly, these conventions. In both *Villette* and *Jane Eyre* Gothic is used but characteristically is undercut.

Jane Eyre hears a 'tragic ... preternatural ... laugh,' but this is at 'high noon' and there is 'no circumstances of ghostliness'; Grace Poole, the supposed laugher, is a plain person, than whom no 'apparition less romantic or less ghostly could ... be conceived'; Charlotte apologises ironically to the 'romantic reader' for telling 'the plain truth' that Grace generally bears a 'pot of porter'. Charlotte almost habitually revises 'old Gothic', the relatively crude mechanisms of fear, with an infusion of the anti-Gothic. When Mrs Rochester first tried to destroy Rochester by fire, Jane 'baptised' Rochester's bed and heard Rochester 'fulminating strange anathemas at finding himself lying in a pool of water'. The introduction of comedy as a palliative of straight Gothic occurs on a large scale when almost seventy-five pages are given to the visit of

the Ingram–Eshton party to mysterious Thornfield; here Charlotte, as often in her novels, falls into the manner of Jane Austen
whom she despised. When Mrs Rochester breaks loose again and
attacks Mason, the presence of guests lets Charlotte play the
nocturnal alarum for at least a touch of comedy: Rochester
orders the frantic women not to 'pull me down or strangle me';
and 'the two dowagers, in vast white wrappers, were bearing down
on him like ships in full sail'.

The symbolic also modifies the Gothic, for it demands of the
reader a more mature and complicated response than the relatively
simple thrill or momentary intensity of feeling sought by primitive
Gothic. When mad Mrs Rochester, seen only as 'the foul German
spectre – the Vampyre', spreads terror at night, that is one thing;
when, with the malicious insight that is the paradox of her madness, she tears the wedding veil in two and thus symbolically
destroys the planned marriage, that is another thing, far less
elementary as art. The midnight blaze that ruins Thornfield
becomes more than a shock when it is seen also as the fire of purgation; the grim, almost roadless forest surrounding Ferndean is
more than a harrowing stage-set when it is also felt as a symbol of
Rochester's closed-in life.

The point is that in various ways Charlotte manages to make the
patently Gothic more than a stereotype. But more important is
that she instinctively finds new ways to achieve the ends served by
old Gothic – the discovery and release of new patterns of feeling,
the intensification of feeling. Though only partly unconventional,
Jane is nevertheless so portrayed as to evoke new feelings rather
than merely exercise old ones. As a girl she is lonely, 'passionate',
'strange', 'like nobody there'; she feels superior, rejects poverty,
talks back precociously, tells truths bluntly, enjoys 'the strangest
sense of freedom', tastes 'vengeance'; she experiences a nervous
shock which is said to have a lifelong effect, and the doctor says
'nerves not in a good state'; she can be 'reckless and feverish',
'bitter and truculent'; at Thornfield she is restless, given to 'bright
visions', letting 'imagination' picture an existence full of 'life, fire,
feeling'. Thus Charlotte leads away from standardised character-

isation towards new levels of human reality, and hence from stock responses toward a new kind of passionate engagement.

Charlotte moves toward depth in various ways that have an immediate impact like that of Gothic. Jane's strange, fearful symbolic dreams are not mere thrillers but reflect the tensions of the engagement period, the stress of the wedding-day debate with Rochester, and the longing for Rochester after she has left him. The final Thornfield dream, with its vivid image of a hand coming through a cloud in place of the expected moon is in the surrealistic vein that appears most sharply in the extraordinary pictures that Jane draws at Thornfield : here Charlotte is plumbing the psyche, not inventing a weird *décor*. Likewise in the telepathy scene, which Charlotte, unlike Defoe in dealing with a similar episode, does her utmost to actualise : 'The feeling, was not like an electric shock; but it was quite as sharp, as strange, as startling : . . . that inward sensation . . . with all its unspeakable strangeness . . . like an inspiration . . . wondrous shock of feeling . . . ' In her flair for the surreal, in her plunging into feeling that is without status in the ordinary world of the novel, Charlotte discovers a new dimension of Gothic.

She does this most thoroughly in her portrayal of characters and of the relations between them. If in Rochester we see only an Angrian-Byronic hero and a Charlotte wish-fulfilment figure (the two identifications which to some readers seem entirely to place him), we miss what is more significant, the exploration of personality that opens up new areas of feeling in intersexual relationships. Beyond the 'grim', the 'harsh', the eccentric, the almost histrionically cynical that superficially distinguish Rochester from conventional heroes, there is something almost Lawrentian : Rochester is 'neither tall nor graceful'; his eyes can be 'dark, irate, and piercing'; his strong features 'took my feelings from my own power and fettered them in his'. Without using the vocabulary common to us, Charlotte is presenting maleness and physicality, to which Jane responds directly. She is 'assimilated' to him by 'something in my brain and heart, in my blood and nerves'; she 'must love' and 'could not unlove' him; the thought of parting from him is 'agony'. Rochester's oblique amatory manoeuvres become almost punitive in the Walter-to-Griselda style and once reduce her to sobbing 'convulsively'; at times the love-game borders on a power-game. Jane, who prefers 'rudeness' to 'flattery', is an instinctive evoker of passion : she learns 'the pleasure of vexing and soothing him by turns' and pursues a 'system' of working him up 'to considerable irritation' and coolly leaving him; when, as a result, his caresses become grimaces, pinches, and tweaks, she records that, sometimes at least, she 'decidedly preferred these fierce favours'. She reports, 'I crushed his hand . . . red with the passionate pressure'; she 'could not . . . see God for his creature', and in her devotion Rochester senses 'an earnest, religious energy.'

Charlotte's remoulding of stock feeling reaches a height when she sympathetically portrays Rochester's efforts to make Jane his mistress; here the stereotyped seducer becomes a kind of lost nobleman of passion, and a specifically physical passion : 'Every atom of your flesh is as dear to me as my own. . . . ' The intensity of the pressure which he puts upon her is matched, not by the fear and revulsion of the popular heroine, but by a responsiveness which she barely masters : 'The crisis was perilous; but not without its charm . . .' She is 'tortured by a sense of remorse at thus hurting his feelings'; at the moment of decision 'a hand of fiery iron grasped my vitals . . . blackness, burning ! . . . my intolerable duty'; she leaves in 'despair'; and after she has left, 'I longed to be his; I panted to return . . .' – and for the victory of principle 'I abhorred myself . . . I was hateful in my own eyes.' This extraordinary openness to feeling, this escape from the bondage of the trite, continues in the Rivers relationship, which is a structural parallel to the Rochester affair : as in Rochester the old sex villain is seen in a new perspective, so in Rivers the clerical hero is radically refashioned; and Jane's almost accepting a would-be husband is given the aesthetic status of a regrettable yielding to a seducer. Without a remarkable liberation from conventional feeling Charlotte could not fathom the complexity of Rivers – the earnest and dutiful clergyman distraught by a profound inner turmoil of conflicting

'drives' : sexuality, restlessness, hardness, pride, ambition ('fever
in his vitals', 'inexorable as death'); the hypnotic, almost inhuman
potency of his influence on Jane, who feels 'a freezing spell', 'an
awful charm', an 'iron shroud'; the relentlessness, almost un-
scrupulousness, of his wooing, the resultant fierce struggle (like that
with Rochester), Jane's brilliantly perceptive accusation '. . . you
almost hate me . . . you would kill me. You are killing me now';
and yet her mysterious near-surrender : 'I was tempted to cease
struggling with him – to rush down the torrent of his will into the
gulf of his existence, and there lose my own.'

   Aside from partial sterilisation of banal Gothic by dry factuality
and humour, Charlotte goes on to make a much more important
– indeed, a radical – revision of the mode : in *Jane Eyre* and in
the other novels, as we shall see, that discovery of passion, that
rehabilitation of the extra-rational, which is the historical office of
Gothic, is no longer oriented in marvellous circumstance but
moves deeply into the lesser known realities of human life. This
change I describe as the change from 'old Gothic' to 'new Gothic'.
The kind of appeal is the same, the fictional method is utterly
different.

Villette

Of the four novels, *Villette* is most heavily saturated with Gothic
– with certain of its traditional manifestations (old Gothic), with
the under-cutting of these that is for Charlotte no less instinctive
than the use of them (anti-Gothic), and with an original, intense
exploration of feeling that increases the range and depth of fiction
(new Gothic).

   As in *Jane Eyre,* Charlotte can be skilful in anti-Gothic. When
Madame Beck, pussyfooting in espionage, 'materialises' in shock-
ing suddenness, Lucy is made matter-of-fact or indignant rather
than thrilled with fright. 'No ghost stood beside me . . .' is her
characteristic response to a Beck surprise. Once the spy, having
'stolen' upon her victims, betrays her unseen presence by a sneeze :
Gothic yields to farce. Technically more complex is Charlotte's use
of the legend of the nun supposedly buried alive and of the appear-

ances of a visitant taken to be the ghost of the nun : Charlotte coolly distances herself from this by having Lucy dismiss the legend as 'romantic rubbish' and by explaining the apparitions as the playful inventions of a giddy lover. True, she keeps the secret long enough to get a few old Gothic thrills from the 'ghost' but what she is really up to is using the apparitions in an entirely new way; that is, for responses that lie beyond the simplicities of terror.

First, the apparitions are explained as a product of Lucy's own psychic state, the product, Dr John suggests, of 'long-continued mental conflict'. In the history of Gothic this is an important spot, for here we first see the shift from stock explanations and responses to the inner human reality : fiction is slowly discovering the psychic depths known to drama for centuries.

Then, when Lucy next sees the nun, she responds in a way that lies entirely outside fictional convention : 'I neither fled nor shrieked . . . I spoke . . . I stretched out my hand, for I meant to touch her'. Not that Lucy is not afraid, but that she is testing herself – an immense change from the expectable elementary response : the *frisson* disappears before the complexer action that betokens a maturing of personality.

Finally, Paul and Lucy both see the spectre and are thus brought closer together : they have had what they call 'impressions', and through sharing the ghost they assume a shared sensibility. Paul says, 'I was conscious of rapport between you and myself'. The rapport is real, though the proof of it is false; the irony of this is a subtle sophistication of Gothic.

The responsiveness, the sensitivity, is the thing; many passages place 'feeling' above 'seeing' as an avenue of knowledge. Reason must be respected, for it is 'vindictive', but at times imagination must be yielded to, like a sexual passion at once feared and desired. There is the summer night when the sedative given by Madame Beck has a strange effect [quotes from chapter 38, 'Imagination was roused . . . into dew, coolness, and glory']. There follows the most magnificent of all Charlotte's nocturnes : that vision of the 'moonlit, midnight park', the brilliance of the fete, the strange charm of places and people, recounted in a rhythmical, enchanted

style (the 'Kubla Khan' mode) which at first reading gives the air
of a dream mistaken for reality to what is in fact reality made like
a dream. This is a surrealistic, trance-like episode which makes
available to fiction a vast new territory and idiom. The surrealistic
is, despite Montague Summers, one of the new phases of Gothic,
which in its role of liberator of feeling characteristically explores
the non-naturalistic: to come up, as here, with a profounder
nature, or a nature freshly, even disturbingly, seen.

The surrealism of Lucy's evening is possible only to a special
sensitivity, and it is really the creation of this sensitivity, in part
pathological, that is at the apex of Charlotte's Gothic. In *The
Professor* the tensions in the author's contemplation of her own
experience come into play; in *Shirley* various undercurrents of
personality push up into the social surfaces of life; in *Jane Eyre*
moral feeling is subjected to the remoulding pressures of a newly
vivid consciousness of the diverse impulses of sexuality; and in
Villette the feeling responses to existence are pursued into sufferings that edge over into disorder. The psychology of rejection and
alienation, first applied to Polly, becomes the key to Lucy, who,
finding no catharsis for a sense of desolation, generates a serious
inner turmoil. She suffers from 'a terrible oppression' and then
from 'anxiety lying in wait on enjoyment, like a tiger crouched in
a jungle . . . his fierce heart panted close against mine; . . . I knew
he waited only for sun-down to bound ravenous from his ambush.'
Depression is fed by the conflict between a loveless routine of life
and her longings, which she tried to put down like 'Jael to Sisera,
driving a nail through their temples'; but this only 'transiently
stunned' them and 'at intervals [they] would turn on the nail with
a rebellious wrench: then did the temples bleed, and the brain
thrill to its core.'

These strains prepare us for the high point in Charlotte's new
Gothic – the study of Lucy's emotional collapse and near breakdown when vacation comes and she left alone at the school with
'a poor deformed and imbecile pupil'. 'My heart almost died within me; . . . My spirits had long been gradually sinking; now that
the drop of employment was withdrawn, they went down fast.'

After three weeks, storms bring on 'a deadlier paralysis'; and 'my nervous system could hardly support' the daily strain. She wanders in the street : 'A goad thrust me on, a fever forbade me to rest; . . .' She observes a 'growing illusion' and says, '. . . my nerves are getting overstretched; . . . ' She feels that 'a malady is growing upon' her mind, and she asks herself, 'How shall I keep well?' Then come 'a peculiarly agonising depression'; a nine-days storm : 'a strange fever of the nerves and blood'; continuing insomnia, broken only by a terrifying nightmare of alienation. She flees the house, and then comes the climactic event of her going to a church and despite the intensity of her Protestant spirit entering the confessional to find relief.

From now on, overtly or implicitly, hypochondria and anxiety keep coming into the story – the enemies from whose grip Lucy must gradually free herself. At a concert she spotted the King as a fellow-victim of 'that strangest spectre, Hypochondria', for on his face she saw its marks, whose meaning, 'if I did not *know,* at least I *felt,* . . . ' When, after her return to Beck's on a rainy night, things are not going well, a letter from Dr John is 'the ransom from my terror', and its loss drives her almost to frenzy. She describes night as 'an unkindly time' when she has strange fancies, doubts, the 'horror of calamity'. She is aware of her 'easily-deranged temperament'. Beyond this area of her own self-understanding we see conflicts finding dramatic expression in her almost wild acceptance of Rachel's passionate acting of Phèdre ('a spectacle low, horrible, immoral'), which counterbalances her vehement condemnation of a fleshy nude by Rubens (one of the 'materialists'). Paul identifies her, in a figure whose innocence for him is betrayed by the deep, if not wholly conscious, understanding that leads Charlotte to write it : 'a young she wild creature, new caught, untamed, viewing with a mixture of fire and fear the first entrance of the breaker in'.

There is not room to trace Lucy's recovery, especially in the important phase, the love affair with Paul which is related to our theme by compelling, as do the Jane–Rochester and Louis Moore– Shirley relationships in quite different ways, a radical revision of the feelings exacted by stereotyped romance. What is finally note-worthy is that Charlotte, having chosen in Lucy a heroine with the least durable emotional equipment, with the most conspicuous neurotic element in her temperament, goes on through the history of Lucy's emotional maturing to surmount the need for romantic fulfilment and to develop the aesthetic courage for a final disaster – the only one in her four novels.

Some years ago Edmund Wilson complained of writers of Gothic who 'fail to lay hold on the terrors that lie deep in the human soul and that cause man to fear himself' and proposed an anthology of horror stories that probe 'psychological caverns' and find 'disquieting obsessions'. This is precisely the direction in which Charlotte Brontë moved, especially in Lucy Snowe and somewhat also in Caroline Helstone and Shirley Keeldar; this was one aspect of her following human emotions where they took her, into many depths and intensities that as yet hardly had a place in the novel. This was the finest achievement of Gothic.

Gothic is variously defined. In a recent book review Leslie Fiedler implies that Gothic is shoddy mystery-mongering, whereas F. Cudworth Flint defines the Gothic tradition, which he considers 'nearly central in American literature', as 'a literary exploration of the avenues to death'. For Montague Summers, on the other hand, Gothic was the essence of romanticism, and romanticism was the literary expression of supernaturalism. Both these latter definitions, though they are impractically inclusive, have suggestive value. For originally Gothic was one of a number of aesthetic develop-ments which served to breach the 'classical' and 'rational' order of life and to make possible a kind of response, and a response to a kind of thing, that among the knowing had long been taboo. In the novel it was the function of Gothic to open horizons beyond social patterns, rational decisions, and institutionally approved emotions; in a word, to enlarge the sense of reality and its impact on the human being. It became then a great liberator of feeling. It acknowledged the non-rational – in the world of things and events, occasionally in the realm of the transcendental, ultimately and most persistently in the depths of the human being. (Richardson might have started this, but his sense of inner forces was so overlaid by the moralistic that his followers all ran after him only when he ran the wrong way.) The first Gothic writers took the easy way : the excitement of mysterious scene and happening, which I call old Gothic. Of this Charlotte Brontë made some direct use, while at the same time tending toward humorous modifications (anti-Gothic); but what really counts is its indirect usefulness to her : it released her from the patterns of the novel of society and therefore permitted the flowering of her real talent – the talent for finding and giving dramatic form to impulses and feelings which, because of their depth or mysteriousness or intensity or ambiguity, or of their ignoring or transcending everyday norms of propriety or reason, increase wonderfully the sense of reality in the novel. To note the emergence of this 'new Gothic' in Charlotte Brontë is not, I think, to pursue an old mode into dusty corners but rather to identify historically the distinguishing, and distinguished, element in her work.

S O U R C E : from 'Charlotte Brontë's "New" Gothic' in *From Jane Austen to Joseph Conrad*, 1958.

Roy Pascal

VILLETTE AND THE AUTOBIOGRAPHICAL NOVEL (1959)

There are certain obvious advantages of the novel-form over the straight autobiographical narrative that I want to mention. It is an advantage to be able to tell of circumstances that occur outside the range of the author's direct experience. Some autobiographies do this, especially when telling us of the author's parentage, but most must necessarily narrow their scope to that of the author-hero's direct experience. The novelist, on the other hand, can evoke events out of his personal range, the inexpressed thoughts of others, he can reconstruct conversations which memory could not possibly retain. The novel's hero, if described in the third person, can be described from all sides. All these advantages are of course pitfalls too, for the imagination can easily lead the writer away from the actual truth. More important is the difference in the whole focus of the work. An autobiography is written by a man who has a certain position, a given reality, usually known to us in advance; he writes about his life with the consciousness of having reached his present position and attitude; over the description of his early life there hovers the knowledge of what he is to become – his motto might be the Pindaric 'Become what you are'. But in an autobiographical novel the author, as in all works of art, is anonymous, so to speak; he does not exist within the pages. He can describe early life without anticipating the future, and can, in principle, evoke the child's experience with complete freshness in itself, without reference to what he is to become. No doubt the distinction is not so absolute as to be categorical, for the aim of an autobiographer may be, in fact, both the reconstruction of the past as it appeared to him at the time, and the interpretation of it as the prologue to the later man. But still, the novel does encourage the writer to greater freedom in this respect.

I am concerned, however, with the difference of purpose rather than differences of expedience or technique. And I propose to discuss three autobiographical novels in order to find what is achieved in them in contrast to autobiographies : Charlotte Brontë's *Villette*, D. H. Lawrence's *Son and Lovers*, and James Joyce's *A Portrait of the Artist as a Young Man*. It will be noticed that all deal with decisive experiences in young people; and I should claim that the essential autobiographical novel is one that centres in experiences which transform and mould a character, not one which merely revolves round a single outstanding real experience. There is the same distinction between autobiographies proper and many travel books, or war books, though these may not only tell us of adventures objectively interesting, but also speak of spiritual experiences of significance.

Villette is the simplest of my three examples. Its theme is the self-fulfilment of a young woman through her job as a teacher, and above all through love. All biographers since Mrs Gaskell have emphasised its autobiographical character, and all fresh material unearthed has confirmed this. Lucy Snowe's character is modelled on Charlotte's, her experiences fit in closely with Charlotte's in Brussels. At the same time, it is obviously not exactly autobiographical. Charlotte was fully justified in writing that she 'only suffered reality to suggest, never to dictate' (E. C. Gaskell, *The Life of Charlotte Brontë*, ed. Temple Scott and Willett, 1924, 374). For instance, Dr John is based on an acquaintance made later, and Polly is perhaps invented, like the 'ghost' of the nun. It would not be hard to show why these figures were introduced, but I would like to concentrate on the alterations in the heart of the story, Lucy's whole situation at Villette and her relations with Monsieur Paul.

In actual life, Charlotte's first visit to the Brussels school was made in company with Emily, and it was part of a plan to prepare themselves to start a school at home with their sister Anne. After the death of their aunt had brought them home, Charlotte returned alone to Brussels, and it is to this second stay that Lucy's story refers. She became more and more homesick, and left Brussels gladly, in order, as she hoped, to be reunited with her sisters at their own school. It seems, as Margaret Lane suggests (*The Brontë Story*, 1953, 157), that it was only on parting from M. Heger that Charlotte suddenly realised how much he meant to her; and her subsequent letters to him make it quite evident that her feeling for him was (or became in absence) profound, almost shattering. In the novel, Lucy has no home-ties, no longing to return; she slowly becomes conscious of M. Paul's affection for her and her answering love. Unlike M. Heger, Paul is of course unmarried, and the only hindrances outside their characters are the differences of religion and the jealousy of his relatives and dependents. These are overcome, and a happy ending is prevented only by M. Paul's death.

Charlotte wrote the book in a period of great distress, when she was often bitterly aware that her circumstances, her physical appearance, and even her character did not entitle her to hope for marriage – before, that is, her brief happiness with Mr Nicholls. Has she simply, in the novel, distorted reality so as to give herself a compensatory if modest satisfaction, after the fashion of many sentimental novelists? Jane Eyre's relationship with Mr Rochester has something of this sort of sentimental compensation, and is the weakest part of that early novel. But in *Villette* Charlotte was involved with truth in a much more inexorable fashion. There is a most illuminating letter written after she had sent the earlier parts of the novel to her publisher, in which the fate of Lucy was not yet decided. The publisher, like Charlotte's father, obviously hoped that Lucy would marry Dr John, the man for whom she evidently had a romantic love; but Charlotte wrote (Gaskell 478–9):

Lucy must not marry Dr John. . . . He is a curled darling of Nature and of Fortune, and must draw a prize in life's lottery. . . . If Lucy

marries anybody, it must be the Professor – a man in whom there
is much to forgive, much to 'put up with'. . . . But I am not leniently
disposed towards Miss Frost [=Lucy Snowe]; from the beginning,
I never meant to appoint her lines in pleasant places.

What this means is that Charlotte was determined to follow
up the inner logic of her characters, in Lucy's case of her own
character. Her own letters and the evidence of her friends tell us
how close are Lucy and herself – for instance, that phrase about
herself as a governess, 'the estrangement from one's real character
– the adoption of a cold, rigid, apathetic exterior, that is painful'
(ibid, 189–90). What she sought to do, in altering circumstances
and events, was to get nearer to the real truth of her own character,
of its hidden capacities as well as its realised actuality. Thus she
deprives Lucy of all home-ties in order that her almost reckless
decision to go abroad should show the reserves of determination
in a character normally forced by circumstances to be passive;
and then, when in Villette, to place her inner dreary loneliness in
an appropriate outer isolation. Thus she allows the love with M.
Paul to blossom – to show her capacity for feeling not merely nega-
tively through the strain of her efforts at self-control and renunciation, but also positively in that gentle radiance of her short happiness. In this sense her novel is truer to her real character than
life itself was, for it unfolds those resources which life seemed
determined to choke. In a merely autobiographical account, these
resources could never have been made plain, however candid
the story might have been; imagination has not distorted the truth,
but has shaped the shapeless. There is an interesting small parallel
to this whole process. In a letter to Emily from Brussels, Charlotte
told of her sudden impulse to confess in the Catholic Cathedral;
in the book she also tells of this incident. But the real account is
told in a way to make it as palatable as possible to her sister; the
imaginary account gives, much freer of personal concerns, what
Margaret Lane calls 'the real tone of the experience' . . .

Do autobiographical novels – I mean of course the best – therefore prevent our knowing the truth which an autobiography pro-

per would show? Do they use improper means, as Stephen Spender says, to win us for the hero, instead of leaving us coolly detached? I don't think either of these questions can be answered with a simple 'yes'. Not only do all autobiographies start off with a prejudice in favour of the hero, but they all give only a partial view of the truth, as historians and biographers know, and many of them indeed are extravagantly biassed. This bias may indeed be the very source of their excellence, if it coherently builds up their world and their character. It may well be that too scrupulous an adherence to factual truth destroys the value of an autobiography. Edwin Muir felt this when he wrote, in his *Autobiography* (1954, 48–9), that if he had adopted the form of the autobiographical novel he would have got nearer to the basic truth of his existence, of life altogether, and it is only a feeling of rectitude that makes him reluctantly 'stick to the facts and try to fit them in where they fit in'. Actually, from the later parts of his account, as from many autobiographies, one does at times get an impression of perfunctoriness, as if the facts reported were not essentially related to him.

What the autobiographical novelist seeks is something general, representative, within his own experiences, the deeper logic within his character, which life itself may in certain respects distort, or within some dominant aspect of his character . . .

s o u r c e : 'The Autobiographical Novel and the Autobiography' in *Essays in Criticism,* 1959.

David Crompton

JANE EYRE AND THE 'NEW
CRITICISM' (1960)

... it has always seemed to me that many books can be found to
be better than they are by by-passing the main issues and concentrating on playing hunt-the-slipper with theme and symbol. Take,
for instance, *Jane Eyre*. The more one goes into *Jane Eyre* the
richer the structural unity of the book becomes. Leaving aside
the more obvious technical devices – the supernatural signs, the
dream omens, the weather symbolism which enacts the theme at
every point – one still has left a character pattern, built up on a
series of parallels and antitheses, which if it lacks the finesse of a
Jane Austen, nevertheless is very effective in developing that 'con-
centration of the area of action' which Edwin Muir saw as the
essence of the dramatic novel. At the lowest level it reveals itself
as a physical separating out into the opposing camps of dark and
light – where light represents conventional beauty of face and
form and dark the reverse. Physically, Jane and Rochester (dark-
haired, dark-eyed and plain) are opposed to the unsympathetic
characters (many of whom are 'given' fair hair and blue or gray
eyes), Mrs Reed, Georgiana, St John Rivers, the Dowager Lady
Ingram, Blanche Ingram, Mason, Bertha Rochester, and even
John Reed (who, after a gross and unhealthy childhood, blossoms
into a 'fine-looking young man'). This opposition is made explicit
in Jane's remark about having a theoretical reverence for beauty
but shunning anything 'bright but antipathetic'. The reason for
it is clear. Conventional beauty in *Jane Eyre* invariably connotes
either the empty head or, more frequently, the hard, shrivelled
heart incapable of feeling, and it is appropriate that the eyes (the

windows of the soul) should be used symbolically to suggest it.
Hence, we find that Mrs Reed has a 'cold gray eye', the Dowager
Lady Ingram a 'fierce and hard' one, Georgiana and Eliza eyes
that give 'an indescribable hardness' to their countenances, Mason
an eye 'large and well cut but the life looking out of it . . . tame
and vacant', and St John Rivers an eye which is 'a cold, bright,
blue gem'. On the other hand, Rochester has 'very fine eyes with
hidden depths' and Jane's eyes 'look soft and full of feeling'. This
opposition is further reinforced in the general characterisation.
On the one hand, it is 'right' that Louisa Eshton and Mary Ingram
should think Mason a 'beautiful man', that Georgiana should
think Rochester 'an ugly man', that Blanche Ingram should react
to the 'black Bothwell' in Rochester rather than to the softness lying
behind the eyes, that Eliza should be attracted by 'the Rubric'
of the Common Prayer Book : on the other, it is equally 'right'
(though Jane Austen would not have thought so) that Jane and
Rochester should talk at length about going to the moon for a
honeymoon.

At a deeper level, this antithesis between surface and depth
is associated with a more fundamental contrasting of the Classical
and the Romantic point of view. Throughout the novel this opposition also has been suggested in the description of the central
characters. Blanche Ingram's beauty is 'Grecian' and *regular;*
she has 'harmonious lineaments' and is 'moulded like a Diane',
whereas Jane's features are *'irregular'* and 'grace and harmony'
are 'quite wanting'. Similarly, St John Rivers, with his 'Greek
face', 'Classic nose' and 'Athenian mouth and chin' is the 'graceful
Apollo' to Rochester's craggy, misshapen 'Vulcan'. A stream of
images suggests the violence of the author's rejection of the Classic
ideal which, to her, is synonymous with coldness, hardness and
emptiness. 'Nothing bloomed spontaneously' in the 'soil' of
Blanche's personality. St John Rivers is a 'statue', 'ivory', a 'cold
cumbrous column'; he is 'like chiselled marble', 'serene as glass',
and Jane is brought under his 'freezing spell'. St John's remark to
Jane : 'I am cold : no fervour infects me' and her reply : 'Whereas
I am hot, and fire dissolves ice' is more, in the wider context, than

Jane exercising her gift for repartee. It is a declaration of the author's faith at least as powerful as that which underlies a novel like *Sense and Sensibility.*

Even if this analysis is allowed, however, its value as an approach to *Jane Eyre* is relatively very slight. Perhaps it might be used to support the view that Charlotte, like Emily, could manipulate the melodramatic framework in such a way that it corresponded with her own intense vision of life. Having made the point, however, one is still left with the fact (which cannot be argued here but is at least generally accepted) that *Wuthering Heights* is a great book and that *Jane Eyre* – whatever its structure – is relatively immature in conception and execution and yields little more from sustained consideration than it does from a single reading. In some ways, of course, it is a remarkable novel, but one feels that the major qualities it has lie outside anything which might be described as the scheme of the novel. In fact, the whole point of this digression has been to suggest that the pursuit of what is interesting but essentially minor can lead to a distortion which neglects both major vice and major virtue...

SOURCE: 'The New Criticism: A Caveat' in *Essays in Criticism*, 1960.

R. B. Martin

VILLETTE AND THE ACCEPTANCE OF SUFFERING (1966)

... Retrospect, we must remember, too often tempts us into seeing a conclusion in what is merely the final work of an artist's life. Beethoven's last quartets, *The Tempest,* Verdi's *Falstaff,* Yeats's late poems : it is seductive to feel that these represent the peaks towards which their creators struggled, forgetting that range after range might have come into their view had time or circumstance not cut off their artistic lives. And so it is with Charlotte Brontë : the basic optimism of *The Professor* and *Jane Eyre* is followed by the bleakness of *Shirley.* As synthesis follows thesis and antithesis, *Villette* takes cognisance of both sorrow and joy, and integrates them into a grave, tragic, awareness of the mixed lot and nature of man and accepts them with neither gladness nor rancour but a serenity that has no precedent in her work. What might have succeeded had Miss Brontë not died in her thirty-ninth year, we can hardly guess (certainly, the fragment of a novel called *Emma* is no indication), but *Villette* remains as the capstone to her artistic life.

In *Villette* there is a full awareness that human justice is fallible, and that even divine favour is partial, but where in *Shirley* there is a sense of religion as providing no comfort in this world, *Villette* is unobtrusively full of hints that Miss Brontë had accepted the traditional view of human redemption as not only transcending earthly life but also throwing over it the comforting awareness that human sorrow is at worst transient. 'I suppose, Lucy Snowe,' the narrator tells herself, 'the orb of your life is not to be so rounded;

for you the crescent-phase must suffice. Very good. I see a huge
mass of my fellow-creatures in no better circumstances. I see that
a great many men, and more women, hold their span of life on
conditions of denial and privation. I find no reason why I should
be of the few favoured. I believe in some blending of hope and
sunshine sweetening the worst lots. I believe that this life it not all;
neither the beginning nor the end. I believe while I tremble; I
trust while I weep.' (chap. 31.)

Rather than appearing oblivious of the suffering of man, as
Shirley seems to suggest, God plans for His creatures in this book
in ways too mysterious for human comprehension. When Lucy
foretells the future for Polly, she speaks, if not in Miss Brontë's
own voice, at least in harmony with the tenor of the whole novel :
'Some lives *are* thus blessed : it is God's will : it is the attesting trace
and lingering evidence of Eden. Other lives run from the first
another course. Other travellers encounter weather fitful and
gusty, wild and variable – breast adverse winds, are belated and
overtaken by the early closing winter night. Neither can this
happen without the sanction of God; and I know that, amidst His
boundless works, is somewhere stored the secret of this last fate's
justice : I know that His treasures contain the proof as the promise
of its mercy.' (chap. 32.) In *Villette* there is still an awareness of
the suffering in store for most men, but it no longer seems purpose-
less; the difference in attitudes is vast.

In the act of accepting the necessity for suffering lies its balm.
In *Villette* Miss Brontë has stopped protesting against the injustice
of a Christian fate that she can neither control nor understand,
and the result is a distinct lessening of the dissatisfaction and agony
that suffuses *Shirley*. The calm acceptance of the inequalities of
life is an indication of her double view that man's duty is to strive
towards perfection at the very moment that he is only too conscious
that earthly reward is never consistent with that endeavour, and
that conventional happiness cannot be counted on a fair wages
for honest striving. It is a tragic view of life, but as in all true
tragedy, knowledge and awareness are themselves an amelioration
of pain, and the consequent dignity of the individual triumphs

over any inclination to self-pity and makes the pity of others unimportant. Tragic awareness precludes the acceptance of happiness exacted at the cost of easy, inferior, or ignoble aims.

This is the only one of Miss Brontë's novels that does not conclude with what is at least a conventionally happy ending to the
plot . . . *Villette* suggests that for a few fortunates of the world,
moral goodness and temporal happiness may exist together, but
for the majority of mankind there is no necessary correlation between those qualities. The children of fortune, like Polly and Dr
John, sail serenely past the shoals of the world, perhaps drawing
little water but never hitting the rocks. The Ginevras and the de
Hamals of the world exist on a lower moral plane but never come
to grief. Even the morally reprehensible of the world meet no
temporal retribution. The last words of the novel are both born
of a painfully achieved tolerance and coloured with irony:
'Madame Beck prospered all the days of her life; so did Père Silas;
Madame Walravens fulfilled her ninetieth year before she died.
Farewell.' (chap. 42.)

Yet this is not to suggest that *Villette* sets forth the world as a
moral anarchy, nor does it suggest ultimate injustice for man. To
be sure, Lucy and Paul never marry, and their one moment of
complete unity is agonisingly brief. Untouched by the smile of
fortune, they are the world's inhabitants who must continue to
strive even while they accept that temporal rewards are not to be
theirs. To perceive happiness is as much as we can expect; if
human aspiration is sincere, earthly reward for it is finally unimportant. Few would wish to repay Lear for his suffering by restoring him to his throne. It may, indeed, be true that when she wrote
this novel, Miss Brontë had come to accept her perpetual severance
from M. Heger and had reasoned herself into believing that the
existence of her love was more important than its fulfilment;
whatever the biographical circumstances, surely what matters to
us is that she wrote in *Villette* a story of suffering and renunciation with meaning far beyond her own experiences in an obscure
Brussels *pension*.

Human injustice in this novel is the parallel in actuality to what cosmic injustice appears to be at first sight. Almost all the characters in the book are unfair to the motivations of others and Lucy herself finds that one of the most difficult attributes of maturity to acquire is that of justice to others. From her initial misjudgment of Polly to her hallucinatory tour of the fête, where she constantly misjudges the other major characters of the novel, she is premature, unfair, and illogical in her assessment of others. Even while she is learning justice herself, she is aware of its rarity in human relations, and when she is asked by the examiners to write on the subject of 'Human Justice', she portrays her as 'a red, random beldame', smoking a pipe and drinking whisky: 'she smoked and she sipped and she enjoyed her paradise, and whenever a cry of the suffering souls about her pierced her ears too keenly – my jolly dame seized the poker or the hearthbrush: if the offender was weak, wronged, and sickly, she effectually settled him; if he was strong, lively, and violent, she only menaced, then plunged her hand in her deep pouch and flung a liberal shower of sugar-plums.' (chap. 35.) . . .

In *Villette* there is a resurgence of Christian faith, but with great importance still accorded to individual choice and judgment, in short, to what Miss Brontë thought of as the Protestant strain of Christianity. Lucy goes 'by turns, and indiscriminately' to the Presbyterian, Lutheran, and Episcopalian chapels of Villette. 'Now, it happened that I had often secretly wondered at the minute and unimportant character of the differences between these three sects – at the unity and identity of their vital doctrines: I saw nothing to hinder them from being one day fused into one grand Holy Alliance, and I respected them all, though I thought that in each there were faults of form; incumbrances, and trivialities. Just what I thought, that did I tell M. Emanuel, and explained to him that my own last appeal, the guide to which I looked, and the teacher which I owned, must always be the Bible itself, rather than any sect, of whatever name or nation.' (chap. 36.) In this novel, for the first time, Miss Brontë uses her anti-Roman Catholic emotions thematically and adequately as she equates Roman doctrine and practices with emotionalism as excesses of the undisciplined aspect of man's nature, the submission of reason and will to the irrational. Christian faith and endurance are so embedded into this novel that it is difficult to abstract passages to illustrate Miss Brontë's thesis without relying on the more conventional exhortations of the text. At the beginning of the chapter called 'Cloud', after telling of the future happiness of Polly and Dr John, Lucy reflects upon her own state: 'His will be done, as done it surely will be, whether we humble ourselves to resignation or not. The impulse of creation forwards it; the strength of powers, seen and unseen, has its fulfilment in charge. Proof of a life to come must be given. In fire and in blood, if needed, must that proof be written. In fire and in blood do we trace the record throughout nature. In fire and in blood does it cross our own experience. Sufferer, faint not through terror of this burning evidence. Tired wayfarer, gird up thy loins; look upward, march onward. Pilgrims and brother mourners, join in friendly company. Dark through the wilderness of this world stretches the way for most of us: equal and steady be our tread; be our cross our banner. For staff we have His promise, whose "word is tried, whose way perfect"; for present hope His providence, "who gives the shield of salvation, whose gentleness makes great"; for final home His bosom, who "dwells in the height of Heaven"; for crowning prize a glory, exceeding and eternal. Let us so run that we may obtain; let us endure hardness as good soldiers; let us finish our course, and keep the faith, reliant in the issue to come off more than conquerors: "Are thou not from everlasting mine Holy One? WE SHALL NOT DIE!" (chap. 38.) The style is perilously close to cant, but its urgency is evidence of the thematic importance to Miss Brontë of the passage.

Miss Brontë's growth as a novelist is nowhere more evident than in her use of the point of view from which *Villette* is told. As she had done twice before, she wrote the entire novel with the main character as narrator, but Lucy Snowe is her first whole-hearted attempt at the use of an 'unreliable narrator'. In *The Professor* she aimed at objectivity in spite of the first-person narration, and almost as if to allow herself but scant identification with the narrator, she told the story through the mouth of Crimsworth. Although he is hardly a success as a masculine character, he does serve to increase the detachment – with nearly disastrous results. Jane Eyre as a narrator swings to the opposite end of the scale, since her adult perceptions and attitudes can, with a few exceptions, be taken as the point of view of the author herself; the identification is almost complete. *Shirley* ... is an attempt to combine the factual quality of a detached narrator with the immediacy provided by a sensibility divided between Caroline and Shirley.

Miss Brontë's frequently expressed feelings of dislike for Lucy Snowe, the narrator and central figure of *Villette,* are adequate indicators that the viewpoints of the narrator and of the author are not intended to be taken as coincident. Throughout the novel we are expected as readers to evaluate Lucy's perceptions constantly, for they are partial or mistaken as often as not. Miss Brontë first gave her the name under which she appears in the novel, then changed it to 'Frost' before reconsidering the change and restoring the original name. 'A *cold* name she must have,' Miss Brontë told Williams: 'partly, perhaps, on the *"lucus a non lucendo"* principle – partly on that of the "fitness of things", for she has about her an external coldness.' (Gaskell, chap. 25.) On another occasion she told Smith that 'I am not leniently disposed towards Miss *Frost* : from the beginning, I never meant to appoint her lines in pleasant places.' (Gaskell, chap. 25.) Lucy's inadequacies (indeed, her whole character) are less attractive than those of Jane Eyre, and we judge them more harshly, as Miss Brontë clearly intended. By the end of the novel Lucy has outgrown most of her narrow views and uncharitable modes of action, but until that point we are expected to make constant comparison between her behaviour and that we might hope for in a more generous, clear-sighted character.

Miss Brontë in *Villette* is once more occupied with the problem of the relationship between the rational and the non-rational faculties. Lucy, like Jane Eyre, is torn between these conflicting claims, but unlike Jane she is not initially attracted by the warmth of passion or dismayed at the chilliness of its lack. As a girl she is almost without sympathy for others and incapable of love, having none of the generous spirit that so often nearly causes Jane to go too far towards the dangers of passion.

In the early scenes at Bretton Lucy is initially disdainful of affection, and it is only long after Polly has arrived there with her father that Lucy feels the first slow stirrings of the unawakened, or stifled, feeling of compassion that lie hidden ...

This first section of the novel is one which has frequently baffled readers who fail to see that its primary function is to establish Lucy's character, not those of Polly and John, and who therefore feel that Miss Brontë's focus changes during the course of the story. Actually, of course, the characters of Polly and John are being established as well, but what is reported of them is not meant to be swallowed whole. Our natural reaction as readers is to demand black and white, to feel that what we learn of these two important persons must be either completely trustworthy or wholly false, but Miss Brontë is attempting something more difficult, the establishment of a certain triviality in Polly and John at the same time that Lucy's inadequate sympathies are condemned in her own words.

That Lucy is something of a prig is adequately shown at Bretton, but the hints of the bigger nature beneath really await their development until she goes to live with Miss Marchmont as her unwilling companion. At the level of foreshadowing, Miss Marchmont stands as a portent of Lucy's future life, both in the loss of her own lover and in the decency and honesty that inform her superficially unattractive character.[1] More importantly, however, Miss Marchmont provides Lucy with the opportunity to see how wrong her own first impressions can be and how easy it is for her to be unjust. 'Closer acquaintance, while it developed both faults and eccentricities, opened, at the same time, a view of a character I could respect. Stern and even morose as she sometimes was, I could wait on her and sit beside her with that calm which always blesses us when we are sensible that our manners, presence, contact, please and soothe the persons we serve.' (chap. 4.) Miss

Marchmont's religious sense also stands as a model for that which Lucy comes to accept by the end of the novel: 'We should acknowledge God merciful, but not always for us comprehensible. We should accept our own lot whatever it be, and try to render happy that of others.' (chap. 4.) . . .

The death of her mentor makes Lucy, like Jane at Lowood, anxious to leave the circumscribed life she has hitherto led and to try her wings in larger surroundings . . .

With Lucy's involvement in life, the problem of justice and kindness to others broadens out into the question of the identity of other human beings, who they are, and how one is to know them, as well as how to treat them. Inevitably, this poses for Lucy the more important problem of self-knowledge, of finding out her own identity. The attempt to discover who she is becomes in part an attempt to find out for herself how much allegiance she owes to the reason, how much to passion and imagination. These two parallel problems of identity and of the importance of rationality occupy the rest of the book, crossing and recrossing, occasionally fusing into a joint question, so that it is difficult to untwine the two threads and examine them separately.

Lucy's mounting experience of passion, the imagination, illusion, and the rest of the non-rational faculties are developed in a series of big scenes, almost set-pieces, reminiscent in their self-contained, theatrical quality of the 'Eden' scene in *Jane Eyre*. The culmination of this group of scenes takes place at the midnight fête at the end of the book, but the recurrent background to them is the *allée défendue* in the school garden, suggesting by its name both the prohibition against its use and the forbidden love of the nun said to have been entombed there alive at the foot of Methusaleh, the ancient pear tree. The sense of venturing into forbidden realms frequently colours what occurs in the secluded walk [continues with a detailed commentary on 'this group of scenes', including the scene with John after the appearance of the box of violets in the *allée*; the night of Madame Beck's fête; Lucy's hypochondria and confession to Père Silas; and her experience of 'Vashti's' acting] . . .

It would be a falsification of both plot and theme in the novel to suggest that Lucy's love for John follows a linear course up to the Vashti episode, and that then she switches direction and heads equally directly towards the final love scene with M. Paul in the Faubourg Clotilde. The novel simply is not that schematic, and there are several indications that Lucy finds John dangerously attractive throughout her life, even if the feeling she has for him operates at a much less mature level than her love for Paul. She tells Polly bluntly that she seldom looks at John's masculine beauty because 'I value vision, and dread being struck stone blind'. (chap. 37.) . . .

Probably in no other Victorian novel is there such an adult recognition that a woman's sexual attraction to one man may persist beyond the growth of love for another. Mature love may succeed mere physical excitement, but it need not destroy it. Small wonder that Miss Brontë's contemporaries found her novels dangerously outspoken.

In the second half of the novel, as Lucy learns a new kind of love, the method of exposition becomes less theatrical. The 'big scenes' of the school play, the confessional, the gallery, the concert, and Vashti's performance have all been cast in terms of the artificiality of the theatre or art (the frequent references to the theatricality of the Roman Catholic church are sufficient evidence that Miss Brontë saw much of it in terms of play-acting). In the latter half of the book there are but two repetitions of this kind of scene, the visit to Mme Walravens and the long night of hallucination at the carnival.

Before these two scenes, however, come the last two visitations of the nun. The first of these occurs when Lucy is burying her letters from John (and her hopes for a future with him) at the foot of Methusaleh, where the body of the original nun and her forbidden feelings are interred. (The likeness between Lucy's symbolic act and Paul's reference to the grace of his earlier passion is obvious.) The nun's last visit occurs when Paul has told Lucy implicitly that he loves her, by saying that they are born under the same star and that their destinies are intertwined. Both visitations come at moments of heightened emotion, but the second time Lucy sees the apparition in company with Paul, who feels as she does, apprehensive but unafraid, aware that whatever the nun may represent is something that they share. Affection and reason may rob even the supernatural of its terror, passion of its dangers [continues with a detailed commentary, first on the visit to Madame Walravens and the night of the carnival as illustrating further stages in the theme of 'reason-v.-emotion', and then on La Terrasse and its part in developing Lucy's 'self-knowledge and knowledge of others'] . . .

Everything at La Terrasse that seems conducive to its becoming home to Lucy is summed up in the punning significance of the name Bretton. In this novel, where things are seldom what they seem, the name becomes ironic, for Lucy is to find identity, family, and home where all at first seems alien: 'I was conscious of rapport between you and myself,' Paul tells her. 'You are patient, and I am choleric; you are quiet and pale, and I am tanned and fiery; you are a strict Protestant, and I am a sort of lay Jesuit: but we are alike – there is affinity. Do you see it, mademoiselle, when you look in the glass? Do you observe that your forehead is shaped like mine – that your eyes are cut like mine? Do you hear that you have some of my tones of voice? Do you know that you have many of my books? I perceive all this, and believe that you were born under my star. Yes, you were born under my star! Tremble! for where that is the case with mortals, the threads of their destinies are difficult to disentangle; knottings and catchings occur – sudden breaks leave damage in the web.' (chap. 31.) . . .

The house in the Faubourg Clotilde becomes at last the emblem of the identity towards which Lucy has been groping throughout her life, for it is her true home, and in it she has found definition. Neither English nor totally Labassecourien, the little house has finally resolved the polarity of La Terrasse and the dark house of the Rue des Mages, the worlds of the unfeeling reason and the irrational imagination, the Puritan severity of Protestantism and the warm piety of Roman Catholicism. Externals no longer count; reality has taken the place of appearance. The meaning of 'identity' has become a kind of pun : individual identity can be found only in identity with another. 'He deemed me born under his star : he seemed to have spread over me its beam like a banner.' (chap. 41.) ...

In the hushed isolation of the little house all barriers between Lucy and Paul finally fall : differences in religion, language, nationality, age, and background all become mere externals with no final meaning. The ultimate unity between the lovers is fore-shadowed throughout the book by their slow and painful attempts to learn toleration of each other's religion. Lucy knows to the end that 'God is not with Rome', and Paul can never totally understand Lucy's 'strange, self-reliant, invulnerable creed', but she learns that '*this* Romanist held the purer elements of his creed with an innocency of heart which God must love', (chap. 36) and Paul is 'made thoroughly to feel that Protestants were not neces-sarily the irreverent Pagans his director had insinuated'. (chap. 36.) As Lucy has not been able to believe in great differences be-tween the Protestant denominations, so Paul finally expresses the pettiness of differences even between Protestant and Roman Catholic : 'How seem in the eyes of that God who made all firma-ments, from whose nostrils issued whatever of life is here, or in the stars shining yonder – how seem the differences of man?' (chap. 36.)

' "Remain a Protestant," ' Paul tells Lucy before leaving Vil-lette. ' "My little English Puritan, I love Protestantism in you. I own its severe charm. There is something in its ritual I cannot receive myself, but it is the sole creed for "Lucy".'

'All Rome could not put into him bigotry, nor the Propaganda itself make him a real Jesuit. He was born honest, and not false – artless, and not cunning – a freeman, and not a slave. His tender-ness had rendered him ductile in a priest's hands, his affection, his devotedness, his sincere pious enthusiasm blinked his kind eyes sometimes, made him abandon justice to himself to do the work of craft, and serve the ends of selfishness; but these are faults so rare to find, so costly to their owner to indulge, we scarcely know whether they will not one day be reckoned amongst the jewels.'

H

(chap. 42.) The simple meal served on the balcony of Lucy's new home becomes almost a sacramental experience of a shared religious sense that lies beyond sect.[2]

With her final clear-eyed recognition of her own nature and that of Paul, with the question of her identity solved, Lucy has changed from the cold, self-regarding Miss Snowe to the fulfilled spiritual mate of her tutor, assured of her place in the universe. The ambiguous ending, with its unwillingness to trouble sunny imaginations by speaking directly of Paul's death, is Miss Brontë's last refusal to bow to the dictates of romantic fiction.[3] The spirit of love is more important than 'union and a happy succeeding life'. Reality, as Lucy has finally learned, is what matters, not appearance.

SOURCE: *The Accents of Persuasion,* 1966.

NOTES

[The following notes are the author's.]

1. Lucy's presentiment at the sound of the spring wind serves to foretell Miss Marchmont's death, and it also establishes the mood of prescience and foreshadowing that makes credible the relevance of Miss Marchmont's life to Lucy's future.

2. Although this is the most conspicuous example in the book of a fairly common usage of shared meals as an indication of personal harmony, throughout Miss Brontë displays a somewhat unusual interest in the reconciliatory, even amatory, powers of food. The child Polly shows her love for her father and Graham by wheedling special goodies for them; Lucy expresses her preference for Ginevra by sharing her own portion of breakfast with her and by drinking from the same cup. Lucy and Paul are several times reconciled by gifts of food; Lucy's rebelliousness as she is preparing for the play is healed by the breakfast that Paul provides; his offer of friendship is often expressed by chocolate comfits and shared brioches.

3. Mrs Gaskell tells us that Miss Brontë's father specifically asked that the novel have a happy ending, but 'the idea of M. Paul

Emanuel's death at sea was stamped on her imagination till it assumed the distinct force of reality; and she could no more alter her fictitious ending than if they had been facts which she was relating. All she could do in compliance with her father's wishes was so to veil the fate in oracular words, as to leave it to the character and discernment of her readers to interpret her meaning' (Gaskell, chap. 25). In a heavily facetious letter to George Smith, Miss Brontë indicated that drowning would be a happier fate for Paul than marriage to 'that – person – that – that – individual – "Lucy Snowe" ' (*LL* IV 56).

R. A. Colby

'LUCY SNOWE AND THE GOOD GOVERNESS' (1967)

... At the time she was writing *Villette*, Charlotte Brontë observed in a letter to her friend and former teacher Miss Wooler: 'Schools seems to be considered almost obsolete in London. Ladies' colleges, with Professors for every branch of instruction, are superseding the old-fashioned Seminary. How this system will work I cannot tell: I think the College classes might be very useful for finishing the education of ladies intended to go out as governesses; but what progress little girls will make in them seems to me another question.'[1] Her own novel harks back to the 'old-fashioned Seminary', recalling for a new generation a system of education then in process of being superseded by institutions like Queen's College.[2] Like Fanny Price before her and Maggie Tulliver after, Lucy Snowe is 'going out' as a governess, but we see her actually practising her vocation.

Some chapters (particularly those entitled 'Madame Beck' and 'Isidore') are so packed with detail about school administration and classroom procedure that they read like source material for Matthew Arnold's *Popular Education in France* and *Schools and Universities on the Continent*. There were abundant novels about English schools, such as Harriet Martineau's *The Crofton Boys*, Mrs Marsh-Caldwell's *The Previsions of Lady Evelyn*, Mrs Gore's *Peers and Parvenus* and Frank Smedley's *Frank Fairleigh* – and many more to come. But the foreign school was relatively new fictional territory ...

Villette, as is well known, grew out of Miss Brontë's renewed and again unsuccessful attempts to publish her first-written novel, *The Professor*. Her return to the scene of that novel happened to coincide with new concerted efforts to establish national schools in England, efforts which caused educational reformers to look with envy across the Channel. A book much discussed at this period, particularly in George Henry Lewes's *The Leader*, which Miss Brontë was reading, was her friend Sir Joseph Kay-Shuttleworth's *The Social Condition and Education of the People in England and Europe* (1850).[3] Kay-Shuttleworth, then Secretary to the Committee of the Privy Council on Education, pointed to continental countries, particularly France and Germany, as models for the establishment of liberal education for children ... Lucy Snowe pointedly observes that the Pensionnat Beck ... is 'a foreign school, of which the life, movement and variety made it a complete and most charming contrast to many English institutions of the same kind' (chap. 8) ... but the bigotry Lucy encounters among her students, along with their resistance to learning, make this particular school fall somewhat short of Kay-Shuttleworth's ideal ...

Another immediate appeal of *Villette* to its own generation certainly was its intimate account of a young woman finding her vocation : 'I know not that I was of a self-reliant or active nature, but self-reliance and exertion were forced upon me by circumstances, as they are upon thousands besides', writes the heroine (chap. 4). A book like *Education as a means of Preventing Destitution,* advertised in the first edition of *Villette,* crystallised Lucy's situation ...

Villette, whatever its superficial resemblance to such period inspirational literature as Mrs Burbury's *Florence Sackville; or, Self-Dependence* (which also chronicles a young lady's obstacles in 'finding herself'), is of course something more than the career-woman's vade mecum. Lucy's course of teacher training involves an education of her mind, sensibility and imagination, and these expand in a large environment of events and ideas. 'You will see that *Villette* touches on no matter of public interest', she wrote to George Smith late in 1852. 'I cannot write books handling the topics of the day; it is no use trying.'[4] She was contrasting her forthcoming novel specifically with a current best-seller called *Uncle Tom's Cabin,* but undoubtedly was thinking also of her difficulties in assimilating military, economic, and social history in her previous novel *Shirley* ... But ... she shows that she was quite aware of the political and religious intrigues of her own times, and *Villette* reverberates with the current rumbles of Church and State.

The years immediately preceding the publication of *Villette* were particularly turbulent ones for the English Church, when so many adherents of the Oxford Movement seemed to be following Newman to Rome ... In 1850, just after the publication of *Shirley,* anti-Catholic feeling was aggravated by the so-called 'Papal Aggression', when the Roman hierarchy was restored to England with the appointment of Cardinal Wiseman as Archbishop of England by Pope Pius IX. This move, intended to unify and inspire English Catholics, was popularly interpreted as a campaign of proselytism. Newman, now established at the Oratory of St Philip Neri in Birmingham, published his *The Present Position of Catholics in England* in an attempt to clarify the significance of the Pope's decision. Lewes, in *The Leader,* welcomed the 'Aggression' as a challenge to his countrymen. Charlotte ... wrote to congratulate him on the article, confirming his conviction that religion must be active in men's hearts and affairs and expressing her own belief that the Church can do its work 'quite as well in a curate's plain clothes as in a cardinal's robes and hat'.[5]

Much of the tension in Lucy Snowe's situation derives from her being a Protestant in a Catholic country. In Labassecour she is beset by a 'Papal Aggression' in miniature [quotes from chapter 9, 'The opinion of my Catholic acquaintance ... impossible to do otherwise', and from chapter 15, Lucy's encounter with Père Silas] ... She makes it clear that the Church of St Jean Baptiste attracted her for the same reason that in London she was moved by the sight of St Paul's – as a religious sanctuary considered apart from denomination ... At this point Lucy is in the perplexed state of the heroine of Elizabeth Sewell's *Margaret Percival* (1847) upon stepping inside the cathedral of Rouen [quotes from *Margaret Percival*, chapter 11, 'We live in an age . . . open to us as our homes'] . . .[6]

Alongside the pulpit war of the early 1850s a war of the pen was being waged on the political front more directly involving England with France. In one of the issues of *The Leader* that debated the Catholic question, Sir Francis Head's alarmist book, *The Defenceless State of England* was reviewed . . . as a 'new romance' . . . Nevertheless, Louis Napoleon's *coup d'état* of December 1851 revived the rumours of aggression. Miss Brontë commented to Miss Wooler in 1852,

As to the French President – it seems to me hard to say what a man with so little scruple and so much ambition will *not* attempt. I wish, however, the English Press would not prate so much about invasion; if silence were possible in a free country – would it not be far better to prepare silently for what *may* come . . . Wonderful is the French Nation! . . .[7]

Conflicts of State as well as Church enter, not surprisingly, into Lucy's adventures in Labassecour. With a playfulness aimed no doubt at the Francophobia of some of her readers, Miss Brontë magnifies the Pensionnat Beck into a political battlefield.

Madame Beck, to Lucy, seems to have been intended for greater things than a Pensionnat de Demoiselles [quotes from chapter 8, 'That school offered for her powers too limited a sphere . . . superintendent of police']. Her stealth and furtiveness in prying into the affairs of her staff is likened to secret diplomacy. Later . . . she adopts the tone of the chauvinist ('Bon! But let me tell you . . . tant soit peu rebelles'). The bellicose language is taken up by Lucy as she faces the fierce second division class . . . The ease by which Lucy quells this classroom war should have effected a comic catharsis for those of her readers who had feared another attempted Napoleonic invasion . . . Lucy's confrontation of Paul Emanuel in class on the day of his fête is carried on as a mock war . . . Monsieur Paul's verbal 'invasion' of England consists of a lengthy blast against English women. At first Lucy is determined to ignore this tirade, and not to betray any reaction to it, but her equanimity wavers [quotes from chapter 19, 'I grieve to say I could not quite carry out this resolution . . . "Vive l'Angleterre, l'Histoire et les Héros! A bas France, la Fiction et les Faquins!" '].

With this jingoistic outburst on Lucy's part, the Professor's bombardment of insults ceases. But Lucy realises that she has played into his hands . . . In fact, it leads to a new admiration on Lucy's part for Monsieur Paul – a breakdown of her habitual fear and disdain for him – that eventually ripens into love . . . The Battle of Labassecour is settled amicably. Since it takes place in Belgium it might be called Lucy Snowe's victory at Waterloo (a battle that had been revived in readers' minds recently by *Vanity Fair* and her own *Shirley*. Indeed, not too long after this episode Lucy likens Monsieur Paul to Napoleon himself. (chap. 30.)

Practically speaking, *Villette* is a reliving of a mental and moral ordeal, 'the actual thoughts and feelings of a strong, struggling soul . . . the cry of pain from one who has loved passionately, and who has sorrowed sorely,' as Lewes wrote in a review[0] . . . Some of her letters to Miss Wooler enter with painful detail into aspects of psychopathology that are explored in *Villette* – loneliness, hypochondria, living with an elderly cripple (in her case, the invalid, nearly blind father, the Reverend Patrick Brontë). In one letter she describes a state of profound melancholia that she herself experienced[9] . . . This 'waking Night-mare' is transferred to Lucy Snowe and objectified into a universal despair.

To her 'studies of character', as she describes Lucy's psychological probings, Miss Brontë brings an insight into human nature that she thought Jane Austen lacked[10] . . . As the Reverend Mr Brontë's daughter, however, imbued with *The Pilgrim's Progress* and the Bible, she was hardly indifferent to the character of the Christian Heroine. But she tended to see the struggle for holiness as a war within the self, and the passions therefore interested her as human instincts to be conquered rather than indulged. She appears never to have forgotten the lessons taught in Isaac Watts' *The Doctrine of the Passions Explained and Improved*, a treatise she read in her

youth at Haworth Parsonage,[11] which bears the motto, attributed
to Solomon: 'he that hath no Rule over his own Spirit is like a
City that is broken down and without Walls' ... Such is the
wisdom transmitted to her readers by Lucy Snowe, the Christian
Heroine incarnated in the Good Governess.

The governess-heroine, a fictional type who emerged in the late
1830s and 1840s alongside the spoiled lady of fashion, was one
whom Charlotte Brontë could readily re-create in her own image.
Like William Crimsworth, the hero of *The Professor,* her heroines
have to work for a living and 'master at least half the ascent of
"the Hill of Difficulty" ' ... The lady tutors of the Female Education novels of the early nineteenth century tended to be unob-
trusive, like Madame de Rosier, the genteel émigrée of Maria
Edgeworth's 'The Good French Governess' ... Miss Taylor, who
has served Emma Woodhouse for sixteen years 'less as a governess
than as a good friend', retires into matrimony on the first page of
the novel. The governess of the Bertram girls and Fanny Price is
barely mentioned. Many ladies seem to have assumed, along with
Mrs Murray, one of the employers of Agnes Grey, that: 'The
judicious governess knows ... while she lives in obscurity herself,
her pupil's virtues and defects will be open to every eye; and that
unless she loses sight of herself in the cultivation, she need not
hope for success' (*Agnes Grey*, chap. 18) ...

The governess had been speaking out for her rights as a human
being at least as far back as Lady Blessington's *The Governess*
(1839), a society novel turned social tract ... Emily Morton, in
Elizabeth Sewell's *Amy Herbert* (1844), sublimates her frustra-
tions and humiliations in her devotion to guiding young Amy in
Christian thought and conduct. The heroine of Mrs Sherwood's
Caroline Mordaunt (1845) is also a teacher of 'vital Christianity'
to her young charges. Agnes Grey expresses mainly disillusionment
with her profession, but her stoicism and moral courage make her
narrative a kind of conduct book and guide to the novice entering the field.[12] Jane Eyre is no more the pattern governess than
she was the model Edgeworth–Holland–Sherwood child at Lo-

wood Hall.[13] The moral of her story is that she is a woman first and a governess second ... Rochester is no handsome prince and Thornton Hall is no castle in the air; nevertheless a certain vestige of the romantic heroine clings to Miss Brontë's first governess heroine.

With Lucy Snowe, Charlotte Brontë reverts to the rugged path that she had set out for William Crimsworth in *The Professor* ... She is never rescued from the necessity of earning her own bread. The only money she inherits is a hundred pounds from her deceased mistress ... The love of her life is an ugly middle-aged man, and nothing, practically speaking, comes of it ...

In *Villette*, then, Miss Brontë tries to follow William Crimshawe's advice that 'novelists should never allow themselves to weary of the study of real life' with no concession to wish-fulfillment ... *Villette* conveys an unusual sense of actuality because it is pervaded by its author's recent recall of her London adventures, as well as her experiences in Brussels, which are transferred to Labassecour, her country of the mind. Many critics attribute the intense realism of the book to the intimacy with which Charlotte Brontë reveals herself in Lucy Snowe. Certainly in Lucy we find the governess heroine completely deglamorised. Also her role significantly changes.

Among literary governesses Lucy Snowe is closer to Maria Young of Harriet Martineau's *Deerbrook* (1839) than to Lady Blessington's Clara Mordaunt ... Maria Young is intellectual but morbidly shy, concealing strong emotions and an intense inner life beneath an unattractive appearance and a diffident manner ... The germ of a memorable character is contained in Maria Young ... It was left to Charlotte Brontë to move the self-sacrificing young spinster from the periphery to the centre of the story. *Deerbrook* foreshadows to an extent the mood of *Villette,* a cry of the heart, a reaching out of one anguished soul to another ... Lucy Snowe ... carries her moral wisdom beyond the walls of her *externat de demoiselles.* In other ways too she moves beyond Maria Young, for she finds release and fulfillment ...

With Lucy Snowe, the Good Governess develops into the travel-

ling Instructress. The reading public had already made her
acquaintance in a popular novel that Charlotte knew well, Julia
Kavanagh's *Nathalie* (1850).[14] The story is a forerunner of *Villette*
in a number of respects – its continental school setting, its rebellious
heroine subdued by religion and love, and particularly its principal romance . . . Her [Nathalie's] clashes with the stony Northern disposition of the tyrannical headmistress Mademoiselle
Dantin are a kind of rehearsal for Lucy Snowe's altercations with
Madame Beck . . . Charlotte read *Nathalie* at the beginning of the
year when she began writing *Villette*. The lesser and the greater
novel alike show cultural barriers broken down by a sympathy of
souls, but *Villette* covers far more ground, encompassing politics
and religion as well as temperamental differences. And – more in
keeping with her own life – Miss Brontë's heroine never settles
down with her Monsieur. Nor does she retire from teaching, as
does Nathalie . . .

Although Charlotte Brontë did not sign herself 'A Clergyman's
Daughter' on her title pages, as did many another contemporary
authoress aiming to impress Mudie's more pious subscribers,
Villette could easily have been taken in its time as another example
of exemplary biography by a governess evolved into religious
educator . . . Certainly Lucy Snowe has the audience for pulpit
novels, among others, in mind when she defends her lapse into
despair during her lonely Long Vacation ordeal at the Pensionnat
Beck [quotes, 'Religious reader, you will preach to me . . . you
would have been, like me, wrong']. She shows her readers the way
of the Christian but makes it clear that the path is a thorny one.
But her detailed recording of mental anguish is meant as a spiritual
catharsis for her readers, Lucy's lay sermon reaching out to the
disconsolate as well as to those disappointed in love.

Villette, considered as religious fiction, is a series of steps along-
life's-way, a kind of secular pilgrimage. Its purpose is not far
removed from Sarah Stickney Ellis's much read and influential
moral treatise of the early 1840s, *The Daughters of England,*
addressed to the 'Christian woman (who) has made her decision
not to live for herself, so much as for others; but, above all, not to

live for this world, so much as for eternity' . . . Another example, read and enjoyed by Charlotte as well as many others of her generation, was a first novel, *Passages in the Life of Mrs Margaret Maitland* (1849), in which the twenty-one-year-old author Margaret Wilson (later Mrs Oliphant),[15] speaking with the voice of a Scottish spinster and daughter of a minister of the Kirk, 'of discreet years and small riches', writes for the edification of 'young folk' . . . The heroine of another novel that Charlotte Brontë knew, Mrs Burbury's *Florence Sackville; or, Self-Dependence* (1852), recalls : 'My friends have generally been among the aged. There is something in their wise and passionless calmness that has always been inexpressibly delightful to me . . . One listens with reverence to their experience, learning lessons of wisdom from their lips'.[16] Lucy Snowe is in such a relationship with Miss Marchmont . . .

As a reminiscence of an elderly spinster now at peace with the world looking back over early years of frustration and sorrow, *Villette* bears an especially suggestive resemblance to a religious novel that preceded it by a year, Elizabeth Sewell's *Experience of Life* (1852) . . . Both conceived in their own images precocious, refractory young girls moulded and subdued by religious teaching as well as unattractive strong-spirited young women of intellect and scrupulous conscience who settle into lives of quiet self-abnegation. The title of Miss Sewell's book suggests a spiritual autobiography rather than a work of fiction, and she in fact disclaims any intention to write a tale which is 'only a vignette, a portion of the great picture of life', preferring something closer to 'a real representation of human existence'. Sally Mortimer, the narrator, makes no claim to being a heroine in the sense of having lived a striking or exciting life. She is rather one of those who 'are born unthought of beyond their own immediate circle, and die lamented only by a few; and we pass over their names in the obituary of the day with the strange indifference with which we hear the aggregate amount of deaths in a battle; forgetting that for each individual soul in the vast multitude there has been a special day of trial, a special providence and guidance; and there will be a special day of reckoning and doom'.

Among the obscure anonymous is Lucy Snowe. 'If I failed in what I now designed to undertake, who, save myself, would suffer? If I died far away from – home, I was going to say, but I had no home – from England, then, who would weep?' she ponders as she embarks for the continent (chapter 6). Lucy stresses her drabness and ordinariness. The unromantic Sally Mortimer describes herself in words that could apply as well to Lucy : 'Sickly, plain and indifferently educated, what better could I expect than to live in shade whilst others glittered in sunshine? . . . ' (chapter 4). The unheroic heroine of *Villette,* together with the minimal amount of 'incident' (in comparison with *Jane Eyre*), suggests that Miss Brontë, like Miss Sewell, was trying to move away from the conventions of fiction and in the direction of the true life history. The structure of *Villette* for the most part is loose and 'open', giving the illusion of the 'flow of time' (as Lucy phrases it) rather than of manipulated events. Even the coincidences – such as Lucy's falling in with the Brettons and Polly on the continent – are attributable, in this scheme of things, to providence. Like *The Experience of Life, Villette* attempts 'a great picture of life', encompassing childhood, youth and old age, related to the grander scheme of *The Pilgrim's Progress.* Christiana, Everywoman, and ordinary woman fuse in Lucy Snowe and her experiences.

This self-effacement answers to Miss Brontë's purpose in *Villette,* which, like *The Professor,* is addressed to 'the man of regular life and rational mind' . . . Lucy identifies her plight with the human condition, and from time to time she invites her readers to participate in an act of resignation and humility [quotes from chapter 18, 'Theses struggles with the natural character . . . for patience in extreme need'] . . .

Villette has the intimacy and immediacy of a diary . . . But there is another tale to be considered . . . – the anti-romance embedded in the life-history . . . Despite her avowal, 'Of an artistic temperament I deny that I am' (chapter 7), Lucy betrays this temperament at every turn with her literary allusions and her intense 'studies of character' of the people she meets . . . although Lucy lives externally in the world of the domestic, didactic novel, mentally she dwells in the world of romance and the tale of terror. Superimposed ... upon the story of how Lucy found peace of mind and her vocation is an allegory of the imagination coping with the world outside itself. And with the purgation of the soul comes the exorcising of the imagination.

Certain arabesque and Gothic elements in the story betray Lucy's susceptibility to 'the strange necromantic joys of infancy'. When she awakens from a stupor to find herself once more with the Brettons ... she momentarily thinks that she is back in England, like 'Bedreddin Hassan, transported in his sleep from Cairo to the Gates of Damascus' (chapter 16). Later ... she is reminded of a city petrified 'as if by Eastern enchantment' and the ancient church with its 'dark, half ruinous turrets' evokes in her mind 'the venerable and formerly opulent shrine of the Magi'. The hunchback Madame Walravens looks to Lucy like Malevola, the evil fairy (chapter 26).

Knowing the good use to which Miss Brontë put the story from *A Sicilian Romance* of the concealed wife in a castle, one is not surprised that Lucy's imagination is tinged also with Radcliffian shades. The house on the Rue des Mages where Madame Walravens lives seems to have been moved out of Udolpho; the drugged potion given by Madame Beck to Lucy (chapter 38) ... recalls brews served to many a Gothic heroine ... Of all the Radcliffe romances, *The Italian; or, The Confessional of the Black Penitents* seems to hover in the background of *Villette*, with its confession chamber and its meddling Father ... However, these are mere echoes used for anticlimactic effect, for *Villette* is a story in which the fancy cheats itself[17] ... In her wry way, Miss Brontë makes her readers recognise that evil is at once more subtle and less glamorous than the Gothic tales would lead them to believe ...

The Arabian Nights and *Tales of the East* were still amusing Victorian children as they had their Georgian forebears, and Mrs Radcliffe's tales of terror were then available in cheap reprints with lurid covers;[18] but Miss Brontë's satire was probably aimed equally at the New Gothicism of Joseph Sheridan Lefanu's *Ghost*

Stories and Tales of Mystery (1851), and the *outré* narratives of
... Mrs Crowe (who) startled mid-Victorian readers with *The
Night-Side of Nature; or, Ghosts and Ghost Seers* (1850)... Her
Light and Darkness; or, The Mysteries of Life (1850)... includes
some nocturnal adventures of a somnambulistic monk.

    In that intensely hallucinatory episode of the mid-night fête
... Lucy ... leads readers to expect the 'nun' to reveal
herself, but lets them down: 'Ah! when imagination once runs
riot, where do we stop?' she warns her readers ...

    Lucy Snowe then represents, among other things, the conflict in
the creative imagination between the 'night-side' and the 'day-
side' of nature. She makes clear which side wins : 'All falsities!
all figments! We will not deal in this gear', she declares ... 'Let
us be honest, and cut, as heretofore, from the homely web of truth'
(chapter 29). Instrumental in her rehabilitation is her tutor ...
Paul Emanuel ... He probably derives at least as much from the
French novels that Charlotte read in the 1840s and 1850s as from
her real tutor ... In Balzac's *Illusions Perdues,* which she read and
admired ... , a learned French priest awakens the mind of a sensitive provincial young lady to the humanities and the secular
learning of the Enlightenment. Her favourite George Sand novel,
Consuelo,[19] begins with the heroine's tutelage under the imposing
and irascible but tenderhearted Maestro Porpora, who discovers
and nourishes young Consuelo's genius for song ...[20]

S O U R C E : from 'Lucy Snowe and the Good Governess', *Fiction
    with a Purpose: Major and Minor Nineteenth Century Novels*
    (1967).

NOTES

[The following notes include a shortened version of the author's commentary.]

    1. *LL* IV 39.

2. See Patricia Thomson, *The Victorian Heroine* (1956), chapter 2.

3. See the *Leader,* 3, 17, 31 August 1850 and, for Charlotte's acqaintance with Kay-Shuttleworth, Mrs Gaskell's *Life,* chapter 21 and passim.

4. 30 October 1852, *LL* iv 13–14.

5. 23 November 1850, *LL* iii 183–4.

6. The omitted passages include a discussion of reactions to Charlotte's attacks on Romanism.

7. 17 February 1852, *LL* iii 318.

8. *Westminster Review,* lix (April 1853) 490.

9. Dated '? 1846' in *LL* ii 116–17, but tentatively redated 'late 1852' by Mildred Christian, who is preparing a new edition of the Brontë correspondence.

10. See Introduction, p. 22.

11. An edition dated 'Berwick 1791', bearing Charlotte's autograph, is listed in an inventory of her books in the Brontë Society *Catalogue of the Museum and Library* (Haworth 1927).

12. *Agnes Grey* and *Wuthering Heights* are both, their profound differences aside, memoirs of educated servants.

13. For a retrospective comment on the 'model' governesses of pre-Brontëan fiction see Mrs Oliphant, *Women Novelists of Queen Victoria's Reign* (1897), pp. 17–18.

14. See above, p. 121 n.

15. See above, p. 122 n.

16. Mrs Burley had the same publisher as Charlotte, who wrote favourably to him about *Florence Sackville,* 20, 28 November 1851, *LL* iii 293–4.

17. *The Italian* is read by Rose Yorke and Caroline Helstone (over Rose's shoulder) in *Shirley,* chapter 23.

18. See above, p. 140 n.

19. For Charlotte on *Consuelo* see her letter to Lewes, 12 January 1848, *LL* ii 180.

20. The essay continues with a discussion of the influence on *Villette* of Bernardin de Saint-Pierre's *Paul et Virginie* (a gift from Paul Heger) and Balzac's *Les Illusions Perdues*; it concludes with a restatement of Mr Colby's earlier findings (Introduction, pp. 35–6), i.e. that Charlotte in *Villette* more than anywhere else 'succeeded in reconciling the conflicting elements in her imagination – passion and reason, fantasy and reality, art and nature', and that the book

as a whole foreshadows later developments in fiction through its special balancing of 'romance and domestic history, the tale of terror and the tale "founded on fact", the novel of society and the religious-didactic novel. The French and English novel are also joined in a unique wedding of sensibility and mid-Victorian realism . . . '

SELECT BIBLIOGRAPHY

Miriam Allott : *The Brontës: The Critical Heritage* (1973). Represents nineteenth-century critical attitudes to the work of Charlotte and her sisters.

Phyllis Bentley : *The Brontës and Their World* (1969). A collection of pictures illustrating Yorkshire scenes familiar to the Brontës from their childhood and youth and including an informative biographical survey.

Richard Chase : 'The Brontës : A Centennial Observance' in *Kenyon Review* IX (1947). A well-known essay in revaluation which argues that the Brontës' novels aroused excitement at the time because they 'translated the social customs of the time into the forms of mythical art, whereas many other Victorian novels were translated by the social customs into more or less tiresome canting'. The discussion centres on *Jane Eyre* and *Wuthering Heights*.

Mildred Christian : 'The Brontës', in *Victorian Fiction: A Guide to Research,* ed. Lionel Stevenson (1964). A comprehensive survey of Brontë criticism.

R. A. Colby : '*Villette* and the Life of the Mind' in *PMLA* (1960). Discusses the importance of *Villette* in Charlotte's artistic development and in the evolution of the English novel. See Introduction, pp. 35–6.

Wendy Craik : *The Brontë Novels* (1968). Analyses each of the novels in close detail, eschewing biographical information and giving particular attention to Charlotte's mastery of her novelistic skills. See Introduction, pp. 37–8.

Inga-Stina Ewbank : *Their Proper Sphere: a study of the Brontë sisters as early Victorian female novelists* (1966). Contains a descriptive analysis of each of the novels and discusses the Brontës' relationship with other early nineteenth-century women writers.

Elizabeth Gaskell : *The Life of Charlotte Brontë* (1857). Still the best biography

Winifred Gérin : *Charlotte Brontë: The Evolution of Genius* (1967). The most ambitious modern biography, aiming to trace the influences fostering Charlotte's creative imagination.

L. and E. M. Hanson : *The Four Brontës* (1949, revised 1967). A useful general survey, notwithstanding the conjectural material concerning Emily Brontë.

Andrew Hook : 'Charlotte Brontë, the Imagination, and *Villette*' in *The Brontës: A Collection of Critical Essays,* edited for the series 'Twentieth Century Views' by Ian Gregor (1970). A variation on the theme of Charlotte's reconciliation of conflicting impulses in *Villette,* with the emphasis now laid on Lucy Snowe's hard-won fight for 'the freedom to feel', however fleetingly that freedom is enjoyed.

David Lodge : 'Fire and Eyre : Charlotte Brontë's War of Earthly Elements' in *The Language of Fiction* (1966). An example of the 'myth criticism' of *Jane Eyre,* which aims to modify Richard Chase's interpretation (see above) by suggesting that Charlotte Brontë 'succeeds in uniting the diverse elements of her novel by employing a system of "objective correlatives" . . . ranging from the prosaic and realistic to the poetic and symbolic. At the core of this system are the elements – earth, water, air, and fire; these . . . are manifested in the weather; this leads to images of nature as affected by weather, and . . . finally . . . incorporates the sun and the moon, which affect the weather, and, traditionally, human destiny . . .'

F. E. Ratchford : 'Charlotte Brontë's Angrian cycle of stories' in *PMLA* 43 (1928) and *The Brontës' Web of Childhood* (1941). Seminal studies of the fantasy worlds created by the Brontë sisters.

Norman Sherry : *The Brontë Sisters: Charlotte and Emily* (1969). A succinct introductory primer, emphasising Charlotte's gift for expressing passionate individual experience.

T. W. Winnifrith : *The Brontës and their Background: Romance and Reality* (1973). 'A fresh attempt to see the fiction of the Brontës in the context of the facts of their lives, while severely separating the fact and the fiction in order to avoid the faults of so many Brontë biographers'. Topics usefully covered include, besides the early critical reception of the Brontës' 'Texts and Transmission', 'The Brontës' Religion', 'Prudes and Prudery', 'The Brontës and their Books', 'Snobs and Snobbery'.

BIBLIOGRAPHICAL ADDENDUM, 1982

George H. Ford (ed.): *Victorian Fiction: A Second Guide to Research* (New York, 1978). This substantially revises the first version of the *Guide* (1964: see Mildred Christian's entry, p. 243 above), and the section on the Brontës is completely rewritten.

Robert Lee Wolff: *Gains and Losses: Novels of Faith and Doubt in Victorian England* (New York, 1977). This treats of themes handled in Margaret Maison's book (Note 2, p. 46 above), but in a more thorough and scholarly way.

NOTES ON CONTRIBUTORS

LORD DAVID CECIL, author and literary critic, was formerly Professor of English Literature at the University of Oxford. His best-known works on prose fiction include *Early Victorian Novelists: Essays in Revaluation* (1934) and *Hardy the Novelist* (1943).

ROBERT A. COLBY, of the Library Science Department at Queen's College, City University of New York, has worked extensively on nineteenth-century novelists in relation to their age and is the author of '*Villette* and the Life of the Mind' (see Bibliography) and *Fiction with a Purpose: Major and Minor Nineteenth Century Novels* (1967).

DAVID W. CROMPTON is Principal of Westminster College, North Hinksey, Oxford, and has written on William Golding as well as on the Brontës.

ROBERT B. HEILMAN, formerly Professor of English at the University of Washington and subsequently (1977), Arnold Professor, Whitman College, Wash.; his publications include important studies on Shakespeare, George Eliot, Hardy and Conrad.

ROBERT B. MARTIN, Professor of English, Princeton University, and subsequently residing in Oxford; his literary studies include *Victorian Poetry* (1964), and *Tenhyson: The Unquiet Heart* (1980), and, as Robert Berhard, he is the author of novels and detective stories.

ROY PASCAL, (1904–82); well-known for his studies in German literature (he was Professor of German in the University of Birmingham) his publications also embrace general works on the art of writing, including *Design and Truth in Autobiography* (1960).

M. H. SCARGILL is a member of the Royal Society of Canada and the editor, in association with P. G. Penner, of *Looking at Language: Essays in Introductory Linguistics* (1966).

KATHLEEN TILLOTSON, formerly Professor of English at Bedford College, University of London, is an authority on nineteenth-century literature; her books include *Novels of the Eighteen-Forties* (1954) and, in collaboration with the late Professor John Butt, *Dickens at Work* (1957).

INDEX

Page numbers of extracts quoted are shown in bold type. Characters from *Jane Eyre* and *Villette* are shown in small capitals.